John Strover, MA, spent his early childhood in India. He was educated in England, where he was a Scholar at Cheltenham College and an Exhibitioner at Trinity College, Oxford. He captained the University at hockey, played for England, and for Great Britain in the Melbourne Olympics. He was commissioned into the Essex Regiment for National Service and into the RAFVR when he learned to fly with the University Air Squadron. He taught Mathematics at Harrow School before he was appointed Headmaster of Kingston Grammar School, going on from there to be Headmaster of Warwick School. In retirement he worked for the International Children's Trust, returning to India on many occasions as their Overseas Executive. He has been a Lay Reader for over thirty years. He lives with his wife in Dorset and has four sons by a previous marriage.

Ernest James Strover, 'Puck'.

THE
FAITHFUL
SOLDIER

A Biography of Ernest Strover, from India to the World Wars

JOHN STROVER

The Radcliffe Press
LONDON • NEW YORK

Suffolk County Council	
30127 08176253 1	
Askews & Holts	Oct-2013
355.0092	£27.50

Published in 2013 by I.B.Tauris & Co Ltd
6 Salem Road, London W2 4BU
175 Fifth Avenue, New York NY 10010
www.ibtauris.com

Distributed in the United States and Canada Exclusively by
Palgrave Macmillan
175 Fifth Avenue, New York NY 10010

ISBN: 978 1 78076 3 880

A full CIP record for this book is available from the British Library
A full CIP record is available from the Library of Congress

Library of Congress Catalog Card Number: available
Printed and bound by CPI Group (UK) Ltd, Croydon, CR0 4YY

MIX
Paper from
responsible sources
FSC   FSC® C013604
www.fsc.org

Contents

Illustrations

Preface

Most of the material used in this biography comes from Puck's own writings. The biography is, therefore, to some extent, an autobiography. He enjoyed writing and filled over thirty exercise books, containing about 300 sermons, which I catalogued into various themes. I have included a selection of the sermons in an Appendix as an illustration of these themes and of his way of preaching, and have used excerpts from others, in the text, in order to throw light on the development of his faith and thinking over the years. I have also included in the Appendix his writings on personal experiences of answers to prayer, in full, despite including passages from them in the main text to illuminate the story, as they were powerful influences on his life.

His sister-in-law, Tickie, encouraged him to write about his Prisoner of War experiences. Tickie kept the letters which he wrote to her as a POW and although these were heavily censored they helped to tell the story of what it was like to be starved of freedom and the necessities of life.

Puck's upbringing was a further incentive to put pen to paper as his brothers and sister, encouraged by their mother, produced a monthly 'package' of original writings and drawings. That led on to him writing fully about his own first thirty years.

The British Library unearthed for me all the confidential reports on his thirty years' service in the Indian Army and those reports gave me a continuing picture of his career. In addition I was able to lay hands on the war diaries of his regimental activities in the Mesopotamian campaign, as well as his own reports when he later became Brigade Major.

Puck was in regular correspondence with his brother Martyn, indeed their letters to each other often overlapped, and they were able to unburden themselves to each other. Sadly, not many of these letters have been kept, but I have included one of them in the text as an example of their close affinity and respect for each other. My mother kept his letters to her from Rhodesia and they were useful for piecing together that restorative time in his life.

I am grateful to Peter for writing his warm appreciation of Puck and the memories he has of a man who had a lasting influence on his own life, spent in public service.

The rest of the story is mainly a filling in of gaps from reminiscences and conversations with my mother, who outlived her husband by almost fifty years, and my brothers Paul and Dick, and with my own memory of a father who lived with the times and who, looking back on it, though I didn't realise it at the time, had an extraordinary and varied life as soldier, airman, priest, friend and family man, ranging over two world wars from Victorian England and the establishment of new social values leading up to the 1960s.

An Appreciation

Colonel The Reverend Ernest James Strover was a splendid example of sophisticated muscular Christianity.

It was magical good luck for me, for which I have always been extremely grateful, that at the age of 16, alone in England (my parents being in Tanganyika), I was, for no discernible reason, 'adopted' on sight by Mrs Strover at a chance meeting in East Bergholt in Suffolk. This led to my spending three school holidays, in 1946/47, with Puck and Rosalind Strover and their three sons at Lawford Rectory with its beautiful views over the Stour valley. Their very athletic sons (John, the author of this fine memoir, went on to captain Oxford University, and play for England, at hockey) must have been astonished at the arrival of this strange, bookish, cuckoo in their nest, but they all made me feel 'one of the family' from the start and we have remained friends ever since.

I at once fell under the spell of Puck's moral guidance and personal example. He was universally known as Puck (although I think I always called him 'Sir'), even by his wife because, I suppose, of the twinkle in his eyes, his impishly irreverent humour and his boyish sense of fun.

After returning from a working holiday in Tanganyika, Puck sent me off, at 18, from Lawford Rectory to my National Service with the Army with the words: 'If you go to the lavatory every morning and say your prayers every night, you will come to little harm' – a combination of humour, practicality and faith that was characteristic of him.

Later, after basic and officer training, as I left, aged just 19, as a newly minted Second Lieutenant, for Liverpool to join a troopship bound for Suez, his parting words to me were: 'Always put your men first.' Only once did I see him again when he came, as my guest, to a dinner of the Coningsby Club where he talked with Rab Butler. He was as much at ease in a political discussion with a cabinet minister as with a teenage schoolboy. He left a permanent imprint on me which has stood me in good stead.

On one occasion, he took me into his study, where he worked intensely hard on his sermons and, pointing to an oar with the names of the Selwyn College Eight, won for securing six 'bumps' in the May 1907 races, he said: 'The others were all killed in the War. I only survived because my fighter plane was shot down and I was taken prisoner.' I have no doubt that his religious faith and commitment to the service of others owed much to that.

Those years in a German prison camp, at the peak of his young manhood, and halting his military advancement, must have been a bitter experience for him, but I never heard him utter an anti-German sentiment. He even told me that he came to feel sorry for his German guards!

In the last phase of his long and varied military service, between the wars, and shortly before I met him, he had been a wartime chaplain in the Royal Air Force. He would have been a striking and unique figure in his blue RAF officer's uniform with his 1914 pilot's wings on his left breast, above two rows of military medal ribbons, all topped by a white clergyman's dog collar.

Such a man, with his witty worldliness and his resolute godliness was, as one would expect, a compelling preacher in his pulpits on Sunday mornings. Former brigadiers, retired ambassadors, grim-looking coal merchants and even the producer of the most famous

Rank film of the time, 'The Wicked Lady', who told me that he had never been a regular churchgoer until the arrival of Puck, flocked to hear his sermons, along with admiring villagers and a bevy of pretty girls with designs upon the Strover boys.

In his sermons, although none were of the 'fire and brimstone' variety, Puck did not pull his punches. He would vividly describe and interpret famous stories from the Old and New Testaments and relate them to modern life, drawing on his own lengthy observation of the customs and religions East of Suez. His realistic description of the flogging and crucifixion of Jesus Christ, in grisly detail, brought home the full horror and human evil of the world-changing event, placed emphasis on the integrity and courage of Jesus (the two qualities he most admired) and that He was a flesh and blood man like us, as well as the son of God.

The Commander of British Forces during the desperate wartime defence of Crete, when our men fought heroically against overwhelming German airborne forces, said to me, as we walked out of the church: 'That was the best sermon I have ever heard.'

I remember those Lawford days as a halcyon time for me – a round of parties, dances and tennis – when everyone was at home and Puck was full of vigour. It could not last. We boys were scattered by National Service. The pretty girls married other men, often far from the exquisite Dedham Vale. Puck died. It was 60 years before I saw Lawford Church again, for Rosalind's Memorial Service.

Rosalind lived to be 106, leaving her body for medical research – a last typical act of concern for others. I called on her whenever I could, sometimes several times a year. She retained her memory of those happy Lawford days with extraordinary accuracy and would tease me about my inadequacy at washing up. She often said as I left her: 'You must stand for parliament again.' Like Puck she had a strong sense of public duty. She also shared with Puck an absolute faith in the existence of a beneficent God and of an eternal life in another world. If they were right, they are together now and waiting to greet the four of us because Rosalind often told me that I was her fourth son.

Peter Tapsell

Peter and the Strover family.

Introduction

The Strovers served the British Empire on both sea, land and in the air from the end of the eighteenth century to mid-way through the twentieth century. Captain John Strover, RN, Indian Navy, Puck's great-grandfather, was rewarded by the East India Company for his 'Galant conduct in the capture of the Cape of Good Hope at the battle of Muizenberg' in 1795 when the Dutch fleet were routed. Lt. General Samuel Rogers Strover, Puck's grandfather, was commandant of the Bombay Presidency Artillery and had survived narrow escapes during his life time. Puck's father, Major-General Henry Strover had fought with distinction at Sebastopol and in the Maori Wars, and commanded the British Artillery in Burma. They were men who had risked their lives in the service of the Empire and Puck drew inspiration from them; but not least from his mother who was an extremely adventurous lady, prepared to tackle any opportunity which came her way. She was one of a line of Strover wives who had supported their husbands in the Far East, had overcome extremely hazardous conditions in giving birth to and raising children, yet found the means, not just for surviving in the heat and disease, but also to enhance the lives of those around them.

It was this love of a challenge which motivated Puck into leading Indian troops, to become a pioneer of air warfare and to be a serial escaper from POW camps in the First World War. It led him into a number of scrapes, all of which he was able to overcome through his deep faith, and eventually into Priesthood.

The British Empire was at its height when Puck began his military service in India at the beginning of the twentieth century. The East India Company had acted as an agent of British imperialism in India from the mid-eighteenth century but was taken over by the Crown after the Indian Mutiny in 1857. The scramble for Africa by European countries had started in earnest in the decade when Puck was born so that by the turn of the nineteenth century the British Empire included about a quarter of the world's population and land surface, much of which, notably Australia and Canada, had dominion status.

India, though, was the 'Jewel in the Crown' of the British Empire. It could be said that Egypt's importance had more to do with safe-guarding Britain's communications with India than with reaping the benefits of the Nile valley. Hence the importance of the Suez Canal and protecting it from Turkish and German forces in the First World War. Likewise, subsequent moves into the Sudan and Kenya were more concerned to control sources of the Nile in Uganda and thus protect the Empire's position in Egypt than with adding yet more land surface to her world-wide dominions. Cape Colony, too, Natal, Mauritius and other Indian Ocean islands provided harbouring places for the fleet which served the sub-continent. However, settlers in these outposts of the Empire soon found rich pickings further up country, notably gold and diamonds on the Rand, copper in the Rhodesias and fertile lands for farming in East Africa; and the Empire lured entrepreneurs from the mother country into other parts of the world where fortunes were to be made and climatic conditions were conducive to the European way of life.

The Government of India needed to protect its borders. Afghanistan to the West was a gateway for Tsarist Russia to extend its own empire into India and the attempted occupation of that country by British forces in 1839 which resulted in their total massacre in 1842 was a clear lesson to the authorities that while it may be relatively straightforward to invade Afghanistan it is wholly impractical to occupy the country or attempt to impose government not welcomed by the inhabitants. A further attempt by the British in a second war (1878–80) to instal a friendly Amir in Kabul for fear of Russian invasion was abortive, though honour was retrieved by Lord Robert's inspirational march from Kabul to Kandahar, only to be compared with the heroic stand at Rorke's Drift in 1879 after the annihilation of the Imperial Army at Isandhlwana, a campaign launched to prevent a Zulu invasion of Natal.

The Government therefore resorted to protecting its North West frontier and the Khyber Pass to prevent Russian infiltration.

Further West, Mesopotamia was also a threat when under German and Turkish influence. Following the campaigns in the First World War when a British Expeditionary Force occupied Basra and Baghdad there was an upsurge of Arab nationalism immediately post-war, which had to be put down but which determined the shape of the new Iraqi state until Iraq finally emerged as an independent political entity with Faysal, the British choice and sympathiser, on the throne. British control of Iraq was short lived: there was a need to protect interests in the Persian Gulf and India but also a requirement to reconcile Arab nationalism.

Burma to the East provided a threat, and attacks on British territory early in the nineteenth century started the first Anglo-Burmese war which led to British annexation of coastal regions; and a second war, motivated by commercial imperialism, brought the important port of Rangoon into the Empire. That enabled further incursions into the Far East and the spice and rubber trade in the Malay States (now part of Malaysia) and the establishment of Singapore as a garrison and port. As a British Crown Colony Singapore became Britain's principal naval base in the Far East, commanding the Straits of Malacca which separated the Indian Ocean from the China Sea.

These were the outposts of the British Empire which came within Puck's experience as a soldier. His experiences of being airman and priest were confined mainly to Europe in the First and Second World Wars, and post-war, but spilled over into Baluchistan (now part of Pakistan) where he was a lecturer in Air Strategy at the Staff College in Quetta, and to Rhodesia where, later in life, he got to know the ex-patriate farming community as temporary priest-in-charge of the large parish of Bindura, half the size of Wales.

A succession of Viceroys had ruled India as representatives of its Emperor, Queen Victoria, when the Crown took over control from the East India Company after the Mutiny in 1857. Previously there had been Governor Generals in charge of the three provinces, Bengal, Bombay and Madras, administered by the East India Company yet subservient to the British Monarch, each with its own individual army. The Bengal Army had been partially destroyed in the first Afghan war and it was in that army that the mutiny started. From 1858 until 1894 the Indian Army was a collective term for the armies of the three Presidencies and had its formal existence from 1895 as the 'Army of the government of India', including both British and Indian Army regiments.

Like the Presidency Armies, the Indian Army continued to provide armed support to the civil authorities, both in combating banditry and, in case of riots, rebellion. One of the first external operations of the new unified army was the Boxer rebellion in China from 1899–1901. But there was also a need to pacify local warfaring people and to prevent banditry, both of which involved numerous small scale actions. The force was recruited locally and officered by British ex-patriates. It was based permanently in India, its main role being the defence of the North West Frontier province against Russian invasion via Afghanistan, internal security and expeditionary warfare in and around the Indian Ocean. The British Army in India consisted of British Army units posted to India for a tour of duty and which could be posted to other parts of the Empire or back to the UK. The Commander-in-Chief of the Army of India reported to the Viceroy. Field Marshal Lord

Kitchener was Commander-in-Chief in 1907 when Puck joined the Indian Army. He had instituted many reforms since arriving in 1902 but had crossed swords with the Viceroy, Lord Curzon, which resulted in Curzon's resignation in 1905.

British officers in the Indian Army were expected to learn to speak the Indian language of their men, who tended to be recruited from primarily Hindi speaking areas. When Puck joined the Army of India in 1907 he was attached to the Sherwood Foresters, a British Regiment posted to India, and was required to learn and pass both parts of the Lower Standard of Hindustani before he could join his Indian regiment, the Brahmans in Agra. Later he was to progress, voluntarily, to the Higher Standard in Hindustani and also in Persian. He was a good linguist, speaking French reasonably well and learning sufficient German as a POW to pass as a German soldier when escaping, and Russian to collude with fellow escapees; Arabic, too, learned at Leiden University while interned in Holland at the end of the First World War, which came in useful in Mesopotamia during the Arab uprising.

On first joining the Brahmans in Agra, Puck made friends with a British Cavalry Regiment, the 14th Hussars, commanded by a cousin of his, and was introduced to polo, which became a favourite pastime. He was much tempted to apply for an Indian Cavalry Regiment but realised that the cavalry had no future in modern warfare against machine gun fire; and days of scouting as forerunner of The Intelligence Corps were already numbered with the advent of aircraft. He determined, therefore, to learn to fly as soon as possible and on his first leave home he set about obtaining a pilot's licence. Meanwhile he enjoyed immensely the lifestyle of a young subaltern with all the social and sporting opportunities that went with service in the British Raj and with learning to be a professional soldier.

Puck had tremendous respect for the 'Indian soldier' (called sepoy) under his command and for their officers. Viceroy

Commissioned Officers (VCOs) were ranked Jemadar, Subedar and Subedar Major, equivalent to Lieutenant, Captain and Major in the British Army, but with authority only over Indian troops. Later, in the 1920s, Kings Commissioned Indian Officers (KCIOs) were created from the Indian ranks and these were trained at Sandhurst, as were British officers, and had authority over British as well as Indian troops. It was while Puck was attending the Staff College at Camberley that he was invited to take a party of potential KCIOs from Sandhurst, during the Christmas break, to Switzerland to ski, where he met his future wife, Rosalind. A Non-Commissioned Officer (NCO) in the Indian Army was ranked as 'Naik', equivalent to a Corporal in the British Army. Puck was greatly touched when he received a food parcel from one of his Naiks when he was a POW. The farewell address from his Subedar Major on relinquishing his command of the 4/2nd Punjab Regiment (Chapter 15) reciprocated the love and respect he had for his men.

From the very start of his thirty years' service in the Indian Army, Puck made it his business to understand the Indian people, their way of life, their politics and the way they were governed by the Indian Civil Service (ICS). When stationed at Nowgon, in the midst of a number of Princely States, he was able to assess the roles of the local District Collector (DC) and Political Agent when invited to tour their district with them while on leave from his regiment. He was impressed by the power that was invested in young DCs, mostly the pick of Oxbridge graduates in those days, and the respect and honour that was accorded to them by the people they ruled. Indian tribes and castes were often at each other's throats and so welcomed the peace-keeping administration and legislature that these men exercised, especially when holding local 'Durbars' when any villager could bring up an issue or complaint. In the Princely States the British Political Agent acted as a monitor of the Indian Raja, who ruled by personal touch but had to swear allegiance to the British Crown, which could call in the Government of India to intervene when the State suffered from misrule. These men served India best when they were trusted to govern within their remit.

Unfortunately there had been too much control exercised from Simla and Delhi which had destroyed the confidence of Indians in the British Government in the past. However, the Liberal Party's election victory of 1906 marked the dawn of a new era of reforms for British India. Lord Minto, who had succeeded Lord Curzon as Viceroy in 1905, and the Head of the India Office in Whitehall, the liberal John Morley, were able to introduce important innovations into the legislature as well as the administrative machinery of the British Indian Government. Morley persuaded the Viceroy to appoint the first Indian members to his Executive Council and to his own Council in Whitehall. True liberal that he was, Morley believed that the only justification for British rule over India was to bequeath to the Government of India England's greatest political institute, Parliamentary Government. The Indian Council's Act of 1909 introduced the elective principle to the legislature, even though to only a small minority of Indians enfranchised by property ownership and education. Before this Act India's nationalists had been engaged in agitation 'from outside', but from then on they were engaged in what might be called 'responsible association with the administration'.

Following the First World War, disaffection with British rule was aroused as a result of the 'black acts', as they came to be known, which were peace time extensions of wartime emergencies. More than a million Indian troops had been shipped overseas to assist in the war effort and India's material and financial contributions were hardly less valuable. Indians expected more than a return to a 'native' existence and a leader arose from among them, Gandhi, saint and wily politician. His call for disobedience by boycotting British institutions – schools, courts of law, goods and tax collectors –

landed him in prison and the British Raj resumed its unchecked sway, conservative principles replacing the liberal reforms. But the heart had gone out from the Raj and Gandhi held the moral lead. His political power was in great measure attributable to the spiritual leadership which he exerted over the Hindu masses, who viewed him as Sadhu (Saint) and worshipped him as Mahatma. He chose Satya (Truth) and Ahimsa (Non-Violence) and assured Indians that these two weapons would bring the mightiest Empire the world had ever known to its knees.

Puck lived in and served British India throughout this turmoil and his sympathies were very much with Gandhi's belief that politics and religion could not be separated. India is a very spiritual nation and he could not have served with Hindus, Muslims and Christians without becoming acutely aware of the power of the Holy Spirit. Indeed, after thirty years service in India his conscience beckoned him into the Church. The only problem was that there was a reaction in the Anglican Church against liberal theology which met with much criticism on the ground that it narrowed Christianity to the limits of what men believed themselves to be experiencing or, in other words, turned objective truth into subjective feeling. These fundamentalists had gained ground from the Oxford Movement in the nineteenth century and from evangelical tradition, so that after the First World War there was a reaction, even within the liberal camp, against all theologies emphasizing religious experience, which came to be known as Neo-orthodoxy.

Puck's faith arose very much from personal experience, from the power of prayer and from his vision of Christ beckoning to him. So it was not surprising that when he went to visit the Bishop of Chelmsford, a conservative theologian, when home on leave, about being ordained he was turned down on the grounds of being too unorthodox. Off he went to see the Bishop of Birmingham, well known for his unorthodox religious beliefs, who was more understanding and accepted him for ordination – a good choice, as the Second World War was looming at that time and as a result of it the Liberal tradition was revived and the Ecumenical Movement, of which Puck was a protagonist, took off, much to the discomfort of Fundamentalists who, at first, refused to join.

It is ironic that his only incumbency was in the Chelmsford diocese, but that was post-Second World War after religious fervour had been ignited again during the war. Perhaps his greatest contribution to the war effort was as an RAF Padre when he prepared over five hundred airmen for confirmation. That, no doubt, convinced Chelmsford that you didn't need to be too orthodox in order to be a respected and much loved parish priest, and to fill your church for worship every Sunday.

Synopsis of Career

1885	Born Bath, 23 May, youngest child of Major General Henry Strover (1831–1900) and Annie Roberts (1844–1907).
1896	Moved to Tonbridge, where he attended Tonbridge School.
1904–7	Cambridge University Rifle Volunteers.
1907	BA Cambridge (Selwyn College).
1908	28 March: landed in India.
	1 April: attached to Sherwood Foresters as 2nd Lieutenant.
	Studied for Hindustani (Lower Standard), Bangalore.
	Passed Parts I and II, 12 October 1908.
1909	22 August: posted to 3rd Brahman Regt., Agra.
	21 December: promoted Lieutenant.
1910	Passed Hindustani Higher Standard (Parts I and II), Hindi obligatory and Persian Lower Standard, Meerut, January–April.
	April–August: local leave in Kashmir to hunt bear.
1911	January–March: Singapore with 3rd Brahmans.
	March–November: home leave to learn to fly.
	November: rejoined 3rd Brahmans in Singapore as Adjutant.
1913	November: Nowgon, Central India with 3rd Brahmans.
1914	Satara: Great War broke out while on musketry course.
	October: with 3rd Brahmans in Zagazig, Egypt on Active Service.
1915	April: Attached. Royal Flying Corps for training at Ruislip, Middlesex.
	September: Gazetted Captain, Indian Army.
	November: posted, as Flying Officer, to 18th Sqn. RFC, France.
	December: shot down over enemy lines. POW.
1918	April: interned Holland, attended Leiden University.
	November: repatriated to England. Attached RFC.

	April/May: attended Senior Officers School, Aldershot.
	July 1919: posted to 3/23rd Sikh Infantry, India as 2i/c.
	September–June 1920: Officiating Commandant.
	December: Mentioned in despatches for services while POW.
1920	April/May: Mountain Warfare School, Abbotabad.
	August–December: active service in Mesopotamia.
1921	Brigade Major, 14th Brigade while still in Mesopotamia.
	February: Mentioned in despatches and promoted Brevet-Major.
	September: posted to 4/10th Chin Rifles, Burmah, as Company Commander.
	Eight months' leave until May 1922.
1923	January: promoted Major.
	Attended Staff College, Camberley, until December 1924.
1925	January: met Rosalind Mary Atkinson while skiing in St Cergue, Switzerland.
	April: Brigade Major Ambala Brigade, until February 1926.
1926	May: student, RAF Staff College, Andover, until July 1927.
1927	21 April: married Rosalind in Mistley, lived at Upper Clatford, Hampshire.
	20 September: embarked on troopship Dorsetshire.
	20 October: arrived Karachi. DAAG, Baluchistan District, Quetta.
1928	April: officiating Instructor, GII, Staff College, Quetta.
	19 September: Paul born, Quetta.
1929	January: DAAG, Baluchistan District, Quetta.
	April: eight months' home leave. Cottage taken in Dedham.
	November: 2i/c Burmah Rifles, Taiping, Malay States.
1931	2 February: John born, Penang.
	May–August: officiating Commandant, Burmah Rifles, Taiping.
	August: visit to Oberammergau on home leave and attendance at Senior Officers' School, Aldershot, until April 1932.
1932	April: posted to Secunderabad, India as 2i/c 4/2nd Punjab Regiment, officiating Commandant from June.
1933	January: promoted Lt. Colonel and assumed command of 4/2nd Punjab Regiment until September 1936.
1934	March–November: eight months' home leave. 'Aladdin' performed in Mistley.
1935	June–August: two months' leave.
1936	April–August: four months' home leave.

	September: officiating, then temporary AQMG.
	Reconstruction, Quetta.
1937	June: left India on SS Mongolia.
	Took up residence in Barford St Michael, Oxon.
	Retired from Indian Army.
1938	Entered Ripon Hall Theological College, Oxford.
	Ordained by Bishop Barnes of Birmingham.
	Appointed Curate of St Chad's, Sutton Coldfield.
1940	Chaplain at RAF Kirkham until September 1945.
1941	3 July: Dick born, Lytham St Anne's.
1944	Appointed Rector of Lawford, Essex.
1945	September: took up Incumbency at Lawford.
1955	January–March: stayed with Minto Strover and family at Bindura, Southern Rhodesia.
1958	Retired from Lawford and moved to Mistley Wood.
1962	24 December: died at Mistley Wood.

1

EARLY YEARS

Ernest James Strover (Puck, as he was later known) was born in Bath on 23 May 1885, the son of Major-General Henry Strover and Annie Gordon Nevill Strover (*née* Roberts). He was the youngest of the family which lived at 2, Springfield Place, Bath. They were a very happy family living near the top of Lansdown, overlooking Bath from a height of 800 ft, and consisted of his father, a retired General, his mother, his eldest brother Harry born in 1876, his sister Nancy born in 1880, Martyn born in 1882, Arthur born in 1883 and himself.

Puck's father was much interested in philanthropy and walked down to and up from Bath two or three times a week. Most of his kind, who had retired to the 'Queen of Cities', lived in Pulteney Street, the Royal Crescent, Circus or Gay Street, so well known in Jane Austen's books. As they had no conveyance the children had to accustom their small legs to climbing up some very steep roads and paths. If there were several of them together they were allowed to climb by Jacob's ladder through woods and over rocks which were considered by their parents to be dangerous and reputed, according to their nurse, to be haunted by lions. His father was also Church warden of St Stephen's Church and Governor of the

Royal School for Officers' Daughters. Puck admitted to having never really known him and looked on him with great respect and awe and did not remember even going into his study.

His mother, on the other hand, was the most human of creatures. They all loved her. Puck knew that he loved her and understood her better than anyone else. She was very artistic. She played the piano, the organ in the church when she could and the

Mrs Annie Gordon Nevill Strover (*née* Roberts).

violin. She painted beautifully, and in the summer she often went off for the day with the Ladies' Painting Society to paint the lovely scenery around Bath. She also belonged to the Ladies' Archery Society. In the winter she used to speak in the Ladies' Debating Society in Bath.

The routine of the day was imprinted on Puck's memory. After breakfast in the nursery their nurse, Jane, hurried them down to the dining room to which the cook, the housemaid, the parlourmaid and the gardener trooped in. Their father read prayers; then their governess arrived. They didn't like her much but she taught them well. In the afternoon Jane took them for a walk. The eldest brother, Harry, was much older than the rest of them and was always away at school or university and had his own friends in the holidays.

The children had a garden to play in and also a large field which belonged to their father and two other retired generals. In it they made a tennis court, croquet ground and a cricket pitch.

Major General Henry Strover, RA.

That grew and finally became the Lansdown Tennis Club with six courts, and Puck felt, like the other children, that they were being pushed out. However, their father stipulated that they could play in a part of it and special days were reserved for children. Every year they had 'children's sports' and marked the ground out with flags, string, stakes, hurdles and obstacles. They begged prizes from the grown-ups and brought in all the children of their acquaintance. Weeks were spent in preparation, but their parents were always rather ashamed that they took all the first prizes, after they had asked their friends for them. But, as they explained, it was only because they had gone into training, denying themselves sweets and puddings and going for runs before breakfast.

In the winter evenings their mother gave them three choices: they could play cards, make or listen to music or make a wool rug while she read a story from 'Rider Haggard' to them. Nancy and Arthur liked cards; Martyn and Ernest liked the story and rug-making. They were supposed to have it alternately but their mother read so beautifully and 'Rider Haggard' was so exciting that the story usually prevailed. Sadly, music was often left out, although they all enjoyed it but, except for Nancy, did not play. As their mother, and sometimes their father, told them first-hand and thrilling stories about India and Burma, India became their Mecca and it is, perhaps, not surprising that three of them spent many years out there.

For two years they produced every month a magazine entitled 'The Monthly Packet'. One of the brothers, Martyn, illustrated it but they all subscribed with stories or poetry. On the first day of the month it was wrapped up and addressed to their mother, an old stamp put on and placed in the letter box of the front door with a postman's knock. Then one of them burst into the drawing room with the glad news that 'The Monthly Packet' had arrived. With genuine joy, but pretended wonder as to whom the nom-de-plumes represented, their mother read and re-read it with great praise and admiration. There was no apparent enthusiasm on the part of their father who criticised it freely and even corrected the spelling, which they all thought to be very bad form.

One edition of 'The Monthly Packet' in 1898, preserved to this day, contained a 'nonsense rhyme by E.J. Strover', aged 13 years:

> There once was a man of Bristol
> who attacked a house with a pistol
> he took all the gold
> and the silver so old
> and an ornament made of crystal.

Other contributions were a serial story by W.D. St Tudor (Harry), a serial story by C.G. Ross, Riddles and Answers and a prize competition.

The 'Packet' became the 'Wanderer' after the family went their separate ways and the Christmas edition of 1906 contained newsy and topical articles: 'The Duke of York's visit to Gibraltar' by Swallow (Martyn); 'Manners of the Present day' by Black Swan (Mother); 'A Junior Pro' by Wilfred Tudor (Harry, by then a practising doctor); 'A duologue in one Act' by Cyril Ross; and 'Saturday on manoeuvres in Baluchistan' by Swallow (Martyn, by then stationed in India).

Their father believed in discipline. Every morning, after prayers, Nancy had to practise scales on the piano for an hour and father's study was next door so that if she stopped he came in to ask the reason. Her playing became so automatic that she put a book up on the music stand and read it while she played. Puck only remembered one beating from his father and that was when Martyn and he got hold of their father's and grandfather's swords and fought a duel on the lawn. A letter from his wife to Martyn in 1905 describes him as 'a quiet man who tended to slide into the background in society rather than be forthcoming – strange in a Major-General – but who had a few close friends'.

The chief entertainment in the house was a 'Drum' which in the nineties in Bath corresponded to a modern cocktail party. Not only each sitting room but also at least two bedrooms were made to accommodate guests, the beds being made into divans. The largest room was filled with chairs and the guests listened to music. The dining room, which was most popular, was jammed with guests, the tables groaning with food. A few of the most charming guests found their way up to the nursery in which Puck and his brother, who were considered to be too young to join the crowd, were playing with soldiers and a fort which blew up by a spring. When the fort blew up one beautiful lady collapsed on the floor and fainted, to their enormous delight. She acted so well that her husband had to get some water from the night nursery and sprinkle it over her. The best part of the 'Drum' for them was the food which was left over. But Puck remembered the beautiful dresses of the ladies with their bustles and the men in their morning coats, frock coats and top hats. As they looked out of the nursery window, at the end of the evening, the coachmen drove up the carriages to the front door and the gay, courtly, happy crowd disappeared down the hill, the horses' quarters hunched beneath them and the coachmen undoubtedly praying that their brakes would hold.

Sometimes they went out for the day in a 'brake' – a large conveyance holding the whole family and friends and picnic baskets. Their father was too busy to come with them, but their mother who inspired it, loved the 'expeditions', as she called them. Having arrived at some beautiful spot with a panoramic view, she would say: 'Isn't it lovely?' and sit down and paint while the children spent hours playing rounders. Then an enormous, luscious meal was consumed before making their way home, singing songs and roundelays.

Every Christmas they acted a play in the drawing room for the benefit of a large number of guests. Their mother produced the play, dressed them, painted the scenery, issued the invitations and made them act whether they could or not. She had a small stage and footlights made in the drawing room and often played the piano softly in the background. Their father looked upon the whole thing as an intense bore, his study being converted into a green room. The invited guests were then entertained to refreshments in the dining room. It was a good way to entertain them but Puck suspected that the family enjoyed it more than they did. Later on they held performances on two nights in order to get all their guests in.

Their mother, although enjoying life to the full was becoming anxious about the education of the three younger boys. They were at a good Preparatory School and would normally go on to Bath College. But Bath College was not really a Public School and not a very high standard of education. Furthermore it had proved to be too far a distance away from home for Harry to walk every day. Their father could not bear the thought of leaving Bath, could not afford to send them away to a boarding school and considered Bath College good enough. Destiny, supported by their mother's determination won. In 1896 Martyn won the Mathematical Scholarship at Tonbridge School, Kent. It had a very good reputation at that time and was well endowed so that day-boys were educated at very little expense. Their mother's wishes eventually prevailed; father sold the house and rented a house in Tonbridge, to which they all moved. It was a great sacrifice for their parents, especially their father who hated doing it. He had left all his interests and his friends behind him in Bath, and was bored and unable to adjust.

They continued family life there as usual. They were a very games-playing family and made most of their friends with those who played the same games. Cycling was the fashion of the time. They had all saved up Christmas and birthday presents from Godparents and, by the insistence of their father, some of their weekly pocket money in the Savings bank, and they bought their own bicycles. Family and friends rode round the beautiful villages of Kent.

In 1898 their father suddenly fell down dead. It was a tremendous blow for their mother. She was left with three boys to educate and the fourth, Harry, not yet through University, and a very small income. She rose to it with wonderful fortitude. They moved into a small house with one servant and their mother had to cook and do housework for the first time in her life. The years told on her physically but, spiritually, she seemed to gather strength. In spite of the hard times they used to hire a boat frequently and their mother loved being rowed up into secret bits beyond the distance of ordinary boaters and to come hurtling down stream with the river in full flood. She took all sorts of risks and enjoyed them as much as they did, just as in earlier days when they all went for a ride she always arranged to hire a horse that bucked. Even later when confined to a wheel-chair she let them tow her on their cycles tearing round the country at breakneck speed compared with other forms of travel before a car was known. Puck remembered one day on the river she had taken letters to read at leisure and she opened one to learn that a distant connection had died and money which had been left to their father's mother at last came to them. It made a huge difference and they promptly moved into a bigger house and got a resident maid. Within a year Harry was practising as a doctor and Martyn had passed into Woolwich. But another blow shook their mother to an extent from which she never recovered. Arthur, who was training to become an engineer, had appendicitis. Nowadays it would be an easy operation, but at that time the doctors did nothing. It turned to peritonitis and he died in great pain.

Puck's ambition from an early age had been to join the Army. Not only his father but also his grandfather had been a

General and the brother who was closest to him, Martyn, was also destined to become a soldier. It was a huge disappointment to him therefore that on leaving school he failed the medical for entry into Sandhurst, after passing in on academic grounds.. His mother had hopes of him being ordained and sent him to Selwyn College, Cambridge in 1904 where he read Mathematics. She left Tonbridge and went to live with Harry in West Hartlepool where he was building up a successful practice.

Puck had a very happy time at Cambridge but enjoyed himself too much and did not work very hard. He felt very much drawn to being a clergyman but also felt that he was not good enough. The family Army tradition was strong and Martyn, coming home on leave, made him long for the profession of Arms. Besides, it seemed to him, as to most young Englishmen at that time, that the British Empire was a wonderful thing to live for. He fed his mind on Kipling and decided that he must go out to India and rule Indians as his forefathers had done. His mother was disappointed but backed him up loyally. In the summer vacation the two of them used to take rooms in a village on the Moors. She would

Selwyn undergraduates. Puck, second left.

The Selwyn second eight crew. Puck seated at left.

paint and he worked at his books. She was by then very delicate and bought a trailer to go on the back of his bicycle so that he was able to take her around the beautiful countryside. They often stayed with her brother-in-law William Brown who had a lovely place, Awncliffe Hall at Mount Grace in Yorkshire. Later he sold it and bought a house in Thirsk.

Puck's mother wrote :

> He is trying to work two hours each morning but I fear that he is not very keen on it, and says that he is no mathematician. But I do hope he works at college, though I wonder very much that he passed his 'Littlego' the first term as I hear it is very hard thing to do and heaps fail. There seems to be so much amusement at at Cambridge I hardly know how they manage to do any work.

Much of his time was taken up by rowing. He held the champion cup for sculls in 1906 and rowed in the College second eight which,

Cambridge University Rifle Volunteers at summer camp on Salisbury Plain. Puck seated at right.

in his last year, secured six bumps in May Week. Undoubtedly the exercise improved his health. Having arrived in Cambridge with a diagnosed weak heart he was proving that this so-called condition did not preclude strenuous exercise on the river.

Then in his last year, the blow fell. His mother died, completely worn out. Her magnificent spirit, fortified by her strong faith, maintained her frail body unto the end of her work. They had been very close and he felt her loss deeply. Furthermore he suddenly realised that he had to stand on his own two feet with very little money, with a degree to get, with Army examinations to pass in addition and, biggest hurdle of all, a medical board which had failed him three years before. He was a corporal in the Cambridge University Volunteer Corps and had to get a good recommendation from them. He worked as he had never worked in his life before. Within eight months he got his degree, passed the Army exams and had been promoted to Second Lieutenant.

But the biggest hurdle was still to come: the Army medical board, which had failed him three years before on account of an enlarged and weakened heart. His exertions on the river clearly had paid off, for after a very rigorous examination and despite all the information on his previous failure before the board, the President said 'Well if you die within a year after you go to India, I'll make it hot for you when we meet again.' He was jubilant and sent a cable out to Martyn in India.

2

THE YOUNG SUBALTERN

Puck landed in Bombay in March 1908 and immediately joined the 1st Sherwood Foresters in Bangalore on the unattached list (for Indian Army) as Second Lieutenant. His first assignment was to learn Hindustani and by October of that year he had passed Parts I and II of the language and that enabled him to qualify for attachment to an Indian Army regiment. He described his fellow officers as being 'very pleasant but too much addicted to spit and polish and drill for my liking and without any training in Mountain Warfare, which was necessary to guard the NW Frontier, surely the first job of the army'. Stationed in Agra was a British Cavalry Regiment, the 14th Hussars. It was commanded by Lieutenant-Colonel Brown-Synge-Hutcheson VC who was a cousin of his uncle Willie Brown. He described him as:

A typical and very good-looking cavalry officer, a very good commanding officer and a bachelor who arranged to put me through a riding school which was very tough and nearly killed me but taught me to ride. I was much tempted to apply for Indian Cavalry but did not feel that I could afford it. Furthermore I felt that, delightful as the life of the Indian Calvary was in peace time, in war their days were numbered. What could horses do against machine guns? What use were they on the frontier? For fighting they were most vulnerable and useless. For reconnaissance the future was in the air. I remember in a lecture to officers on reconnaissance the lecturer said that the Observer, who had to sit on the petrol tank behind the pilot and hold onto a strut would squeeze the strut so hard from fright that he would squeeze the wood into pulp. Nearly everyone threw scorn at air reconnaissance because aeroengines failed so often, but I determined, on my first leave home, to learn to fly.

So he applied for Indian infantry in the Northern Army. After his first year with the Foresters his CO reported: 'He has initiative, energy and self-reliance, is of active habits and fond of sport, and is well up to the standard of his rank professionally. In my opinion the retention in service of 2nd Lt. E.J. Strover, unattached list IA, is in every respect desirable and likely to be advantageous to the Army.'

Very soon after this he went down with enteric fever and was certified temporarily unfit. As soon as he had recovered from his illness in August 1909 Puck was posted to his first Indian Army Regiment 3rd Brahmans, stationed in Agra as a Double-Company Officer, and arrived there with the temperature at well over 100 degrees in the shade. He felt 'the heat, the smells, the interest and excitement – real India'. He wrote:

The Brahmans were the highest caste of Hindu, the priest caste though the men were not priests, but all of them land-owners from the country around Delhi and Agra. As there were only two regiments of Brahmans we were able to pick and choose and their average height was over 6 ft. They had beautiful features like Greek gods, broad shoulders tapering down to small hips and long legs. Some had beards and whiskers which they rolled neatly round a loop of string. They made fine soldiers but their religious customs were a nuisance. For instance each man cooked his own midday meal every day. Having washed and taken off most of his clothes he drew a circle round himself and built a small clay oven. He could not go outside that circle until he had cooked and eaten his food. No man could be enlisted unless he had at least one rotiar, a near-relation who was allowed to cook his food. They promised that, in war, they would cook and feed together but we were told by Army Headquarters not to force them because of political repercussions, the Brahmans being the highest caste and having great influence in India. There were four double-companies, each commanded by a British Major or Captain, with a British Lieutenant as his 2 i/c. Each company was commanded by an Indian Officer, a Subedar, with a junior Indian officer, a Jemedar, as his 2 i/c. My Subedar was the finest looking man I have ever seen. He was 6ft 4ins and I was glad to ride a horse on parade because it was embarrassing to give orders to a man who towered above me. Twenty-four years of serving under British officers had enabled him to understand completely the British sense of humour. I found him therefore easy to get on with although it was nearly a year before I had mastered their language.

Puck felt that he was of very little use because he could not yet speak the language. As the commands for drill were all in English he concentrated on drill until they were all bored with it but, at least, they became very smart and proud of themselves. He would never get to know the Indian officers until he could talk with them, and his Company Commander told him that they would never give their trust and loyalty to him until he could speak their language well so, during the very hot weather a 'Munshi' or teacher came to his bungalow in the afternoons to teach Hindustani. It was 112 degrees in the shade and they sat under a punkah, pulled by a punkah-wallah sitting outside on the verandah with the end of the string tied round his big toe. His Munshi was a fascinating old man with a fund of Indian and Persian stories and a big English vocabulary – a strange mixture of classical English and slang. The other essential, he was informed, was two polo ponies. He pleaded poverty and was advised to start with one, not necessarily a fast and expensive one but one easy to hit a ball from. Having acquired one he spent hours on its back hitting the ball from all angles. By the end of 1909 he had been promoted full Lieutenant and his CO reported: 'Has been with the Regiment a few months only – keen and works hard and I consider him a promising young officer, he is a good rider and plays polo.' During the following three months he went on an intensive language course while the regiment was in Meerut and passed Hindustani Higher Standard Pts I and II, Hindi obligatory and Persian Lower Standard.

All British officers were mounted which made life much more pleasant in peace time and enabled them to do wide reconnaissance in war. Half of them were on leave when he arrived and he sometimes had to command a double company when the British commander was taken for duties outside the regiment. His Company Commander had just returned from famine relief work in South India and told him the most heart-rending accounts of the starvation there owing to the failure of the monsoon. He had brought up supplies of food all through the hot weather, working day and night, but did not appear to be any the worse for it.

Regimental life continued. Every Saturday morning at 12 noon the regiment assembled round the open space outside the Orderly Room for the weekly Durbar. The Colonel sat in a chair under a tree, supported by all the British and Indian officers sitting behind him, while the remainder of the regiment squatted on the ground. The prisoners were brought before him and the Colonel, who had disciplinary powers much greater than that of a British Regiment, tried each case. Then came the 'Azzis' or complaints which any man could bring forward. As nearly all the men were landowners these were mostly concerned with land disputes which were difficult for them to deal with when they were away with the regiment. The Colonel heard each one patiently, sometimes gave advice and usually gave orders to a clerk to prepare an 'Azzi' to be sent to the Deputy Commissioner. The Durbars were well worth the two hours spent on them; they did an incalculable amount of good to the happiness and contentment of the regiment, its discipline and the good feeling between British officers, Indian officers and the men. It was in accordance with the long-treasured customs of the people of India. After the First World War it was discontinued mainly because of the lack of knowledge by post-war officers of the language and customs of the Indian people and the time taken up by the Durbar. Thus the Indian Army and all the fighting races of India suffered in consequence. The spirit of the regiment was wonderful: the mutual trust between British and Indian officers, the amazing keenness and loyalty. A favourite way for sepoys to amuse themselves in their free time was for a group to go off to the parade ground and drill each other for two or three hours.

On his first spell of leave Puck went up to stay with his brother Martyn who was with a mountain battery at Jutogh in the Simla hills, 7,000 ft above sea level. He wrote:

It was wonderful to feel and breathe the cool air and see the green everywhere with English wild roses, bird's eye, campion, aster and many others covering the banks by the road. The five officers of my brother's battery were all picked. One was Dowding, afterwards Lord Dowding who organised and commanded the Fighter Squadrons in the Battle of Britain. The men were big, strong and active. I was allowed to go with them during their training. It was delightful to see how the mules with their guns got up these rocky, precipitous hills and down with men helping them by holding on to their tails. The speed with which they assembled the guns and got into action and the accuracy of their fire made me feel as Kipling says of the enemy 'can't get away from the guns'. But they always had to be on a war footing in case of a raid by Pathans.

When I got back to the Regiment the monsoon had broken and the heavy rains had flooded the country, but the temperature had come right down. The rains played havoc with the mud-built houses in the villages and many a man brought me a telegram from his village: 'house fallen down, please come'. I got leave for as many as possible. Once the rains had ceased the Colonel came back from his leave home and we got down to the rifle ranges to teach the sepoys how to shoot accurately. He was very popular with the regiment and with the other regiments and civilians in Agra but I had often heard it said of him, outside the regiment, that he went home every year in the summer, came out in the winter for the shooting and used the regiment as beaters. When I first met him I was trying to make the men hit the target at 1000 yds. He shook hands and was charming and very good-looking with a big moustache. He watched the men missing the target and very pleased with themselves if they hit at all. His only remark was: 'Give me a rifle'. He lay down and fired one shot which hit the target low right. He then put in five bulls-eyes. The men gasped. He said: 'Do that', and walked away. I have never forgotten this lesson of 'example being better than precept'; it undoubtedly raised the standard of shooting in the regiment. His policy was that in war infantry must be able to march and shoot. This was in line with 'Kitchener's Test' for every regiment, which consisted of a march of fifteen miles followed by an attack over two miles on a position covered with targets and iron plates using live ammunition.

Puck with his polo ponies Pat and Silent Meg.

The Young Subaltern

The next week he ordered the 15 mile march. Every British officer was mounted, the Colonel on a beautiful Arab, but as soon as the march began he dismounted and walked at the head of the column. The adjutant felt that he had to do the same. I was determined to follow his example and some of the other officers also dismounted, but the Majors and senior Captains remained mounted because they knew they were unable to walk the whole way. It was very rare for a man to fall out and then only from genuine illness. It was a lovely cold and crisp morning and I thoroughly enjoyed walking with my Brahman Subedar discussing Hinduism and the Mahabarath and Indian customs. We marched at four miles an hour for ten miles to one of the lakes (jheels) of which there were plenty in the country. There we halted and the men ate their haversack rations and drank their water. For the officers, breakfast was ready, a large white tablecloth spread out under a tree, and the mess sergeant had sausages, bacon and eggs sizzling. Then we marched home through new country. I must have been very fit because I usually played polo in the afternoon.

3

SPORT AND SOCIAL LIFE

Polo gave Puck many friends. Most men in Agra kept one or two polo ponies and as they nearly all had the same speed every one had fun. Furthermore they all got to know each other very well. There was no British Cavalry Regiment there. Much as he liked the British Cavalry he felt that they had ruined polo in India. Not content with Arabs, country-breds and even Australian walers, they brought out thoroughbred English ponies at enormous expense, and no one else could get near them.

They played polo on three afternoons a week. On the other three afternoons they played hockey with the men. The Colonel was very keen on polo and encouraged and helped him to buy good ponies, lending him money from the officers' Loan Fund. Being anxious to get the best, he bided his time. Opening the 'Pioneer' one morning at breakfast he saw that the son of the Begum of Bhopal was giving up polo on medical advice and was selling his three Arab ponies. The matter was of the most supreme urgency to buy them before others came to the scene. The Colonel gave Puck and another officer, Whitamore, a week's leave and told them to buy a couple of ponies for him. On arrival at Bhopal they were met by a guilded coach drawn by four Arabs with postilions and outriders with spears. The crowds in the streets appeared to enjoy the spectacle and they were cheered on their way until they arrived at the Guest House which was luxuriously furnished and equipped with electric light and fans. The Prime Minister called on them and said that all the ponies would be on the polo ground after tea for them to try. He hoped that they would stay for a few days and he would show them all the improvements which had been made in the last few years. When they reached the polo ground the sight which met their eyes would have gladdened the heart of any horse lover. Twenty-four Arabs, greys, chestnuts and blacks, each saddled and bridled, with polo sticks and balls were waiting for them to try. After long inspection Puck selected a big grey with strong, long quarters, short back and sloping shoulder named 'Romani'. He was the best ride he had ever had, very fast and perfectly trained. They each rode all the ponies several times before they made their decisions. It took three days.

One afternoon they were taken round the town by the Prime Minister in the gilt coach. He proudly showed them the dam which had formed a big lake sufficient to irrigate a very large area, the new tarmac road and the electric plants which lit up the Palace and the chief buildings. On the second day he informed them that the Begum would like to see them. He explained that, although the Begum would see them, they could not see the Begum because she would be in purdah. The Sovereign of Bhopal is always a woman and she was then in purdah although she emancipated herself later on. The Prime Minister escorted them through the palace guards over soft carpets to an inner sanctuary where, from behind a curtain, a charming feminine voice greeted them and hoped that they were comfortable and had been shown all that they wanted to see. They thanked her for her hospitality and she told them what a blow it was to her son to have to give up polo which he loved so much. Puck congratulated her on the modern improvements to her State which obviously pleased her very much and she said that they must meet the British engineer who was responsible.

They left Bhopal with the ten best ponies. Two Indian Cavalry officers arrived as they left and were not very pleased to find that they had skimmed the cream. The 3rd Brahmans, although an Infantry regiment, was now as well mounted as most Cavalry regiments and they started to practise for the tournaments. With the Colonel so keen it was not difficult to get time to practise.

Agra was a small station with a garrison of two regiments and a Field Artillery Battery, a Commissioner, Public Works Officer, Police Superintendent and a Banker. There was great excitement when thirteen English girls arrived for the winter season, at a time when a white girl was a rarity. The station woke up socially and the wives organised dances, parties, moon-light picnics and even mixed cricket matches. With some difficulty Puck broke in two of his ponies into a trap and bought a second-hand but third-rate trap which he had painted with bright colours. He drove it down to the polo ground and remembered, more than forty years afterwards, the Colonel's fury: 'What the hell have you bought this trap for? Poodlefaking! I know; Poodlefaking!!' repeating the word with the utmost contempt, red in the face and addressing everyone within earshot. However, he was forgiven when Romani's speed helped them to win the first round of the tournament.

Puck got a very good horse, cast off from a Cavalry Regiment because of his age and was able to join in the pigsticking. He wrote:

> This was the most exciting sport I have ever known. The first time I joined the Agra Tent Club we started off at 5 a.m. to a meet about 5 or 6 miles down the road. It was bright moonlight and we passed near the Taj Mahal. This, rising from the ground mist looked so beautiful and ethereal that I waited behind the others to drink in this wonderful sight which is rightly known as one of the Wonders of the World. When I caught up with the others dawn was just breaking and they were discussing tactics with the headman of a village who had about thirty beaters.

The country was dotted with areas of long dry grass and, beyond that, an open dry plain stretching for miles but more areas of grass in the distance. The beaters spread out parallel to the road. There were twelve of us mounted with long spears and we divided into three heats of four ahead of the beaters, one heat near the right of the line, one to the left and the third well ahead in the centre. We moved slowly forward in front of the beaters, our heat being on the right of the line. The beaters shouted, hit stiff canes with their sticks and used rattles. After about twenty minutes a 'sounder' (boar, sow and piglets) broke into the open. It is of course the boar, who does damage to the crops and who fights so magnificently, which we attack and never the sow and piglets. We waited until the sounder was well clear of the grass and then the Captain of our heat gave the signal by lifting his spear high in the air. We four galloped as hard as we could. Gough of the Gunners, who had a very fast horse, soon led and I on my eighteen-year-old was well behind. As Gough caught up to the boar he jinked (shot off at right angles) and Gough, whose horse naturally could not turn so quickly at full speed, was left shooting ahead.

Then Hay, an Indian civilian, became the nearest pursuer. As he came up alongside and bent down with his spear in readiness the boar turned into him and attacked his horse's forelegs. Hay caught him with his spear which went right in and, at the same time, pulled up his horse who stood staunch and firm. Then, as I galloped up, I saw the most extraordinary sight: the boar literally drove his way through the spear determined to get at the horse with his huge tusks. Hay still held him off, leaning down lower and lower until his hand was within a few inches of the pig's head. In this perilous predicament Hay said in an extra slow and rather bored voice: 'Somebody come and give him a dig'. Gough was the first and got his spear into the boar's heart which collapsed, dead. I was the last to arrive, too late to be of any use. This picture remains in my memory as my first experience. The beaters came up delighted. These Hindus love pork when the boar is wild, and they cut out the 'tushes' (tusks) as a trophy for the Sahibs.

It was the most exciting sport I had ever known. It had the element of danger because, if the boar cut the horse's legs and felled the horse, as sometimes happened, he would attack the rider on the ground and cut him badly with his large 'tushes'. Once a boar is involved in a fight he will not stop until he has killed his opponent or been killed himself. It needs quickness of eye and steadiness of hand and arm and great nerve and judgement of speed.

Another excitement was the arrival for three days of the Crown Prince of Germany and his large staff in magnificent uniforms. They liked the Crown Prince: he played polo with them and constantly missed the ball, calling out, 'Ach I am so bad.' They were sorry to hear that afterwards he earned for himself a bad name by chasing an Indian Princess. At a dinner given in his honour one of his staff who sat next to Puck said, 'I am amazed at the way in which you English hold India. I go to a place where there are ten million Indians and find three Englishmen who are governing them and no troops. If Germany held India we would need ten times as many troops as you have.' Puck couldn't help saying, 'Perhaps for that reason you will not try to take India.' The German laughed and said, 'We do not want to fight England – never.'

Even then in 1910 the war clouds were beginning to appear and quite suddenly the regiment was ordered to Singapore, much to their sorrow. All reports said it was a small island, devoted to commerce and no polo, so they sold all their ponies. It was with a sickening feeling of despair that he parted with Romani, although he sold him for more than double his cost to one of the best cavalry teams. He had never met his like. He was faster than any pony he had met on any ground and yet he could play him on slow chukkas without touching the reins. He used to follow Puck round and once put his head into the mess dining room on a guest night.

After they had sold everything they received orders that their departure was delayed for six months. Whitamore and Puck got two months leave to Kashmir. They took the train to Rawalpindi and then hired two tongas, a small two-wheeled cart pulled by two horses, to take them and their light kit up to Srinagar. The driver sat on the front seat and they sat behind, facing the rear. Every few miles the ponies were changed. They drove for about six hours and then stayed for the night at a Dak bungalow. As they climbed up to above 3,000 ft the air became beautifully cool, the hedges full of dog roses. The road wound the river Jhelum and in the evenings, when they halted, they promptly went down to the river to fish for mahseer (a large salmon with a hard mouth).

On arrival at Srinagar they had a houseboat waiting for them and were joined by 'Mac' who had gone ahead. Then in the utmost comfort and leisure they were punted and paddled down the river by skilled boatmen. Spreading on either side of the Jhelum were fields of long grass covered with blue irises. Beyond them the mountains, clothed in dark pine forests and topped with snow, cut like cameos against the blue sky. Puck amused himself by sketching (for private, not public benefit!). On the way they lunched with their Colonel and his wife at a lovely spot named the Nassim Bagh (beautiful garden). They admired the scene and the Colonel said: 'Yes, but I can't spend all day admiring the view. I've hooked a few fish but there is nothing else to do.' They said that they were off to shoot bear and he said he would love to join them but could not leave his wife. Much as they liked his wife they felt that marriage was a terrific 'thorn-bit'. After three days they crossed the Wuln lake by night. In the middle of the night the boatmen began to shout and rush about the deck. Puck went outside to enquire the reason and they shouted that a storm was brewing. They pulled up the planks at the bottom of the houseboat and extracted from the bottom large boulders which were presumably the ballast. Over these they fastened ropes and threw them into the water, making fast the ends of the ropes to the houseboat or holding them in their hands, thus making primitive anchors. They soon found how right the boatmen were. The storm struck them in a deluge and the waves rocked them until their beds and tables were thrown from side to side. The wind catching the house part of the boat would have capsized it but for these boatmen, soaked through and hanging on grimly throughout the night.

At dawn the storm ceased as suddenly as it had begun. The boulders were replaced and they proceeded slowly with the tired men to the other side. As they approached the shore they saw twelve ponies and an equal number of natives who appeared to be of a different race. They all wore beards and thick homespun clothes. These men had been sent for in advance to take them up into the mountains. They each had four ponies and men: one man was the 'Shikari', or huntsman, one the cook, the third looked after four ponies and the fourth was the shoe maker The shoes were made of twisted grass. They were very light and gave them a secure grip on rocks and hard snow. They only lasted two days. All four helped the ponies up and down the steep places and pitched the camp. Puck took over his four men and ponies who packed his kit and a '450 high velocity' rifle which gave the Shikari great joy. His Shikari had a face like a hawk. He said that he was the seventh generation of Shikaris, and Puck liked him at once for his efficiency and lack of subservience.

They started at once for the Traubal Pass (14,000 ft), the Walia lake being 5,000 ft. As they were unaccustomed to climbing and had been sitting in tongas and houseboats it was a very stiff ordeal the first day. The Shikaris, however, insisted that they must camp that night at 9,000 ft, so they pushed along slowly and steadily. Puck felt, perhaps, it was his early training in Bath, that he did not get as exhausted as Whitamore and 'Mac'. They had to halt often while they rested. Suddenly they reached the snow line and pelted each other with snowballs. From there to their camp was an exhausting climb, but they camped at last, clearing the snow for their tents. Puck remembered waking up the next morning to see 'Haramokh' with its square head floating above the clouds and all the snow turning pink with the sunrise. All that day they climbed and finally camped on the other side of the pass with a long valley opening out below them and the river shooting down in rapids and cascades. The Shikaris asked them to decide which mullahs (valleys) they wished to shoot in. The shooting rights were simple; the first to camp at the bottom of a mullah has the shooting rights of the mullah as long as he is in it. There were two mullahs to choose from: Bara Gagai which was 14 miles long with ample room for two guns and Chota Gagai, only 6 miles long for one gun. They tossed for them. Whitamore and 'Mac' went to Bara Gagai and Puck went to Chota Gagai. So they parted and were not to meet for a month

Puck wrote:

I felt very light-hearted and full of enthusiasm as I trekked off with my four men and ponies. My Shikari was very happy because, he said, we had the best mullah. We crossed the river and headed down the valley for four hours until we came to a mountain stream, a tributary winding down from snowy heights to the North. This was our mullah and at the entrance it was very beautiful, with many grassy slopes, forget-me-nots, starwort, anemones and gentian. Deciduous trees gave us shade as we ate our lunch. Then up and following the stream until deciduous trees once again gave place to pine woods. Here we camped knowing that the shooting rights of the mullah were ours.

Next day we left the camp and the ponies in charge of one man and climbed the mullah, two men carrying our stores and three small bivouac tents. As we climbed we found that the summer thaw had left bridges of hard snow over the stream which we were able to cross in safety. They all became hard snow again with an occasional patch of grass and a few rather stunted pine trees. We halted on a fairly level sheltered spot beneath some rocks. Leaving the two men to clear the snow, pitch the tents and cook a meal, my Shikari and I went forward. Although I was carrying a heavy rifle I found that my grass shoes gripped the hard snow perfectly. The mullah became rather precipitous and the Shikari asked me to be very careful. Steadily we climbed a peak near the summit and here I scanned the country with my field glasses. All I could see was snow and rocks and pine forests and it did not seem that any game could find any means of subsistence at this height. Suddenly the Shikari gripped my knee. He pointed below and, about half a mile away some animal was crossing the snow. He said: 'After me Sahib' and immediately tobogganed down the steep slope of the hill on his behind, hitting a snow drift at the bottom. I followed expecting a jagged point of rock at any second. Struggling out of the snow drift I followed him up a small mullah, over a ridge and down again. Then we climbed another steep slope, the Shikari whispering 'Quickly, Sahib'. At the top of this we lay beneath a knife-edge and, slowly lifting our heads, saw a magnificent red bear about 50 yards below us, scratching at the snow. As he could not see us I waited to get my breath and then fired. He fell over and over, finally pulling up and galloped into the fringe of small trees. As it was getting dark and I had been warned of the danger of following up wounded red bear, we decided to return to our bivouac.

Next morning, at first light, we went to the place in which he had disappeared. My Shikari began to track. At first there were marks in the snow but later we came to a rocky surface. This was revelation to me. He would show a pellet of mud or a drop of blood, an occasional foot mark or a broken twig. After two hours we found him dead. He was a very fine specimen – the biggest of the year. I did not want to shoot another red bear and the chances of seeing another were very small as they are becoming rare, so we left our own mullah and went back over the Tragbal pass to the valleys overlooking the Waiar lake, where black bears are to be found. This was the most lovely park-like country. I pitched my camp in a broad green valley with trees of mulberries, a stream winding its way through the banks of wild flowers. In the evening my Shikari and I climbed the hills and, with a full moon, searched for black bear which often climbed the mulberry trees for the fruit. We paused under one large tree and my Shikari whispered that a bear was in the branches. I could hear the grunts above me and could see a vague black mass. It was an exciting moment. I fired into the middle of this blackness, heard a roar, and the bear fell almost at my feet, but immediately rushed down the hillside. I confess that I felt some relief because he could easily have despatched me. I told the Shikari that we must finish the bear off as he was obviously wounded. We got back to the camp in the early light of the dawn and I called for breakfast. As I was enjoying my poached eggs a young Kashmiri came running down the hill and shouting 'Baloo, baloo'. He explained that there was a large black bear in the jungle at the foot of the hill, half a mile away. Seizing my rifle and cartridges I called to the Shikari and three boys to follow me. On reaching the place I saw a large flat-topped rock at the lower end of the patch of jungle. I climbed this and directed the five men to throw stones into the jungle above me. After a very short time there was a 'woof-woof' and the bear came out going hard up the hill to my left. It was too far for a shot and I followed him as hard as I could, calling to the men to come with me. On reaching the ridge I saw him disappearing into a thick wood in the next valley. I sent the men to the top again to throw stones, but the bear would not come out. I, therefore, decided that I must go in. I took the Shikari in although his only weapon was a stout stick, but his quick eyes would be invaluable. We crept slowly through until we came to a clearing. Here, with my rifle at the ready, I scanned the black rocks above me, when the Shikari suddenly called out 'Sahib'. Whisking round I saw the bear on its hind legs and arms outstretched within a few feet. I could not miss and killed it with a single shot. It had a wound in its side and was obviously the same bear which I had encountered before.

The next day two men came to see me from a village a few miles away to beg me to shoot a black bear which had been making depredations in their village. They said that it had killed a woman and several goats. Telling my men to strike camp and follow me I went off with these villagers until I came to a fair sized village. The men knew where the bear usually hid during the day and I asked for volunteers to drive the bear towards me. There was no need, because the whole village turned out, including all the small boys armed with sticks. I impressed on them the necessity for silence until they had got round the bear and the drive commenced, told them where I would stand, and left the rest to them, leaving my Shikari with them to organise the beat. I waited for an hour until I heard the beat begin and then hid under the shadow of a rock, remaining motionless. After a short time I saw a large bear coming straight towards me. I waited until he was passing close to me and then killed him with one shot. When the villagers came up they belaboured the body with sticks until I stopped them. They then slung it on a pole and brought it into the village chanting a song. The villagers told me that there was a Sahib in the next valley. As I had not seen a white man or spoken English for nearly a month I went to see him. He was a large, delightful gunner named Twistleton-Wykeham-Fiennes. He told me that he had been in Kashmir on leave four years running and had not shot a bear. With one red and two black bears I felt that I was indeed fortunate.

Time was running out and Puck had only three days left to meet his friends on the Woolar lake, so he moved fast, over lovely country, stopping only to camp when he came to a village. He sensed that these villagers were better off than those in the valley of the river Jhelum, but they had the same story of rapacious Hindu landlords. It was a story of greed, tyranny and extortion. Since then, successive British political officers have done their best to ameliorate the conditions of the Mohammedan peasantry, suffering under the rule of the Maharajah and his nobles and landlords. When India was given self-government, Puck's sympathies were entirely with Pakistan over Kashmir and he was surprised that Pakistan did not go in and take Kashmir, just as Nehru went in and took Hyderabad (a Hindu State ruled by Mohammedans).

On arrival on the shores of the Woolar lake he found the houseboats waiting for them, but the other two, Whitamore and 'Mac' had not arrived. He wallowed in a bath and shaved his beard, which was partly red, and was just enjoying his tea when his friends arrived, also with beards. They had been unlucky and had only seen one bear in the distance and considered that he had been particularly fortunate, though they were very charitable. The luxury of a house-boat after camp and bivouac was delightful and the three grew fat and lazy on the way home. In Srinagar, plague and cholera were raging, so they paid off their men and Puck took his skins to a famous shop to be cured. With great regret he said good-bye to his Shikari whom, he said, frankly wept on departure.

Puck wrote later:

No one who has not been in India can realise the touching affection and loyalty of Indians. It has to be experienced to be believed. I have heard Englishmen say that when an Indian does something for you it is because he expects to get something out of it. That is not so. When I was shot down in France in 1915 and became a prisoner in Germany a Brahman Naik (Corporal) in my regiment sent me two food parcels, each of which must have cost him a month's pay. He certainly never expected to see me again. The stories of the loyalty and self-sacrifice of Indian servants during the Indian Mutiny have often been told.

There is one story which is true but not generally known about the Indian Mutiny. A firm of Indian bankers had promised to deliver a large sum of money by a certain date at a town in the United provinces. On the way the money was captured by mutineers. A young Cavalry officer coming up with a squadron of cavalry scattered

Puck with his three bear skins. Shikari seated right.

45

the mutineers and recaptured the money. The Indian in charge begged the officer to escort him to his destination. He said that the reputation of the firm of bankers depended on it. It was a long detour and the officer had been warned that large numbers of mutineers, far superior in numbers, were between him and that place. Nevertheless he was so touched by the pleading of the Indian that he decided to do it. He fought his way through and delivered the money on the date. A few years later the officer was being married in England and a very valuable present arrived from this firm of bankers. Sons and daughters grew up and always, when they were married, a wedding present mysteriously arrived from the same source.

4

SINGAPORE AND LEARNING TO FLY

The regiment went to Singapore and enjoyed all the freshness and novelty of entirely new surroundings and a new life. Everything there was civilised and luxurious after India, but they soon found that it was no place for soldiering and no place for polo. It was hot and sticky and the men hated it. The officers cheered them up by saying that it was only for two years and kept them busy, but they had no wives or families and no other Indian regiment to compete with. Before they left India they were inspected by the Commander-in-Chief, Sir O'Moore Creagh. He was a thorough Irishman and Puck suspected him of blarney, but he said to the Colonel: 'Shore it's the foinest regiment I've ever seen in my life! After Singapore you can ask me for any station.' They kept his promise in mind.

Puck made many good friends among the civilians, with the Buffs who were stationed alongside them, and with the Navy and the Dutch Navy who were sometimes in harbour. He also made friends with some Germans and liked them very much. They had a magnificent club known as the Teutonia Club; but one night he got a shock. He was at the bar of the club and had to walk through a room in which there was a German dinner

47

party, in order to reach the stables and find his trap. As he walked through the room the Germans were all on their feet with their glasses raised and calling out together: 'Am Tag'. Puck asked one of his German friends what it meant. He was silent and thoughtful. After being pressed he said, 'many Germans think that there will be war in Europe very soon'. That impressed him much and he thought long and deeply on the subject. The worst tragedy for him would be to be left in India or Singapore when England would be fighting in France against Germany. He was due for some home leave and had read with great enthusiasm of the establishment of a civil school of flying on Salisbury Plain and Brooklands. He determined to take his pilot's certificate which would help him to fly in France when war broke out. He told Hutcheson, who was always experimenting with model aeroplanes. They agreed to go together and learn to fly. They sailed in a P&O in March 1911.

On the way out Puck went to the first Air Display at Rheims. He had a letter of introduction to a Frenchman who knew most of the early pilots and showed him their machines and took him up. The French in 1911 were much in advance of England. Their machines were lighter and their engines more reliable. They had already evolved a seaplane known as 'Le Canard' – the duck. Bleriot, who had flown the channel the year before had now a more reliable monoplane, but very light. Puck met two famous English aviators, Graham-White and Sopwith. The French were certain that Germany would invade them in a few years and they realised the value of the Air Arm for reconnaissance. Even they did not then visualise it as an offensive weapon but one 'to see without being seen'. They knew that they would have to fight in the air. They hated and feared the Germans, and regulations were enforced to eliminate German spies as far as possible. Puck just had time to see the awe-inspiring and majestic beauty of Rheims Cathedral. The next time he saw it it was a shell.

Puck took eight months' leave, the first ninety days of which were paid. All his spare cash of £125 he used to pay for his flying course. But before he started on it he spent time with his elder brother Harry and his wife Tickie and their family, and with his Yorkshire cousins at Mount Grace. Apart from Martyn, who was in India, his relatives were dead against him learning to fly. His uncle said that it didn't much matter if he killed himself, but if he was maimed for life he might have to keep him! His cousins tried to marry him off to an heiress instead, but, he wrote, 'I did not think she would want to share my wandering life and, realising my own susceptibility, I slipped off to Salisbury Plain with Hutcheson to start the flying course organised by the Bristol Biplane Society.'

Puck wrote:

Our instructor was a Frenchman called Jullerot. The French were ahead of us in flying and there were only five Englishmen capable of instructing in flying. The machines were Bristol biplanes similar to Maurice Farmans, with an elevator fore and aft, and the engine behind. The instructor sat in front with the joy-stick and rudder and nothing underneath him. The pupil sat behind on the petrol tank, holding onto a spar with his left hand and his right hand over the shoulder of the pilot, feeling the movements of the joy-stick There were no instruments and the speed was judged by the wind in one's face. If the wind died down you knew that the machine was stalling and you promptly put the nose down. Generally, we were advised to keep the front elevator about a foot above the sky-line. We were only allowed in the air when the wind had died down. I enjoyed this flying immensely: it was absorbing in those days when we were all learning together; we knew nothing about air currents and air pockets, of spins and side-slipping and vol-planes. All we knew was that it was very dangerous and fatal to make a bad mistake.

The day arrived when Jullerot said that I could fly by myself. This meant using the rudder for the first time. Jullerot said that, sitting behind him on the petrol tank I was to make two or three landings after which he would get out and I should go on at once. I confess to a feeling of trepidation similar to that before the bumping races at Cambridge, only more acute. It was a perfect early morning and we had the best machine. I took off and made three landings and after the third Jullerot got out and I transferred to his seat, my heart in my mouth. Jullerot merely said, 'voila' and waved his hand on. I let the engine rip and raced over the plain until the wind in my face felt strong enough to lift her. Then off the ground and up and up slowly but surely. A big bump over Stonehenge – there always was and no one ever knew why – steady! I righted her but found myself circling to the left. For the first time I used the rudder, but banking slightly with the ailerons at the same time. Round she came beautifully and I gained confidence. It was the dangerous right-hand turn. In those days the torque of the engine and propeller sent the elevator upwards when one turned to the right, but I had remembered to keep it down.

Now for the left-hand turn – easy. She responded like a sailing boat. I brought her round and headed for home. Must land against the wind. This meant another turn when we were over the hangars. A left-hand turn, I decided, then down and down in a vol-plane. There was no throttle and I had to keep the engine going by switching it on and off. Here's the ground – steady – gradually closer – bump of air – steady again – NOW. I felt the wheels touch down and sent up a prayer of thanks. Keeping the engine going I turned and taxied to the hangar. There was Jullerot. I knew how critical he was and awaited his verdict. 'Bravo!' he said and I was happy. He gave me leave to take out an aeroplane whenever I liked. This was my summit of joy. I spent all day there, helping the mechanics with the engines, testing the rigging and doing repairs. The long, fine summer evenings gave us plenty of time to fly.

The other pupils were Newall, who became Chief of Air Staff; Smith-Barry who broke both his legs in an air crash in France and afterwards ran a flying school which made their fighter pilots superior to the Germans; Johnson, who was killed; and Hutcheson.

Newall, Hutcheson and Puck were all flying solo and each had a machine. Newall received a wire offering him the Adjutancy of his regiment, 2nd Gurkhas. It had been his ambition and he was undecided what to do. Hutcheson had one of his bad attacks of malaria which he had contracted in India. Ambition claimed Puck. With Newall and Hutcheson out of the way he would be the first of the Indian Army (except one Massy) to get his pilot's certificate. But he crushed that thought and advised Newall to refuse, which he did.

In September they all got their pilot's certificates (International Aviation Certificate, issued by the Royal Aero Club) – Puck was no 145. He promptly went to the India Office and asked the military secretary if he would attach him to the Air Battalion. He said that Puck must first get an extension of leave from his regiment. He wired for it but only received in reply the order to

Pilot's licence no 145.

rejoin on the expiration of his leave. He knew that his old Colonel would have encouraged him to join the Air Battalion, but he had gone and a new Colonel had been appointed.

So ended a most interesting leave and Puck rejoined his regiment in Singapore with Hutcheson in October. The new Colonel was very efficient and drove the regiment hard. It was probably all for the good but they were never so happy and never had such good relations between all ranks and, in particular between British officers and Indians as under 'Colonel Warren Sahib' who knew the value of constant personal touch and the absolute necessity of British officers knowing the language thoroughly. No regiment could be efficient if it is not happy, no matter how strong the discipline, the drill, the spit-and-polish and the up-to-date training. Before leaving the regiment, Colonel Warren had written of Puck:

> A well educated officer, possessing a University degree. Good tempered, fond of riding and playing polo regularly when in India, but too expensive in Singapore. Shows tact and judgement when dealing with natives. Energetic and self-reliant. Is powered of common sense. Is active and fond of games. Is at present in England and is going with a course of aviation in Bristol. Up to the standard of his rank. Not yet passed for promotion to higher rank. Quite a useful junior regimental officer.

Puck found on arrival in Singapore that he had been appointed Adjutant – that, he thought, was really why his extended leave had been refused. It was an all-absorbing job and he enjoyed it thoroughly. The people in Singapore were very hospitable – overwhelmingly so – and in return they gave two dances in their own mess which nearly ruined them. The regiment remained there for another year and the new Colonel clearly thought well of him, writing:

'A capable, energetic hardworking officer. Has power of command and initiative. Shows tact and judgement in relationships with

Indian ranks. A very good temper. Keen on aviation and possesses a pilot's certificate. Anxious for employment with Flying Corps about to be raised in India. Passed for promotion to Captain. Up to the standard of his rank.'

Not all went well for him there for he fell in love with the Colonel's daughter, and she dropped him!

5

INDIA PRE-WAR

In 1913 the regiment was sent to Nowgon in Central India. It was the last on their list of stations for which they had applied, but it turned out to be a most interesting posting because it was surrounded by Native States, each ruled with a rod of iron by an autocratic but usually popular Raja, Maharaja, Maharana or Raj. They were rich in variety, charm and colour, and quite different to British India which was ruled by regulation and by a bureaucracy which was often too remote from the people. An added bonus, as far as Puck was concerned, was that he could once again mount himself for polo.

Two of Puck's polo friends were the Deputy Commissioner and the Political Agent for the district. At the invitation of the DC and with permission from his Colonel he was able to go on a tour of the district, on horseback, with tents and a retinue of servants when they camped outside groups of villages. There, the DC held courts in the open, giving his decisions from the bench in front of all the villagers. His decisions were always accepted. Every Indian had the right to bring up a grievance which could be enquired into publicly and, if just, could often be rectified on the spot. That is what every Indian likes. He wants to see his paternal government in action where he lives and know that justice will be given. Quick communications can be of great value if they are not abused by too much red tape. Sadly, by 1913 the telegraph, telephone and railways had made it easy for Simla to keep control, and Whitehall to control Simla, so that District Commissioners and their Deputies were tied to their desks and too much of the personal touch had gone. The members of the Indian Civil Service (ICS) were, in those days, the pick of Oxford and Cambridge and served India best when they were trusted. Puck knew from many sources that too much control from Delhi and Simla destroyed the confidence of Indians in the British Government, which found itself 'sliding down the slippery slope of hostility, sedition and lawlessness', as he put it. It also began the deterioration of the ICS.

Not so in the Native States; the Rajas ruled by personal touch; they knew what the people wanted and they impressed by their great courtesy and dignity, qualities which appeal to all Indian hearts. Whitehall and Simla looked upon the Native States as backward because they had not made the same material progress as British India. But they received something of a shock when they were told that these Indian States were much happier. Puck soon discovered that the Indian moves spiritually in regions wider than are known to the British but, materially, he likes limits and he heartily dislikes the drab monotony forced on him by the Government with its distant, impersonal rule.

There is nothing Indians love more than a Tumesha or Show. They liked to see the Raja dressed in his gorgeous robes with jewels in his turban, sitting in his gilded carriage drawn by beautiful horses with plumes and with outriders in chain mail armour. Above all they liked the traditional Durbar when the Raja sits in the Great Hall of audience, or out in the open court and all, even the humblest of them, can have access to him. It was a remedy for injustice and it curbed the officials. It gave the Raja an opportunity to speak to his people and to learn from them their wants and preoccupations. It was a safety valve and cleared the air, just as it did in the regiment under Colonel Warren Sahib when Puck joined it in Agra. Unfortunately their present Commanding Officer did not understand the regiment and had little influence compared to their last CO.

There were, of course, Rajas who were too easy going and left their country to the mercy of their officials. That is where the Political Agent came in: he knew their language and understood a chance allusion in the local patois, so when a State suffers from misrule he could get the Government of India to intervene. A Council was then appointed, reforms were introduced and there was a thorough overhaul of the finance and administration of the State. The Raja might be deposed but such instances were rare.

The Political Agent (PA) dealt with a number of small Native States, each ruled by a Raja or Maharaja. Some of the States were very backward, although to a visitor like Puck, they were very picturesque. When he and the PA went to see the Maharaja of Chittapur they were met at the nearest railway station by a State Carriage, drawn by two horses and two camels. There were outriders in chain armour with lances. They were driven through thronging crowds to the Guest House which was well built with modern conveniences. The crowd seemed to him to be poorer than the Indian crowds in the British Provinces. The majority looked under nourished and many were dressed in rags. When he spoke of this to the PA he agreed with a sigh. He was doing his best. He had initiated public works to irrigate a considerable amount of land and a hydro-electric scheme which would eventually bring in electric power. The revenue was very small and it would take some years to increase it. Of course, in Western eyes, the Maharaja spent too much of the revenue on maintaining his Court, but his people were impressed by it and would not like his standard to be lower. The Tumesha was all important to them and the money saved by abolishing it could not bring any noticeable prosperity to the people and would weaken their unity and law abidingness. The Political Agent's job was to keep an eye on the revenue and to see that it was spent wisely. That he did by his own personality. Of course he had the power of the British and Indian Army behind him and everyone knew that. But a Political Agent with a strong personality was essential with those hereditary and self-confident Princes, who had the most charming manners, but cared little for the poverty of their people.

There were some very enlightened monarchs, notably the Maharaja of Travancore and the Gaekwar of Baroda. In a later period of his service he met the Nizam of Hyderabad whom he described as: 'A most extraordinary Prince and probably the richest man in the world for cash at his immediate disposal'. The resident there told him that the coffers in the palace held 150 million rupees' worth in gold, guarded by 50 sentries. There were also a large amount of notes, some of which had been eaten by ants! In addition there were unaccountable masses of jewels, yet he, himself, was a miser. He dressed in a poor and simple costume and went about in an old Ford car. His methods of increasing his revenue were hereditary. There was an old custom named 'the Nazar' or 'Appearance'. Anyone to whom the Nizam appeared in his palace had to fork out a 'goldmore' (a large sum of money). He would, therefore, sometimes give a dinner party to the officers of his army. After he had 'appeared' to them and sat chatting amiably at the head of the table, they each gave a 'goldmore' which was swept into his coffers. He also saw to it that flowers were sent to all the nobles and officials for their birthdays, for which each returned a 'goldmore'.

Years later, when Puck was commanding a regiment in Secunderabad, the Viceroy, Lord Willingdon, came down to visit Hyderabad and the Nizam really lavished hospitality on his guests. One hundred and twenty people, who included Puck and, by then, his wife, were invited to dinner and each had gold plates, knives, forks and spoons. Golden candelabra were spaced at intervals in the centre of the tables and the food and wine were insuperable, yet the furniture was ugly Victorian stuff. The roofs of the palace were covered with thousands upon thousands of tiny oil lamps with a fairy-like effect. Some years before, the former Viceroy of India, Lord Halifax, had intervened over the corruption and inefficiency of the State and had sent four selected men to administer it. They had done a great deal towards cleaning up the State but much was still needed to be done. Puck had great respect for Lord Willingdon, who had been Viceroy of both India and Canada, and his ability to spread good will wherever he went and to make men cooperate.

Puck wrote:

We had the most wonderful shooting in Nowgon – duck, snipe, black partridge, buck, cheetah and sometimes a panther. I often went out shooting with my orderly and it was curious to see the villagers salaaming, not to me but to my Brahman orderly and calling him 'Maharaj'. They treated me with respect but they treated my orderly with reverence. However, we were chiefly concerned to make our Brahmans into soldiers. Every Regiment in India had to undergo Kitchener's test and was judged by the way it stood up to it. The test was to march twenty miles in six hours, and then attack for two miles across country, finishing up by shooting with live ammunition at targets of iron plates on a hill. In Agra our magnificent men came through this test with very great credit. That was chiefly due to Colonel Warren who insisted on a twenty mile march each week. He, himself, marched with the men and would never ride. He also insisted on a high standard of musketry. I have seen him put in five bulls-eyes at a thousand yards. But our present Colonel could not march or shoot and the regiment missed the example. Consequently we fell below the Agra standard.

In the hot weather of 1914 Puck was sent to Satara for a musketry course. While he was there the Great War broke out and officers began to be ordered on service. They were a happy, jolly crowd of subalterns and they gave every departing friend a send-off to the railway station, riding his tonga ponies down the hill. To his joy, he was ordered to rejoin his regiment which was posted to Egypt.

6

FIRST YEARS OF
THE GREAT WAR

The obvious line for natural defence of Egypt from the West was the Suez Canal, served by a rail link all the way from Port Said via Ismailia to Suez. The Suez Canal had been described as the 'jugular vein' of the British Empire, being a vital line of communication between Europe and Asia. After the declaration of war with Germany garrison troops in Egypt had to be strengthened. The alliance with Russia freed Indian troops for service in Egypt and elsewhere and in August 1914 two infantry divisions and a cavalry brigade were to be despatched from India to relieve British troops who were being sent to France. These two divisions were ordered on to Marseilles without disembarkation in Egypt and the British garrison was replaced by a TA division and another infantry brigade.

Germany had a strong influence on the Turkish Army, maintaining its HQ in Baghdad, and there was belief in the German/Austrian alliance as being invincible. The Sinai desert was a barrier which kept the Turks in Palestine at arm's length, but it had been reported in September that a small body of armed Bedouin had crossed the frontier at Rafah, about 100 miles East of Port Said. On 30 October neutral Turkey joined the 'Central Powers' and Great Britain formally declared war on Turkey on 5

November 1914. The defence of the canal from land attack became an added commitment.

The Canal zone was divided into three sectors for defence: Suez to the Bitter Lakes (Sector 1); Devesoir to El Ferden (Sector 2); and El Ferden to Port Said (Sector 3), with Headquarters at Ismailia. The supply depot at Zagazig was 50 miles to the West of Ismailia on the main line to Cairo. Puck's Regiment, the 3rd Brahmans, was posted to Sector 3 with the rest of their Brigade (22nd Infantry) stationed in Sector 2.

Puck wrote:

We arrived at Zagazig in the Egyptian delta in October. Now was our chance to make our men give up the caste prejudice of every man, or his near relation, cooking his own food. It was essential for active service that the men feed together and that cooks prepare the meals. The Colonel put it to the Indian officers who replied that if they did it they would lose caste and the priests, when they reached India, would cast them out.

We were very soon ordered to the Northern bank of Port Said and I was sent with my machine guns and a Company to a redoubt three miles ahead. The whole area between this and Kantara, which was twenty miles away, had been flooded by cutting a channel to the sea, leaving a strip of sand about 300 yds. wide on the sea shore. This went up North and was the route to Syria. My redoubt was placed there to stop any Turkish troops advancing on Port Said. I also had twelve cavalry troopers, four of whom went forward on reconnaissance every day.

As soon as we arrived I told Subedar Ramesar that this individual cooking would handicap us very much and that if we could not feed together we should never be employed, during the whole war, on any important duty. I said that it was my wish that two men should be appointed as cooks and that they should all feed together. He looked very serious and said that he would talk with the men. I knew that I could trust him to do everything possible to carry out my wishes. The next morning he said that if I gave the order the responsibility would be lifted from the men. I therefore ordered the Company and the machine gunners to assemble and we had a Durbar. I told them that they knew how much I respected their religion and their customs, but that I was determined that the regiment should gain Izzat (honour) in this war. That would be impossible if each man continued to cook his own food. If I gave the order for cooks to be appointed and to feed together it would be my fault that their caste was broken. There were murmurs of approval all round. I therefore gave the order for this to be done. I never had any trouble while I was there.

Soon afterwards we received a report that a section of the Turkish Army was moving slowly down the coast from Syria and was now only one hundred miles away. Another Company was moved up from Port Said and my Double Company Commander took over command. A week later one of our aircraft, of which we had a squadron, reported an enemy camp about twenty miles North on the coast. Obviously they were coming down on us. I asked for leave to go out and reconnoître with the cavalry troopers. It was referred to the General at Kantara who gave me leave but said that I was not to get involved in any action.

So my chance had come. I got a good horse from the cavalry and rode fifteen miles along the open coast line. The country then began to be broken up into hilly sand dunes and we had to move forward slowly and carefully. After a few miles I saw through my field glasses what appeared to be a large camp of brown tents. One of my troopers said that they were fishermen's huts, that at certain times of the year fish abounded here and men came down here for a few weeks. We moved forward slowly in pairs but there was no sign of life. Then we saw that they were straw huts shaped like Arab's tents and all unoccupied. I immediately wrote out a message giving this information and sent back a trooper with it. With the others I rode slowly home. The horses were terribly thirsty. Forty miles in this heat without a drink was enough to kill a horse which had not been trained to it. It was dark when we got back. The next day I received a letter of thanks from the General saying that I had relieved him of great anxiety.

A few days after, the Turks attacked Kantara but had such a hot reception that they went back. They then tried to cross near Lake

Timsah. They had dragged pontoon boats across the sand for 150 miles and they got them across the canal. But the fire was too hot for any men to cross and they finally sheered off and retreated back to Palestine. Our cavalry pursued but became bogged down in the sand. Afterwards we heard that the Turks had been assured that when they advanced on the canal the Egyptians would rise against us from the rear. Whatever the intention of the Egyptians were, the presence of 50,000 Australians at Cairo was sufficient to intimidate them.

About a week after this General Cox made a sweep round with his cavalry from Kantara, returning by Port Said. His object was to capture or drive away the pockets of Turks which were left. He gave me an order to move out with twenty camels, carrying water, and my four troopers and meet him by those fishermen's huts where we would bivouac for the night. Again, he warned me not to get involved in any action. Accordingly I started in the dark because I knew that the camel's speed would not be more than two miles an hour. We arrived at the huts at about 3 p.m. but there was no sign of any human being. Leaving my camels with two troopers I moved forward to rising ground and saw a village half a mile ahead. I studied this with my field glasses and saw many women and children and some old men, but no young men. One of my troopers who spoke Arabic and knew their habits said that the young men would all have joined the Turkish army. As my horses were thirsty and there was a big well in the village I decided to move forward. Telling the troopers to keep their rifles ready and drawing my revolver in case of any ambush we moved forward to the well.

The old men received us hospitably and without fear, and the women were not in the least shy. We watered our horses and moved forward to some rising ground. From there I could see some cavalry approaching but was unable to distinguish whether they were friends or foe. We concealed ourselves and waited. At last I was able to see Indian cavalry coming forward, extended in a long line, followed by a long mounted column with flank guards. It was now nearly five o'clock and I did not want the horses to go further so waited for their arrival on the top of the rise. A good looking young officer wearing a turban cantered up to me with a few men. He was obviously commanding the vanguard. 'Are you the fellow who has brought the water?' he asked. I told him where the camels were and he moved on, and the whole advance guard moved past me. Close to it was the General and his staff. I rode forward to meet the General. He had a very stern face. 'Where are the camels?' he barked. I told him that they were two miles away. 'How far have you come?' 'Twenty-five miles', I replied. 'Much too far', he said, 'why didn't you stay with the camels?' I felt rather crushed but thought it better to put on a bold face, so said that my horses were very thirsty so I had to come to this well. 'Besides', I said, 'it is five o'clock and it will be dark in two hours. I came forward to hurry you up'. He glared at me but only gave orders to the staff captain to go forward with the advance guard and get the evening meals ready and take the mess cart with him. The villagers produced some troughs and we very soon watered a large number of horses. Then we rode on to the camp and found the headquarter mess tables with a clean white cloth and tea all set with camp chairs round it.

The General became very cheerful and chatty and poured some whisky into my tea. Didn't I need it! We discussed the war and he said that Winston Churchill was right. Gallipoli was the place to go for, but it must be a surprise attack. They told me about the Turks' attack on Kantara. One young cavalryman, who was a great polo player, had charged the Turks with his squadron and lost his right arm and many men. The General said it was 'damned stupid, cavalry charges are 100 years out of date'. We spent a very happy evening and bivouacked under the stars. Next day we rode back and as we parted from them at my redoubt I could not help wishing that I was with the General and his staff.

Not long after that a message came from the War Office saying that there were three officers serving in Egypt who had pilot's certificates. Were they willing to join the Royal Flying Corps? Puck felt 'what wonderful luck'. The Colonel ordered that he should go to Port Said to speak to him. As he rode in to the regiment the men were all spread out, each cooking his own dinner. He reported to Maxwell, the adjutant, and told him that his men were all feeding together. Maxwell said the Colonel wouldn't allow it: he was afraid of political troubles in India. He advised Puck to take the opportunity because they would never get into the front line with the present CO. Hutcheson was also included. To Puck's surprise the Colonel was very decent and said that he would not stop him if he was keen to go.

7

ROYAL FLYING CORPS

Puck wrote:

So it came about that in a month's time we were on board a ship at Alexandria, bound for England, home and beauty. I said farewell to the 3rd Brahmans for ever, but with a great heartache when I left my beloved men. The first landing at Gallipoli had just taken place and the ship was full of wounded. The Captain did not like it at all. He had not enough boats to take the wounded if we were torpedoed. Furthermore it was before the days of convoys and many ships, moving singly, had been torpedoed especially as they neared England. He was rather superstitious and became more than ever depressed when we sat down, thirteen officers at every meal!

While we were entering the Bay of Biscay a wireless message in code arrived from the Admiralty. We had no code on board and several of us spent a day trying to decipher it. The Captain eventually asked for the message in clear. It came: 'Enemy submarines near you; proceed to nearest port'. We went full speed to Queenstown in Ireland. We could not have made for a more dangerous harbour because the Lousitania had been sunk outside the day before. As we raced for Queenstown that moonlit night I went up on the bridge and the Captain said that a submarine had been chasing us. I do not know if it was his imagination but we made the harbour safely at dawn. There we waited until our orders came from the War Office to go to Ruislip for flying training. [This was No. 18 squadron formed in May 1915 at Northholt.] I still remember the beauty of Southern Ireland in the early summer in contrast to the sandy desert of the Suez Canal.

At Ruislip we had to dig up hedges, fill in ditches, build aeroplane hangars and huts before we could start training. Our machines were Maurice Farmans and Henry Farmans, both with the engine behind, and Moran fighters. I loved the Henry Farmans. They were so easy to manipulate, like a handy polo pony.

In those days of the RFC there was a gulf between the officers and the men. The officers did all the fighting and flying and took all the risks whether in the fighting area or at home. The men were in safety and comfort and did all the maintenance. The officer would climb into his aeroplane, do his flying morning and evening, and then go back to the mess. Both Hutcheson and I felt that this was not in accordance with our regimental traditions. We got to know the men and the engines. Hutcheson was particularly good at engines and spent his spare time in the workshops. I spent more with the men and got up games and concerts. We were all to go out to France together and the sooner we got to know each other the better. The Gilbeys who lived at Swakeleys, a large house in the vicinity, were very kind to us and I felt that their house was like a home.

By September most of the officers had their 'wings' and we were transferred to Norwich. There we were made into a fighting squadron and equipped with the new 'Vickers Gun Bus' [the Vickers FB5, a two-seater bi-plane of the 'pusher' configuration], the first aeroplane to be armed with two machine guns. The engine, which was a rotary 'mono-s-Pape', was behind with the propeller so that there was a clear field of fire for the gunner in front and the pilot, seated between him and the engine, also had a machine gun to fire over the gunner's head. There was a sheet of steel under our seats which made the machine heavy but which I was to be very grateful for.

At Norwich I was used as a 'ferry pilot', that is to say that I was sent down to Farnborough and other aerodromes to fly these aeroplanes up to Norwich. The engines were not always reliable and twice they failed and I had a forced landing, which I survived by sheer good luck.

On the first occasion it was a lovely July day and I was rejoicing in the beauty of the landscape and the feel of the aeroplane when the engine suddenly stopped. Below me was standing corn on all sides. I had always heard that it was a certain crash to land in standing corn but there was no alternative. Fortunately there was a fairly strong wind. I flattened out with the wheels touching the top of the corn and put the nose up as she sank. She just ran a few yards in the corn and stopped. On examining the engine I found that the 'high tension wire' had become disconnected and did not fit properly. And now, it being a Saturday afternoon, people began to appear from all directions treading down the corn and flocking round the aeroplane, many of them not having seen one before. The usual banter took place: 'Like me to take you up George?'; 'Think I'd keep one foot on the ground'. A kind young man with a car asked if he could help. I asked him to take me into Norwich where a garage soon put a proper terminal on to the high tension wire. But I could not get out until the corn had been cut.

On another occasion, when flying a new aeroplane up to Norwich the engine stopped when I was over Norwich Cathedral. I just got to the edge of the aerodrome which was on a cliff. There was not a drop of petrol left: it must have been leaking badly. On a third occasion, after flying above a storm for an hour I judged that I had reached Norwich but dared not come right down into the cloud for fear of hitting a building. I therefore circled until there was a rift in the clouds and a field could be seen. I promptly landed but ran into a ditch.

One lovely summer morning I was instructing a young pilot when the engine stopped and I had to land in Wroxham Park between trees. I found that the magneto had fallen down. A passing cyclist lent me some tools and we managed to get back, only because the wind had freshened and just lifted us over the trees at the edge of the Park. Life was full of surprises with these engines. On my cross-country flight I was always, almost sub-consciously picking out large fields on which, at any moment, I might land.

Evidently Puck's forced landings caused much mirth among his fellow pilots (as the cartoon on the next page illustrates). The cornfield forced landing must have been on Wong Farm, Great Melton. A correspondent recalled the incident in a letter to Puck's widow, Rosalind, after he died in 1962, in which he reports from the Church notes of Great Melton:

> A long memory: on Saturday afternoon, Oct. 16th, 1915 an aeroplane made a forced landing on a field on the Wong Farm failing to find its way to Mousehold Aerodrome. The airman was Lt. Ernest James Strover who later was shot down over Germany, became a prisoner of war, and, after the war got married and (later) was Ordained, became Rector of Lawford in Essex and has just died at the age of 77. How many can still remember his forced landing in Melton?

The correspondent's uncle remembered the incident as, apparently did a number of others.

Soon after this Puck's squadron (No. 18) moved over to the Western Front. He wrote:

> In November the great day arrived on which we were to fly to France. I was sent to Farnborough to get the last new aeroplane and join the rest of the squadron at Folkestone. The lorries with all our equipment had already been shipped across. Next day twelve of us started, each carrying a passenger and wearing an inflated inner motor tyre tube in case we fell into the sea. Of the twelve two, after climbing to 6,000 ft, found their engines failing and went back. One fell into the sea and was picked up by a destroyer and one just got over to Cap Gris Nez. The rest of us arrived safely at St Omer and joined the rest of the squadron. As I landed I heard the guns booming in the distance and was thrilled to be in the real war at last.
>
> We were sent to Aire and our task was to patrol the line and shoot down German aeroplanes. These orders frankly confused the

Mons. Le Commandant Strover looking for a suitable place to make a forced landing.

minds of military authorities who, accustomed to land warfare, did not fully realise that the air has height and depth as well as length and breadth. A pilot can rarely see another aeroplane in the air unless it is fairly near his own level or fairly close, even on a clear day. When there are clouds evasion is easy. Often as I cruised about searching the sky I considered how particularly fortunate was my lot. Two years ago I had spent my savings of a year's pay shooting in Kashmir. Now the gracious Government gave me the best of aeroplanes and two men to look after it, while all they asked in return was a sport which knocked big game hunting into a cocked hat. When I compared my luck to the wretched infantry below I felt ashamed of my luck.

The Squadron H.Q. was billeted in a chateau, the men sleeping in barns and on straw. They were very cheerful and the only complaint I ever heard was that the rats' feet were rather cold! I have often noticed that the worse the conditions the happier the British soldier or airman becomes, provided that he feels he is doing a good job of work. When he is in barracks with every comfort he is always grumbling. But, if marching along with the rain pouring down on him and the prospect of bivouacking in the open, he is cheerful and singing and cracking jokes. The officers of the three flights were billeted in the cottages. In my billet the French women were tremendous workers. They were out in the fields at dawn and never seemed to rest until they went to bed. But, on Sundays when they went to Mass, they dressed up and looked charming. I believe that the word is 'chic'. France has always fascinated me and I felt glad that we were protecting her from these hordes of brutal Huns who, without a shadow of excuse, had launched this murderous and bloody war on her.

The French soldiers of the first War were deeply patriotic and self-sacrificing, but they took the war light-heartedly and enjoyed themselves when they were not fighting. Our 1st Army had just taken over this part of the line from Armentières to Lens from the French and a British officer whose battalion had taken over from a French battalion gave me the following vivid description of it. It is perfectly true and illustrates the characteristics of the French troops. On the morning fixed for the taking over the British Colonel and Adjutant met the French Colonel and Adjutant who showed them round the trenches. The British Colonel remarked on the fact that there were very few French troops holding the line. The French Colonel said laconically, 'C'est midi, ils prennent leur café.' 'But,' persisted the British Colonel, 'suppose the Germans attacked at this moment'. 'They will not attack', was the reply, 'I can assure you'. Then they got down to the trench map and the Adjutant asked about the portion of the front-line trench which he had not seen. 'Unfortunately', said the French Colonel, 'it is in the hands of the Bosche'. Before they left they asked how many men were posted as sentries and the French Colonel counted them up: 'There is Alphonse, and Louis and Pierre etc. – about seven all told.'

That night the British battalion came up and took over the trenches and the French streamed out. The British were very anxious about the section of trench which the Germans held and had built barricades on both sides and posted men with bombs. About 3 a.m. they heard the cries of 'A la bayonette' and a rush of French troops from their rear came over their trenches and charged the section held by the Germans. When the tumult and the shouting had died down the French Colonel, covered with mud and blood, came to the British battalion H.Q., bowed low to the Colonel and said: 'Now I have the honour to hand over the trenches complete'. He took the British Colonel and Adjutant over to the trench from which the dead and wounded were being carried away. The British Colonel said, 'Well done, that was magnificent. I congratulate you.' Then, looking around and seeing very few French soldiers, he said: 'But where are the men who have done this magnificent deed?' 'Ah', said the French Colonel, 'C'est fini. Ils prennent leur café.' Before the war the French Army was trained to attack. 'L'attaque, l'attaque, toujours l'attaque.' But their generals did not realise the power of machine guns in defence. Consequently the flower of the French Army was lost in 1914 and 1915, and France has never recovered from it.

Day after day we patrolled the First Army front. Occasionally we saw a German aeroplane but, when we approached them, they dived down. The first encounter was mine. One sunny day I went up feeling particularly happy that something was going to happen. I took my favourite observer and gunner. After patrolling for an hour I saw a German aeroplane, a Taube, below. I dived at him and he immediately dived to the ground. At that moment I heard a machine gun firing behind me and the engine started to splutter. I immediately turned and saw another German aeroplane above me. Although he was above I got on his tail and fired my own machine gun at him. Down he went and I do not know what happened to him. My own engine had obviously been hit, protecting me, and was only firing on 5 or 6 cylinders (out of 9). We were miles over the line but luckily there was a strong East wind blowing from Germany and, although we were losing height, I felt confident that we should get back. Nevertheless, it was with a sigh of relief that we crossed the lines, having lost 3,000 ft. It was only a few miles on to Aire and we made the aerodrome. As I made out my official report I realised that I had been 'had for a mug' and said so as it might be useful to other pilots. The first Taube below me was obviously a decoy and the Kilber, above me, came out of the sun where I could not see him. We found the bullet holes in the engine. So much for my first encounter, I had learned something.

An RFC Communique No. 22 substantiates this story: 'On 28.xi.15 Lt. Strover and 2nd Lt. McKenna (Vickers, 18 Sqn.) encountered two hostile machines, a DFW and an LVG. They dived at the LVG from 9,600 ft The hostile machine turned East, nose diving very steeply. At the same time the DFW fired at the FB5 Vickers from above but, when attacked, turned and disappeared Eastwards.' Puck had been promoted Captain on 1 September 1915 but his new rank was not gazetted until April 1917, presumably why he was still being referred to as Lieutenant.

This was the beginning of the 'The Fokker Scourge' and the reign of Manfred von Richthofen ('when I have shot down an Englishman my hunting passion is satisfied for a quarter of an hour'). Operating in numbers the Fokker quickly proved too fast and manoeuverable for the 'gun buses' which had been gaining a fair number of successes during late summer 1915 and early autumn, but by November these aircraft were clearly outclassed. It would be April 1916 before more appropriate aircraft (FE 2Bs) arrived to re-equip 18 Squadron.

Soon after this event there was a tearing hurricane of a wind from the West and the Squadron Leader would not allow his pilots to go up because, with unreliable engines, they might easily be forced to land in German territory. Puck busied himself with studying the reason for engine failure and discovered that the large British 'obdurator ring' was not made of the right alloy and would not expand with heat in the same way as the French piston rings. He was then sent to Paris to bring back a French machine. He found it very pleasant to be put up at the Ritz at Government expense, but was longing to get back to his squadron as day after day passed and the weather was too bad to fly. At last, one morning dawned with a clearer sky and he decided to go, taking with him a dozen bottles of 'Cliquot' champagne for the squadron mess. The clouds were low and thick and, although he had a straight railway line to follow to the North he was constantly enveloped in cloud and no instruments, not even a compass. Fortunately the weather cleared just before St Omer and he was able to touch down without mishap. On the aerodrome he met the great Trenchard who asked him if he had come from Paris, in his great booming voice. He told him that he must be a fine pilot to get through this storm. Puck said that he was a lucky one. The fact was, he admitted, that he was not an especially good pilot but had great faith in God and knew that he should get through. He rather wished that he had told him that. The squadron at Aire were delighted with the champagne but decided to keep it until Christmas.

A pilot's service on the Western Front averaged out at about six weeks before he was shot down. Puck did not last that long and he wrote of his miraculous escape from death as follows:

On December 28th 1915, when I arrived at the aerodrome, there was a strong gale blowing towards Germany. Hutcheson said that it was foolish to go up. I was given the choice to decide. Frankly I was afraid to risk it but all my life I had trained myself to do the things of which I was afraid. It is a stupid policy. How would we all be in existence to-day if our ancestors had not run away from danger? So I crushed down my cowardly feelings and taking up a new gunner was soon over the German lines. At 8,000 ft the wind was so strong that, in patrolling the line, I had to keep my back towards Germany and constantly look over my shoulder. Over Lens I received a burst of anti-aircraft shells, bursting too close to be pleasant. It was near the end of my patrolling time and I put down my nose and made for home. Then I told myself it was cowardly and, as I turned, I saw a Taube doing a figure-of-eight below, obviously observing for Artillery fire. I went down at him and in a few seconds he was within range and my observer fired. Down went the Hun and down went we pursuing in headlong rush. But fast as we were, he was faster and soon shot out of range. I put up my nose and looked for the other because German aircraft, at that time, usually hunted in pairs. But no vestige of life disturbed the serenity of the skies. Such was a pilot's life. Perfect peace and calm, suddenly broken by a few seconds which demand instant thought and action, succeeded by peace again. I discovered, however, that the strong West wind had blown me for miles over the German lines and I was near Lille. I steered West, moving slowly against the powerful wind. Suddenly the anti-aircraft guns began to burst behind me. In those days 'Archie' was always bursting harmlessly behind. I laughed happily and putting the nose for home, took up the speaking tube and told the Air Mechanic Holden, that we were set for home as fast as the wind would let us. A few minutes of straight flying and then 'Donk' 'Donk' 'Donk' 'Crash', shells bursting all around us. Another burst and then a crash behind. The old Bus heaved over on its side and with joy stick right over I was only able to keep her straight. Worse than that the whole machine jerked up and down as the propeller, half of which had gone, slowly turned over. There was a strong smell of petrol and my first thought was of fire. There were, of course, no parachutes in those days. The aeroplane was jerking so much that I could hardly reach the switch. But I switched off at last and then with joy stick hard over to the right and right rudder full on, I kept her nose for home. Then she began to spiral. Holden, my gunner, looked back at me with a face of terror. I nodded and smiled but felt far from happy. The spirals increased and we rushed to the ground. Then I prayed as I had never prayed in my life before. Through fear? Undoubtedly – but that is one thing which makes us pray. It certainly did me. As we neared the ground something made the aeroplane right itself and we touched down – or rather crashed down because there was no undercarriage. We were thrown forward and something bumped my head.

The next thing I remembered was being carried, not too gently, by a chattering mob of German soldiers. Someone was pulling my field glasses which were round my neck. I held on but they were jerked out of my hand. Then a voice said in my ear: 'Êtes vous blessé?' I answered 'Maloom nahin' being the best foreign language I could summon at the moment. Then I was thrown into a cart and Holden beside me. Holden said he was unhurt but that the aeroplane looked like a 'dog's dinner'. He said that the Germans fired at us with rifles when we were near the ground and that some shots had hit the steel plates underneath. The first shot from 'Archie' had crumpled up the engine and smashed part of the tail. The next shot had broken a part of the left wing. Our own escape was miraculous. I lay back and thanked Providence with all my heart for our life and prayed that we would get an opportunity to escape back to our lines. At the same time I had a very reverent feeling of awe and thankfulness that I was still alive: surely I was kept alive for some purpose [see Appendix I, 'Personal experiences of answer to prayer'].

As the cart trundled along the cobbled road shells occasionally burst in the fields to right and left. We were West of Lens and were being driven towards that town. Some of the houses on the outskirts had succumbed to shell fire and many roofs had been demolished in the town itself. It struck me as very curious that French citizens appeared to be carrying on their normal routine regardless of the deadly destruction which might, at any moment, befall them. Streets were somewhat empty but shops were open and appeared to be fully stocked. We drove up to a house in the main street and a German officer with three soldiers escorted us into a room on the ground floor, where he presented us to two German officers, a Major and a Captain. All were ceremoniously polite and solicitous for our welfare. They brought us food and water and produced an interpreter who asked if there was anything we wanted. I had heard stories of the different methods of gleaning information from prisoners and suspected that their solicitude prefaced an enquiry. It soon came. We gave them our names and squadron but I told them that I could not give them any further information. To my surprise they did not press for it but my mechanic, Holden, astonished me by his wonderful imagination. He told these stolid, serious, gilded German staff that we had thousands of aeroplanes being built in England, that shortly we should have 300 squadrons in France, many of which would be able to bomb Berlin. The German interpreter translated sentence by sentence to his staff, who uttered guttural exclamations of astonishment at these wonderful revelations. Holden was enjoying himself enormously and I had the greatest difficulty in restraining my mirth. Finally, however, he overreached himself in describing our latest machine as capable of doing 200 m.p.h while firing a 6-inch how [howitzer. Ed], like a machine gun, and he was told to stop. Their punctilious manner, their consideration and their dignity gave me a very different opinion of the German to that which was prevalent on our side of the line.

Shortly afterwards we were taken out and put into a motor car with the interpreter and two soldiers. We drove Eastwards to a village named Henin Lietard. As we drove the interpreter regaled us with a description of the battle of Loos. He was a bumptious young man and explained how difficult it was for our Generals and staff to compete with the Great General Staff who were always aware of our attacks for weeks before they took place. With the amateur's confident criticism he predicted that it was impossible to make a surprise out of an attack on either side. In the little village of Henin Lietard we were handed over to the Hanoverian Hussars whose guard occupied a house on the village street. An officer explained to me through an interpreter that it was an order to search all prisoners, but he would accept my word of honour that I handed over all documents in my possession. As I had nothing but a few letters from home which had arrived that morning, I accepted. They read the letters and gave them back. Holden was taken to another room.

It was then that an extraordinary event occurred. I was looking out of the window, wondering what my chances of escape might be, when down the village street two very smart officers of the Hussars were marching with grey-blue cloaks, lined with scarlet, breeches, boots and spurs. The nether man did not do full credit to the upper man and a British Cavalry Officer would have shuddered at their outfit. They came into the guard room, clicked their heels and bowed and I followed their motions feeling as if I were playing a parlour game Then one of them looked hard at me and said in perfect English: 'Surely we have met before.' We finally decided that we had met in Singapore in 1912 where he had dined in our mess and had ridden in a paper-chase which we had held (even then with badly cut breeches!). His name being Meyer.

Nothing could have exceeded his kindness, consideration and sincerity. He got leave to take me to the house in which he was billeted and where he gave me all the comfort which was at his disposal. Later on, when I was interned in the unpleasant prison of Lille, he obtained a special permit to come over and see me and bring me food and books. During my time in Germany, I came across the worst side of the German, but the pictures which I like to keep uppermost are those of Meyer and other officers near the front line whose simple patriotism, kindliness and courtesy are some of the attributes of a great nation.

In the afternoon Meyer brought down the officers of a squadron of the German Flying Corps who were stationed at Lille. They offered to drop a note over the lines to my people and my squadron. I wrote a note to each and I heard afterwards that they were received within two days. They were a cheery lot of souls. We spoke in French and they regaled me with stories of fights in the air. One of them was the pilot with whom I had had an encounter and who had trapped me with a decoy. We had a good laugh over it and I charged him with running away when I turned on him. He quoted the old English saying: 'He who fights and runs away lives to fight another day'. The whole thing seemed so incongruous: here we were, the greatest of friends with the camaraderie of the air which existed among the early pilots and yet, if we had met again in the air we would cheerfully have tried to kill each other. I spoke of this and they told me something of their loyalty to their country, their strong patriotism. They asked me if we hated Germans. I told them that such a thing as hate could not exist in British officers. They were chiefly anxious to know when I thought the war would end. I told them, five years, at which they smiled and shook their heads.

At the same time they did not like flying on bad days and they hated fighting. One thing which they said showed me the essential difference between our Flying Corps and theirs. They said that their Squadron Commander was always ordering them to fly. That, they said, was easy but he did not fly himself. Their admiration for him, however, was obvious as was also their discipline. In our Flying Corps we fly because we like it. If a pilot is not keen to go up he conceals the fact. Our feeling of sport carries us through. Our discipline is poor. A Squadron Commander in the R.F.C. would be admired because he flew and was a stout and good fellow. If he were a disciplinarian he would be disliked and pronounced a 'hot air merchant'. They were full of admiration for our Flying Corps but said we were foolish to go about singly. They admitted that man for man they were no match for us but that they could defeat us by moving in pairs.

I was very much surprised at their admitting their inferiority and I told them that Immelman (who at that time was recognised as a great fighter) was a most intrepid pilot and a magnificent shot. Our whole conversation was very much like that of two rival football teams after a match. They were sick to death of war. They said that we should never have fought each other and that it was entirely the fault of our 'verdampte' politicians who never visited each other and never attempted to see each other's point of view. I said that it was a thousand pities that England and Germany had to fight each other. Together we could keep the world in order. We parted the best of friends before I was taken over to the guard room for the night. In spite of the atmosphere of the guard room I slept heavily, waking only when I felt myself, periodically falling through space.

8

PRISONER OF WAR

Puck wrote:

Next day Holden and I were taken to Lille citadel by a guard of one N.C.O. and four men. As we marched through Lille I was surprised at the emptiness of the streets. Shops were open but the streets were mostly deserted except for a few women, chiefly dressed in mourning. It was rather a contrast to Lens which, inspite of the shelling to which it was daily treated, appeared to be carrying on a thriving trade.

Lille citadel, built by Vauban, looked a most formidable place to attack; but my point of view was how to get out. They locked me in a room with walls six feet thick, stone floors and barred windows. I got leave to have Holden in my room so that I was sure he was properly looked after. Food consisted of one slice of black bread (war bread, fourth class) made of potato, a little rye and sawdust and a cup of coffee made from acorns, for breakfast. This was the recognised diet for prisoners. One couldn't blame them because they were already short of food. But it was impossible to keep fit on that diet or to have strength enough for hard exercise. In prison camps we lived on parcels from England, which were nearly always delivered intact through Holland and I never heard of a case of a German stealing our parcels.

Every day a little German padre came to see me and brought copies of the English papers. Anything in our papers which was derogatory to Germany he had underlined in blue pencil, which he said 'hurt him very much'. I asked him if he had ever considered how Germany had hurt Belgium and France and England for no good reason whatever. I suspected him of trying to get information and I let him do the talking. I asked him for books. He said the French nation were so narrow-minded that the shops could not produce any English books. I asked for French novels but he said that they were very 'schlecht'. I told him that they would beguile the boring hours of jail very well. He eventually produced a couple of lurid novels and Longfellow's poems. To prevent my brain from becoming completely torpid I learnt 'Hiawatha' by heart and never want to hear it mentioned again. On the third day Meyer appeared with tinned sausages, chocolates, cigars and books. How I blessed him. He was in a great hurry as his Regiment had been dismounted and ordered to the trenches. Yet he had given seven hours of his scanty time to see an enemy prisoner. He had been employed by a firm in Singapore and after the war I wrote to the firm telling them how well he had treated me. I never heard any more and fear that he was killed.

After six days we were taken to the station and put into a train. There I found Garth, one of the original members of the R.F.C., who had been brought down two days before me. There were about twenty British soldiers in the carriage who had been caught on patrol on different parts of the front. There was no dejected bearing among them. As we left the station they waved to the civilians on the platform: 'good-bye Eliza', 'good-bye Missus Brown'. Shortly after we started a German officer walked into the carriage and placed himself in a commanding aspect at the corridor door. It was a long carriage, badly lit with gas. The German N.C.O. jumped to his feet and said 'Achtung' (Attention). No-one took any notice except one British soldier who called out 'all tickets please'. This was greeted with a roar of laughter which annoyed the German officer. He strode forward and stood in a threatening attitude in front of this man who looked up with an innocent face and said "Ave you come to see about the gas?' The roar of laughter which greeted this was too much for the officer who left the carriage growling out orders to the N.C.O. The N.C.O. was very angry and shouted out various orders in German but the nearest soldiers shouted him down. 'There, there, Fritz, don't worry. We 'ain't going to hurt yer'. He eventually subsided in resigned despair. During the whole time I was in Germany I never saw a British soldier or officer show the slightest sign of fear in front of Germans although I have seen them bayoneted. Before the good-humoured friendliness of 'Thomas Atkins' Germans invariably melted.

After 24 hours travelling we reached Munster. Here I had to explain Holden's real rank and he was put into the men's lager [camp. Ed]. I heard no more of him until I was repatriated to England in December 1918. I am glad to say that he avoided the mines and, with his usual intelligence, picked up sufficient medical knowledge and German to become the hospital orderly of his camp.

Garth and I eventually arrived at Gutersloh in Westfalia and were ushered into the camp, starving. The British officers in the camp received us with immense kindness. Food, clothing, baths, beds, every physical comfort as well as the joy of being with friends. I felt as though I had crossed the Styx and joined the shades of the departed There were about 200 British officers there, captured at the beginning of the war, many of them old friends. There were only two other officers of the R.F.C. In those days the Corps was small and I knew them both and was delighted to see them because they had both been reported as missing and believed to have been killed. Porter, of the Royal Artillery, a very keen early pilot, and Humphreys, scientist and explorer, who had been with Shackleton on North Polar expeditions and had taken up flying before the war in order to use it for exploration. They got me into their room of four, and were very lively and entertaining.

The camp consisted of twelve enormous buildings surrounded by barbed wire, over a mile round. Sentries were posted every 30 yards outside the wire and it was lit up at night. There were about 700 Russian officers, 400 French as well as the 200 British. The camp was teeming with life. Football, organised by the British, was played all day. Theatricals, usually of a very high standard, were given every week by each nationality in turn. Most British officers were learning languages. It was the custom to keep a pet Russian and Frenchman and to learn and teach each other's language. Of course there were some who had sunk into a condition of mental depression and inertia and who could not be roused by their friends. But such officers were rare among the British. Those who lacked the will power were kept up to exertion by public opinion.

The Russians were very entertaining. To most of us they were a discovery. Some officers treated them as equals, some as inferiors, but I think we all liked them. They varied tremendously from the Petrograd and Warsaw guardees to the Mongolian from Siberia. The guardsmen were the most attractive and could usually speak English and French. It was, therefore, among the guardsmen that I made my friends. They were intelligent and interested in music, art and literature, and their knowledge often put us to shame. They were also interested in wine and women and to a degree which was revolting to the ordinary Englishman. For example the cream of Russian regiments was the Petropavlosk. This was raised by Peter the Great as a boy, from boys. He endowed it so heavily that no officer had a mess bill. When a vacancy occurred for a new officer they chose one for his family, size and appearance. He then came to the regiment for a period of probation for a month. During the first fortnight they made him deliberately drunk in order to see how he behaved. Many other customs were a curious blend of aristocratic pride and barbaric crudeness. As I got to know them better I began to realise how uncivilised and cruel their life in Russia must have been. Some of them possessed estates which were larger than an English county. They visited their estates once or twice a year for shooting parties and left their bailiffs to look after them and to produce the rents. They took no interest in their tenants and did not feel that they were in any way responsible for them or for the wretched conditions under which they lived. While the peasant lived the life of a serf the landlord spent the rents in riotous living and this they believed to be perfectly natural. The peasants were, to them, lower than animals are regarded by Englishmen. Their outlook was at least as callous, as irresponsible and as brutal as that of the French landlords in the eighteenth century.

I was fortunate enough to make friends with one Russian reserve officer from Moscow who was one of the most delightful men I have ever met. He was most intelligent, well read and interested in everything. He spoke English, French and German very well. He said that he gained a great deal from speaking English with me but, in reality, he gave me far more, teaching me Russian. I never met a man with such great love for his country, with such deep sympathy for her sufferings, or as much hope for the future.

One night he introduced me to a room full of his Moscow friends, whom I found more intelligent and interesting than the Petrograd guardsmen. Very shortly, however, I discovered that these were friends of Lenin, the originators of the Revolution. They were receiving letters from Moscow, keeping them in touch with the situation. This was eight months before the Revolution and they knew perfectly well that it was coming. They told me of the appalling condition of Russia, the corruptness, the suspicion, the lack of justice, the callous brutality of the upper classes and the wretched conditions of the poor. They always spoke calmly but took no pains to conceal the utter hopeless state of the country under its present rulers. Most of them spoke with hatred and contempt of the ruling classes. Indeed it would be hardly natural if a great deal of hatred were not mixed with that revolutionary spirit. But my friend and a few like him never showed any sign of hatred. They discussed the danger of revolution and weighed the advantages with the disadvantages. Some thought that revolution would bring such chaos that Russia would take generations to recover. The majority believed that nothing could stop revolution.

The distressing side of their characters was the lack of religion. They had such a complete contempt for their priests who were, they said, insincere and merely the tools of the Government employed to dope the people with superstition. Thus the people were kept as slaves of the rich, and the next life was to be happier for them if they bore their poverty and misery with patience and humility. I told them that I was amazed to find men with such enlightened minds and with such love of their country holding these irreligious views. They all admitted the truths of Christianity but were agreed that their own Church had fallen into disrepute. They took me to their Church which had been established in a building in the camp. The choir of male voices behind the screen was beautiful and the Church was beautiful. Everything which Art could do to help to worship had been enlisted. But the worship of Icons and the superstitious ritual was mere idolatry. If the war had not hastened the Revolution it is probable that some purifying reform would have evolved in their Church.

Puck found it difficult to believe that Communism really satisfied the spiritual wishes of the Russians after both wars, and difficult to believe that the ruling Bolsheviks who composed the Politbureau could have the stupid and hostile ideas with which Europe credited them. For him the Bosheviks at Gutersloh towered above the other seven hundred Russians both mentally and morally. It became clear to him that if Russia could be ruled despotically then it was best that the Government should be in the hands of such men as those, rather than controlled by the narrow-minded and pleasure-loving aristocracy from which the officers of the guards were selected. He found both types of officers most attractive. The officers of the guards, although not deserving of admiration, were more pleasant to play with. There was a simplicity and whole-heartedness about them which he had not found in any other European nation.

Group of British, French and Russian POWs at Gutersloh. Puck in RFC uniform, 'ringed' in centre.

Contact with home was through Puck's sister-in-law, Tickie, married to his eldest brother, Harry, the doctor. She kept up a constant supply of food parcels and news from home. This was no mean feat as both Harry, in the RAMC, and Martyn, still a bachelor in the gunners, were on the Western Front and both had been wounded, ending up in the same hospital at the same time. Food parcels were essential to keep alive, as there was a shortage even for the German captors and civilian population. Many Russian POWs died for lack of it as they seem not to have received parcels from home. Amazingly the parcels and letters got through and an official post-card, received by Tickie through Maastricht, signed by Puck, acknowledged receipt of '2 Loaves in good condition'. A letter from Puck to her, written from Gutersloh, dated 30 April 1916, ran:

Dear old Tickie,

Thank you so much for the regular letters and parcels you are sending me. Don't think I am not getting enough. I am getting all I want, thanks, of everything. The bread from Holland is very good and quite fresh. Will you stop the bread from Switzerland? When you write to May next will you thank her for her parcel... Poor old Martyn, I hope it won't be a long job [reference to a wound?]. Write and let me know how ... [remainder of sentence blanked out]... We are having most glorious weather here. We've got two tennis courts so that one gets a good deal of tennis all told and I am going on with my German lessons. All the badly wounded fellows are going to Switzerland in a few days i.e. those who will be no good for fighting. Tell me in your next letter how Harry is doing. I expect he will love the life. I haven't heard from any of my friends in France but I hear that Hutcheson is engaged !! Funny time to do it. He was home on leave a short time ago and if it is the one I think I'm very glad as she is a good sort and will keep him well in hand. All my friends are married now, or about to be. There is only one bachelor in my regiment. You must look out for somebody for me. About 18 to 21 & very pretty – with money if possible – a sense of humour & fond of a large family & the more feminine the better. Then I shall settle down in England. We don't get many new fellows here now but we've a fairly strong contingent of the R.F.C. Well I've nothing of interest to tell you & if I had I couldn't write it so had better stop. Your loving brother, Ernest.

In a letter to Tickie, dated 5 January 1917, Puck wrote:

I hope you all had a cheery Xmas together, & that you will have Harry home for a bit now. Please thank him for his letter & Martyn for his. I get them all. Thanks awfully for all the Xmas good things. I do not want any more tinned tongue, tinned ham & tinned bacon but would you send me fresh bacon every week instead – it keeps well. Also fresh eggs – some shops pack them well. Will you also send me the following every fortnight in a separate parcel: 3 tins of condensed milk, 2 pounds of butter (or margarine), 3 jam, 3 lbs lump sugar, 1 tin Crawford biscuits. And I also want one large box, only once, which you can send me by American Express containing the following: fifty tins of corned beef (two lbs each), fifty lbs of condensed milk, fifty lbs of lump sugar, and please let me know the price and also the price of the parcel you are sending every fortnight I will tell Cox to send you the money. Tell Martyn that this is for 'dousra admi' … Jolly nice for him to be at home for the winter so long as his wound doesn't worry him for long. I hope Harry is quite fit again. I expect his practice is in a bad way and he will have all his work cut out to get it up again, but he seems to be wanting to get out to France again. We had a very successful Pantomime Bluebeard. There is a lot of talent here. It was written & music composed by fellows here, and the scenery painted and costumes made by others. The Russians have returned from their reprisal camp and my old pal has begun to teach me Russian – which is a dreadful language.

Tickie might well have wondered what such large supplies were for. No doubt Martyn might have got wind of what was up!

9

ESCAPES

Escape was in Puck's mind from the beginning of his captivity. Recalling his escapes for the benefit of Tickie after the war he wrote of the various attempts which he made:

One day Garth came to me with a scheme for escape. Apparently some Russians, who had previously been quartered in our building, had started a tunnel in the cellar. They wanted to continue with the help of four Englishmen. Would I join? Would I not? I would have joined the wildest, most abortive attempt if it gave the slightest chance of escape. The other English were 'Humph' and 'Saggers'. 'Humph' was an excellent character. He had been on a North Polar expedition and his main objective was to do it again. For this purpose he had made himself proficient in geology and surveying and had a meticulous knowledge of fauna and flora. He was also one of the first Englishmen to take up flying, with a view to using it for exploration. Physically he had great powers of endurance. 'Saggers' was a land agent and one of the most cheery souls I have ever met.

We began our adventure by getting a four-bed room together at the top of the barrack. The tunnel had been started by removing a yard square of bricks in the floor of the cellar and cementing them in a wooden tray which fitted into the hole. The earth, or rather sand, below had been removed to a depth of four feet. It was only possible to work at night as the German guards would soon have discovered us during the day. Even then the utmost care was necessary. The surrounding wire of the camp was only twenty yards away from the building and the electric light spaced around this wire shone through the windows of the cellar. Also the sentries outside the wire were near enough to hear any unusual noise. To add to the difficulty, patrols of one N.C.O. and two men visited all the buildings and cellars at unknown intervals during the night. It was therefore necessary for one of us to remain at each end of the building in order to give warning of an approaching patrol. The Russians, in order to help, agreed that one of them should hide in the attic roof every night until it was safe to begin work.

In February (1916) we began our tunnelling. Every night at 1 a.m. we got up, called the Russian and crept down to the cellar in socks. It was very cold and the wretched Russian was always found nearly frozen. He usually explained that his heart was very hot. They were wonderful to work with. Their main idea was to escape back to Russia in time to take part in the Spring offensive. One Russian, in particular, appropriately named Okuloff, could never be stopped from digging. The Russian idea was that each took his turn at digging and passed the sand up in bags. As the tunnel progressed we found that the air became so bad that breathing was difficult. The Russians however explained that the officer who was digging should continue until he fainted through lack of air. As soon as the others saw no life in his body they dragged him out by the heels and he was relieved by another officer. Somehow this never appealed strongly to us and we insisted that the digger only went in for a few minutes at a time.

One night I was digging at the face of the tunnel when a Russian's voice called down 'Come out. The Germans are coming'. I started to wriggle back but it was some way to the entrance. Then I heard a hoarse whisper. 'Stay still, we will shut down'. I heard the tray let in and then silence. The air was very bad and after a few minutes I began to gasp. I felt that I must get out or die. I was close to the tray and could lift it. Then I knew that, if I did, I should betray everyone, British and Russian. I was terrified and gasped, choking to death. Would the Germans never come? In my terror I prayed very hard and suddenly felt relaxed. Soon after, I heard heavy feet above. Then I lost consciousness. When I woke up I was lying on the floor of the cellar. My friends had opened up the tunnel just in time and pulled me out unconscious. I think this was the most horrible experience of my life and I can imagine nothing worse than being buried alive. There is no doubt that I was saved by prayer [see Appendix I, 'Personal experiences of answer to prayer']. If I had struggled for breath I would have fainted sooner and died before they reached me. After that, we British insisted on some sort of pump, even if it were only a pair of bellows and a hose pipe, and arrangements made for quicker warning. The Russians agreed but I think they considered us rather soft.

To get rid of the sand was the difficulty. We took it up to our rooms and stored it in boxes under our beds. Then next evening, after dark, we buried it in the black-trodden sand of the camp. Those nights were full of excitement. More than once one of us, posted as sentry, ran in to give warning of a German patrol. Then the digger was pulled out, the tray of bricks replaced in the floor and the sand swept up with the greatest of speed and accuracy. There were two entrances to the cellar and we always disappeared up through one door as the German patrol came down through the other door. Once the German sentry, who slept in the house close to one cellar door came out, turning on the electric light. Garth gave warning as we hastily cleaned up. Suddenly Garth came running down again to warn us that the German had walked to the other door and would probably come down through the other cellar door. Humph, who was doing a rear guard action with a shovel mistook Garth for the German and dodged behind the cellar pillars in the dark. Garth mistook Humph for the German and did the same. While we ran upstairs with the sand these two remained, dodging each other in the dark. Humph in order to save the tunnel was ready to give Garth his quietus with the shovel. Fortunately Garth recognised his burly figure. Still more fortunately the German sentry never came down.

In our room at the top of the house we often collected a very entertaining and delightful crowd in the evenings. A few prisoners from the London Territorial division had arrived and they included a

Barrister, a Politician, an Oxford Don and a Theatrical Manager. Opinions and experiences were varied and conversation often rose to intellectual heights which were great compensation for imprisonment. Although lights were all out at 10 p.m. our guests often stayed until 1.00 a.m. By the request of the Russians we could not divulge our tunnel. The Russians were afraid that if knowledge became public the Germans might hear of it through careless discussion. Consequently with our late guests and work every night from 2 until 6 a.m. we found little opportunity for sleep. We therefore each took a night's rest in turn and were forced to sleep during the day. However we took part in games and other amusements so as not to arouse suspicion. Thus from the dreariness of captivity, life suddenly opened up intense interest.

We were full of hope and calculated to the time when we should get all the English out by our tunnel. Our greatest allies were the British orderlies. There were a few British soldiers in the camp whose job was to look after the British officers in the way of cleaning boots and cooking. Some of them knew about our tunnel and always gave us any information about the German use of the cellar, or any new orders which the sentries and patrols had received to prevent our escape. Every day two of them went down to the cellar, under German supervision, to fetch cabbages and potatoes which were stored there. Our German Feltfebel (Sergeant) known as 'Whiskers' spent his time looking for possible tunnels. He had discovered two Russians working in a tunnel in another house and had bayoneted one of them in the tunnel. The Russians complained to the Camp Commandant and to show their disgust they refused to go on roll call parade which was held every evening. The whole seven hundred stood away from the parade ground singing 'Volga, Volga, Queen of Russia'. The deep, defiant music was wonderfully stirring and savage. It sounded like a roll of thunder, dying away to a distant echo and then crescendo-ing up to a great crash of thunder again.

The Commandant was full of sense. He treated them like children. He agreed that it was a rotten trick to bayonet the officer in the tunnel, but that of course they took their lives in their hands when they tried to escape. Meanwhile he was Commandant and must please insist on them going on roll call parade. The attitude of the three nationalities to the Germans was interesting. The Russians said the Germans were cruel bullies and would only behave decently under force. The French merely hated the 'sales Boches' on principle. The English looked on the Germans with friendly amusement.

This is an instance of Russian methods. At the beginning of the war Germany created a new rank called 'Feltfebel Lieutenant'. This was an officer promoted from the ranks. The Russians thought that they were Warrant officers and sent captured 'Feltfebel Lieutenants' to soldiers camps. Germany protested that they should be treated as officers, but the Russians made no difference. To retaliate, therefore, Germany took Russian officers of the best families from our camp and sent them to Strohen, a 'Straf' camp near Hanover. They encouraged them to write to their people to inform them. One of them wrote to his sister who was at the Czar's court. He described the filthy condition of the camp and their brutal treatment by the Germans. His sister showed the letter to the Czar who promptly sent all German prisoners, officers, to the worst camps in Siberia. As soon as Germany's officials heard this they climbed down and brought the hundred Russians back to Gutersloh. Russians always maintained that Germany must be crushed and kept down after the war. Otherwise she would be a menace in Europe. Naturally they were thinking of Germany under the Kaiser and the General Staff.

One afternoon, Private Dunne, one of the British orderlies, came to warn us that our tunnel had been discovered and that a German patrol would lie in wait for us that night. It was a bitter blow. All our hopes were centred on it. Later on Dunne came to say that, instead of lying in wait for us, they had put a padlock on both doors. This seemed better. From the German point of view a lock was a lock. Few of the 'Earnest men' as the Landstorm were called by their Commandant, could be spared to look after prisoners-of-war when they were needed at the front. Therefore a lock relieved their minds of the possibilities of anyone getting into the cellar. We were safer than before because no German patrol would trouble to visit us. However, we soon decided that we must start another tunnel, profiting by our experiences. We were unanimous that any future tunnel must be made without the participation of the Russians.

Although the Russian guardsmen, with whom we had worked, were admirable and had our friendship and trust, they themselves, trusted very few of their own countrymen. Every night it had been necessary to conceal two or three of them in our barrack and, sooner or later, they would probably be discovered. And, although they were so gallant and whole-hearted, they were very happy-go-lucky in their arrangements.

We carefully selected twelve British officers and asked one Rogers, who in civil life was a mining engineer, to organise this secret society. Someone suggested that it should be called the Red Hand, which was afterwards deprecatingly named the Pink-Toenail or P.T. (which might also stand for Private Tunnel). There were many difficulties to be overcome. First to get into the cellar. Dunne followed a German into the cellar, made a wax impression of the key. Deane, by means of metal cut from a camp looking glass and a file, eventually produced a key which fitted and turned the lock. We then inspected the stair and found it firmly imbedded by concrete into a brick wall on either side. To cut it out we only had pocket knives and the very blunt German dinner knives. However where there is a will there is a way. Knives were made into saws by cutting teeth and we began again our nightly visits to the cellar. For six weeks we laboured, constantly breaking these ridiculous knives, but always progressing. We found that we could safely work from twelve to one every day as this was sacred to the German dinner hour and no German had ever been known to be absent from his 'Mittagessen 2'. Even in the palmy days before the war this hour was sacred. Now, therefore, when meals were small and few, nothing short of an Air Raid would withdraw a self-respecting Hun from his only good feed in the day.

After six weeks sawing, the step gave way and we wedged it with wood. Then we cut away the bricks behind the step in the two walls in which the step was embedded. Rogers made false masonry to fit the holes created by removing these bricks. Then by removing the false masonry the step slid back underneath the step above it. He then put it on greased rollers so that, although large and heavy, it slid back easily We began to remove the sand below the step. A new method of discarding the sand was discovered. By removing the floor boards in the attic above us we found a space of about 18 inches between these floor boards and the lathe and plaster of the ceiling of our room and the rooms adjoining. We therefore put cardboard over the lathe and plaster, deposited our sand on it and replaced the boards. The sand was taken up in bags under our coats between twelve and one every day. We dug out a chamber below the stair 8 ft x 8 ft. Since the floor of the cellar was four feet below the surface of the camp outside, we began our tunnel 12 ft below the surface.

Roger's genius next turned itself to a fan. This he made from wood and tin. A wheel, revolving on ball bearings inside a box, took air in one end and drove it out of the other end of the box. Geared to a big wheel which was turned by hand its average performance was six hundred revolutions a minute. The ball bearings were from roller skates, the wood from the parcel boxes and the tin from bully beef tins. The exhaust box was continued up under the foundations and under a flight of steps outside the house. The foul air was sucked by a pipe from the face of the tunnel and thrown outside the building. To fill the vacuum thus created, fresh air poured in from the crack in the cellar step. A working party of four was now pushed down every morning at eight thirty immediately after roll call. The step rolled back, the four workers went down and the step was rolled back into place again and sealed with plasticine and dust. The cellar was re-locked and the workers left to their fate until twelve o'clock when the tunnel was re-opened. I remember when we first re-opened it I half expected to find the four workers suffocated. Rogers laughed at my fears and his confidence was justified by the exit of four sand-begrimed but cheerful officers.

As the tunnel progressed a small sleigh pulled by a rope at each end was introduced. A man lying in the tunnel behind the digger took an empty box from the sleigh and replaced it by one which the digger had just filled, giving a tug to the rope as a signal. The third man at the mouth of the tunnel pulled back the sleigh, emptied the box into a sack and sent the empty box back. The fourth man worked the fan.

We had not progressed far before a new difficulty arose. The sand began to flake from the top of the tunnel and Rogers, fearing that we might be buried alive, refused to proceed without bolstering the tunnel with wooden boards. The tunnel was two feet high and one foot six inches wide. Every yard a board was put across the top of the tunnel and a board at the bottom. A prop was then knocked into position at each side to hold up the top. The difficulty, of course, was to find wood. A large amount of wood was brought by the Germans for our theatricals and this was sawn into the right lengths and stored under our beds. But we could not leave it there to run the risk of search by 'Whiskers'. Therefore we cut away the board of a window sill in our room and made a 'cache' by hollowing out the wall beneath.

All day long we were busy. Frameworks of boards had to be sawn to bolster up the tunnel and the lathe and plaster of the ceiling, and reinforced to bear the weight of the sand. All this required wood and we soon exhausted our stocks. We then used some of the boards of the beds on which we slept. After that we discovered that a new house was being opened in the camp for more Russian prisoners and that quantities of bed boards were available. Under cover of darkness we stole enough to complete our tunnel and hid them in the attic above the ceiling. As we were gloating over this find, Dunne came to say that the Germans, having discovered the loss, had threatened to send all the British orderlies to the mines unless the boards were put back. Here was a terrible quandary. Most of the boards had already been sawn into the right size and to return them in this state would give the Germans sufficient evidence to discover our tunnel. On the other hand it was impossible to let the orderlies go to the mines. The German Commandant had given the orderlies 24 hours to restore the boards and as each hour passed and no solution became possible, it seemed that discovery was certain. At seven o'clock that evening Williams, another orderly, told us that a locked room in the new building was full of bed boards. He had seen a German officer open it and seen stacks of boards inside. We had three hours before 'lights out' when Germans came round in patrols. Everything depended on the speed with which Deane could make a key. By this time he was an expert and in two hours he had fitted a key and opened the door. In half an hour we had restored the bed boards. The Germans never discovered the loss of the stack, but it was a near thing.

Our tunnel became the object of our existence. Work upon it was systemised. Every one had his job. No orders were necessary. Regular hours, regular work in regular rotation. Thus it was driven forward in a gentle, upward slope advancing at the rate of two or three feet a day.

Many were the alarms. Once we were nearly discovered by a German boy who somehow got into the house during the dinner hour. The situation was saved by drawing him to the bathroom to discuss the repair of a leaky tap. Once when 'Whiskers' organised a meticulous search and gazed at the very point of our proposed exit outside the wire, we stopped work for a week. But nothing was discovered. Rogers left nothing to chance. In the winter there were big falls of snow and the water level came half-way up our tunnel. We had to close down for a month and during that time we flooded part of the camp and skated. The Russians, who were of course experts, taught us with great care and the utmost friendliness. A great spirit of camaraderie grew up between the Russians and ourselves. Some of us made an effort to learn their appalling language. With a mixture of bad German, bad French and very bad Russian emphasised in English, we spent many happy evenings together.

One of our members of the P.T., Lord Phillimore, who had learned to speak Russian fairly well, was approached by five officers of the Preobajensk Guards regiment who had a plan for an escape. Phillimore was asked to bring one other Englishman into their secret and he asked me. We met in the Russians' room which they shared and they, in perfect English, unfolded their secret. Two of them had discovered an underground tunnel from the German headquarters in the camp leading outside the camp. It was seven foot high, lit by electric light, and used to bring the water and electrical supply into the camp. A Russian soldier, working under the Germans, had stolen the key of the door at the entrance to the tunnel and given it to one of the Russian officers. He had moulded an exact copy of the key, and the Russian soldier had replaced the original key before it was missed. It all seemed to be too easy if we could get there without being seen. I asked if the other British who were working with us could be included but they were adamant about this and were doubtful about trusting the secret to more than five of their own officers. It was here that I began to get a glimpse of the narrowness of Russian societies, their secrecy from each other and their distrust. It was due to this that this enterprise, which might have enabled many to escape, failed ignominiously. One of the Russians brought in three friends who were distrusted by the others. There was a quarrel and the owner of the key threw the key into the stove where it melted. So ended the dealings with the Russians. Phillimore who knew them better than I did said it was typical. It is little wonder that the iron hand of Communism has gripped them and forced them to work without respite or plotting. I felt somewhat ashamed of my escapade and told the other members of the P.T. who seemed to be only amused.

At the end of February 1917 we opened our tunnel and found that the water had caused the sides of our chamber to slip. Thanks to shoring up with timber the tunnel was little damaged. We soon repaired the chamber and got the tunnel to work again. It was very wet and cold but we were young and it did us no harm at the time. We went merrily along and about the middle of March we calculated that we were outside the wire so that everything should be ready for our Spring offensive. All of us were in high spirits collecting food for our journey, copying maps and memorising them. One of our members received a ham from England and on cutting it up found six small compasses and a map inside.

When we were at our highest point of delight news came of the Russian Revolution. Many Russians who had lived in Moscow expected this and some had hoped for it, but to the Guards officers it came as a shock. It came as a greater shock to us because a week later we were told that the English were to be removed from the camp within three days in order not to influence the Russians. I have never known such utter dejection. Our life and thought had been centred on escape for a whole year and our hopes had been very high. Some of us thought that the tunnel must be beyond the line of sentries outside the wire and that we could burst out. We therefore constructed communication by electric wire from a window where we could observe the sentries down to the tunnel. From the face of the tunnel a stick was pushed up through the earth into the air and waved when the sentry's back was turned. It was disappointing to find that we had only reached as far as the line of sentries just outside the wire. In fact the stick waved close to a sentry box. Rogers was against any attempt to break out but finally agreed to take the risk of two breaking through, provided that the sentry was not in his box, but patrolling his beat. We therefore broke through at the face to within three feet of the top, dug a pit for the last three feet of sand to fall into and made a ladder. We then had an election for the two who were to make the break-through.

It was decided that Owen and I were to do it. We spent the rest of the day making our preparations. Owen was to break through and I was to follow. All depended on breaking out quickly and noiselessly and there was a very good chance of us being shot as we got out, especially the last one. As soon as it was dark we got down into the tunnel and crawled to the face with our bags of food. There we waited for the signal in suppressed excitement, each trying to be witty to cheer up the other one. Word came down that it was raining and the sentry was in his box. Hour after hour we waited and I prayed hard that we might get out. At about 2 a.m., word came that it had started to rain again and the sentry was back in his box. So again we waited a long time for our chance, until the voice of Rogers came booming down the tunnel: 'It's no good, it's getting light. You must come out'. My heart sank in despair.

Caricature of Puck deliberating his next escape, drawn by fellow prisoner Doody Wynne, who originated for him the sobriquet 'Puck' because of his 'mischievous spirit'.

So that was the answer to my prayer. All the hopes we had lived on for eight months were destroyed. It was a risk worth taking. But looking back on it now [written 30 years later], I am grateful to an overruling Providence.

The long stay in Gutersloh ended in disappointment. The tunnel was handed over to the Russians, who appreciated it very much, but afterwards Puck heard that within a month the tunnel was treacherously divulged to the Germans by one of their officers. Puck, along with the rest of the British contingent were transferred to Crefeld which, by the accounts of others, had good conditions and the POWs were allowed into town on parole. But soon after their arrival the camp was split up and Puck was sent to Strohen. Strohen was not far from the Dutch border and was described as 'without exception the worst camp' experienced by others who had been moved around. Sanitary arrangements were very bad and the food impossible to eat. The guards were encouraged to be as brutal as possible and many of the stories told by POWs who were interviewed after escape, confirm that prisoners were sent to the cells for very minor offences Soon after arrival Puck was told that he was to be sent, with five other 'criminals' to Augustabad in East Prussia. Augustabad was 350 miles from the Dutch frontier. Once interned in that camp he realised that his chances of escape were very poor. He wrote:

I made up my mind to take the first opportunity, however slight, to bolt. The camp at Strohen was the usual shape surrounded with a barbed wire fence 15 ft high, lit up at night and with a sentry outside the fence every 50 yds. An open drain which carried the slops from the kitchen ran under the wire. It was blocked by some strands of wire, but it might be possible, while the sentry was at the far end of his beat, to swim down the drain, cut the wire and get out. The drain had pretty clean water, but I would have gone down the filthiest drain to get away. My pals were amazingly kind and gave me a meal, which nearly defeated my chance of moving. They arranged a rugger scrum 50 yds on each side of the drain, to draw off the sentries. Smith, known as Crippen, said he would come with me. Heppy lent me the wire-cutters which Charles Fox had sent to him inside a ham. I promised that whatever happened I would throw back these cutters into the camp. Onslow returned my compass and Wynne gave me a railway map. I had collected meat tablets and Horlicks malted milk from parcels from home which ought to last a fortnight, and Strohen was only 85 miles from Holland.

As soon as it was dark the rugger scrums began their turmoil and the sentries went up to them to see what was happening. I got into the drain, pushing my bag of food in a mackintosh which floated in front. Crippen got in behind me and Heppy stood behind ready to warn us if a sentry came near. I got to the wire pretty quickly and began to cut. Suddenly I heard a warning cry from Heppy and, looking up, I saw a sentry only 20 yds away with his rifle at the aim, pointing at me. I got out of the drain dripping with water and told the sentry that I had fallen in. He said: 'You are trying to escape. If you come forward I will shoot'. I expected his beastly rifle to go off at any moment and I said: 'Of course I'm not going to escape, how could I. Put your rifle down'. He didn't put it down so I turned and walked away trying to look dignified, dripping with water and expecting a bullet in my back any minute, and very thankful when I turned the corner of the first house. Crippen had got away. Next morning a hot sun helped me to dry my clothes which an orderly had washed. Heppy could not understand why the sentry returned at such a critical moment. Three minutes more and I should have been away. They discovered the cut wire next day and doubly reinforced it. Nevertheless, six months later two fellows cut their way through and got over the frontier.

This episode seems to have ended in a period of solitary confinement. He wrote:

They let me out of solitary confinement for 24 hours into the camp to collect 'my things', consisting of one suit and a shirt. At mid-day six of us were taken to the station and put into the train. German civilians looked white, pinched and starved. I felt very sorry for the children but I don't think it did grown up people much harm. They were gross over-feeders before the war and it certainly improved their figures. We went through Essen, about 10 miles of factories making guns and ammunition. I marked down several spots where bombs would have a wonderful effect and hoped I should get the chance of dropping them. I believe that continuous bombing of Essen would have finished Germany in 1917.

There were two soldiers in our carriage, one opposite me – I had a seat by the door – and one by the other door. They had their rifles between their knees and told us that they were loaded. My only chance of escape was at night. About 9.00 p.m. we were due to pass a place in North Prussia which was only 12 miles from the sea, by my railway map. If I could get away and get to the coast I might find a boat and sail across the Baltic to one of the Swedish islands. It was rather a forlorn hope but I was determined to take the slightest opportunity rather than languish at Augustabad for the rest of the war. As it grew dark and we neared the place I had selected luck seemed to be with me. The soldier opposite me was asleep. The other was awake but very sleepy. I took my bag of food and was ready. The train began to slow down and the brakes began to grind. The soldier on the other side stood up and turned his back to take something from the rack. It was my chance. I opened the door and jumped out into the dark, forward with the train. My feet touched the ground and I ran forward and fell, but not badly. We were nearly into the station and there were lights. As I fell I heard a rifle go off and a bullet whizzed past me. I picked myself up and ran down an embankment of grass. Someone had jumped after me and was pursuing with howls. On my right was the station, in front a road lit up. My way was to the left, parallel to the railway line along which we had come. I ran like a lamplighter. My store of food which had seemed so heavy now appeared to be as light as a feather. I felt utterly happy and remember thinking that, after all, a fox must have a grand life. Suddenly I went down on my face, 'splosh' into a stream. It was only up to my waist but I lost my bag of food. Groping round I found it but the blighter who was pursuing me caught me up and I saw two people with lights in front, apparently directed by his yells. I got through onto the grass again and doubled to the right. I believe I could have got away but I slipped on the grass and before I was up the blighter was on me. I fought him hard as I could and landed him one in the face, but he hung onto my coat yelling like a jackal till the others came up. Then one took each arm and they marched me back to the station where the train had arrived. On the platform was a crowd of Prussian civilians shouting 'Schveirereil, Schweinhund Englander!' One of them hit me in the mouth and broke two teeth. I was held by both arms but I just managed to catch him with my foot as he jumped away and I was so angry that I think he remembered it.

The rest of the journey I passed with a Prussian soldier sitting on each side of me, separated from the other fellows. When we arrived at Augustabad the Prussian Commandant came out and addressed me. He said that he could not allow me to stay more than two days in his camp but that I must go to solitary confinement in a camp of common soldiers where I would be punished. I was very dirty and stained with blood and two broken teeth, no hat and my clothes smelt still of the drain. I told him that I did not want to come to his beastly camp, it was too far from England for my tastes, and that when we had won the war enquiries would be made as to how British officers were treated. I tried to be very dignified but I must have looked ridiculous.

In the camp were about 50 British officers. They were awfully kind to me and gave me clothes and a beautiful bed to sleep in, with sheets. I slept and slept. It was a most comfortable camp. They seemed to have made themselves almost luxurious. But apparently they had given up all idea of escaping because it was, they said, too far away. Consequently the camp was dead. They were like comfortable ghosts. They were allowed out for walks provided they gave their parole not to escape. I dare say they were sensible but I could not have stood it for long and was glad when I left.

My escort was a chatty N.C.O. and two soldiers. We went to the station by the shore of a lake surrounded with woods and hills, perfectly delightful. As we rounded a corner we came across several girls bathing. They looked so pretty and charming that my escort had to drag me away.

The new camp, Parchim, in Bavaria was enormous. About 70,000, mostly Russian and French soldiers but about 1,000 English. My cell was in the middle of the camp, about 12 ft by 6 ft A small barred window showed me the sentry outside. Beyond that a wire fence with the usual sentries and another fence beyond that. I looked onto a hut full of Russian soldiers. One was standing outside with his arms folded, looking at the ground. He remained like this for two hours. Another came creeping out. As he came the sentries laughed and pretended to aim at him. He ran round the hut looking terrified. I asked my gaoler about them and he said they were all mad. Every day I saw three or four coffins being taken out. These were Russian prisoners who had died. I asked the German guard commander why the devil they didn't look after them better. He said they had no food because of our blockade and they couldn't starve their soldiers in order to feed their prisoners. He said that the British and French got parcels from their homes, but that the Russians got nothing.

When I was taken into the camp to have my bath, which I insisted upon every day, I met these Russians and was able to talk to them as I had learned a little Russian. They were fine looking fellows but nearly starved, simple and accepting their fate like an Oriental. I don't think I ever felt so sorry for people in my life. There seemed to be nothing for it. I could not blame the Germans. Their own meals were pretty scanty. We had to use the blockade, but it is a horrible weapon. Over 100,000 Russian prisoners died in Germany. I talked to some of our own men. They had parcels from England and were pretty cheery. As usual they had the Germans feeding out of their hands. Two German soldiers would march out 50 of our men to the fields to pick potatoes. Our fellows would say: 'Come on Fritz, get a move on'. Then the Germans wanted men to go down the mines and tried to get hold of those who were miners in civilian life. They lined them up and asked them what their profession was before the war. The first one said he was a 'hair-pin painter', and this was solemnly written down by the Hun. The next said he was a 'domino-spotter'! 'They gave me a slice of black bread in the morning and the same in the evening, but at mid-day a good meal of vegetables with occasional meat, for which I had to pay. The gaoler opened the door and a Russian brought it in. The second day he showed a note under his hand. I put my hand on it and read it as soon as the door clanged and was bolted. The note was from a Romanian officer in the cell next to mine who was there for being rude to a German officer. It was written in French and in German because, he explained, British officers do not care for foreign languages but I might, perhaps, understand one of them. In it he described how he was taken prisoner. 'I had the honour, he said, to lead a charge on a German position. Everyone can testify to my courage. I was alone in front of my men shouting brave words to my comrades "debout, jamais couche". The bullets whistled around me but unhappily my flesh had not the honour to receive the lead. My glorious regiment – we took the position – so brave, Ah so brave! Then the Germans counter attacked and I was hit over the head with the butt of a rifle'. Every day he wrote me long letters. I wish I had kept them. They were exactly like Conan Doyle's 'Brigadier Gerard'. Once, as I was being brought in from an hour's exercise he was coming out. He dashed forward shouting 'mon brave Anglais' and threw his arms around my neck and kissed me on both cheeks. Fortunately the German soldiers pulled him away.

They gave me lots of books in my cell, both English and German. But I saw a chance to escape. The floor of the hut was about one and a half feet above the ground and if I could saw through the floor I might get away. I started by purloining a table knife signalling to the Russian waiter not to give me away, which he did not. With another knife I cut teeth into this and made a saw. I then started to saw through the floor boards under my bed, cutting inwards so that, when sawn through, the boards would still rest on the remainder of the boards from which they had been cut. It took ten days to cut through and then I found a space to crawl through under the floor. To get away I had to crawl under on the other side of the hut and then climb over two barbed-wire fences between the sentries. The sentries here were spaced about 100 yards apart and there seemed to be no chance. I was held up to begin with by a mound of earth up to the floor. As German soldiers came into my cell at odd hours of the day I could only work at night. At night a sentry came in once, sometimes before midnight, sometimes afterwards, one never knew. He stood at the door and flashed a torch at me and the blighter usually woke me up. To circumvent this I made a dummy in my bed. I had my flying cap still with me which, when stuffed, was the shape of my head. I cut off my hair which was very long and stuck it to the flying cap by means of Horlick's malted milk. On the pillow it looked exactly like a head turned to the side with a sheet up to the ear. Clothes in the bed looked like a figure and unless the sentry looked closely it might pass.

Then as soon as 'lights out' went I got down and grovelled in the earth under the bed. After about an hour I heard the door open and a soldier tramp in. I saw the light through the floor boards and waited expecting a bayonet into my behind at any minute. Then the footsteps and the door slammed and was locked. For three nights I dug but the way out was terribly blocked. My pyjamas were filthy and I left them under ground. On the fourth day the Commandant came to see me and said that they had decided to let me off with three weeks instead of a month. I said that, as a matter of fact, I was enjoying myself learning a lot of German from his men and from books. I should be charmed to enjoy his hospitality for another week. The old man was delighted. He said he had never had a request like this before, that he was a great admirer of England and liked his prisoners well. However, orders were orders and he would send me off tomorrow. I asked where and he said Strohen. I was delighted. Strohen was only 85 miles from the frontier and most of my 'criminal' friends were there. Surely we should get out.

I had my usual escort of one N.C.O. and two men. We had a long journey and stopped a day at Hamburg. The N.C.O. said that, if I would give my 'parole' not to escape, he would let me go into the town and would dismiss the soldiers, but come with me himself to see that I was not molested. I said that I would give it for the day only. The town looked dead. Half the shops shut, the other half with very little in them. The people white and haggard without life. The wharves empty with lines of empty ships. No one took notice of me. I talked to Germans in shops. They all had the same point of view. They were sick to death of the war. When would it end? No one could win it and all countries would be ruined. When the war was finished, they said, there would be another war in Germany – a Civil war. It was the Junkers who started the war and who were keeping it going, the higher ranks drawing lots of pay and keeping well away from the front line. Everywhere I heard the same thing, in trains, from my escort, from the guards, the sentries. Their spirit seemed to be broken in September 1917 with the winter in front of them.

In Strohen I had a wonderful reception from all my old friends. One of our German escort had returned with the story of my escape from the train, much exaggerated. Some of these sentries were in sympathy with every attempt to escape though they did not dare to show it, and dared not to speak to us when a sentry was near. We were warned that German soldiers were 'earnest' men, carrying out their patriotic duty; they were marksmen with the rifle and fired on escaping prisoners with the intention to kill.

The place where I had cut the wire was now guarded by an extra sentry and more wire. There was no possible outlet which I could see, especially as we were now locked in buildings at night under the regime of the new Commandant 'Niemeyer'. I soon concluded that the only hope was to disguise oneself as a German soldier and get through a gate by daylight. I chose Gray of the R.F.C. who had escaped before, and Bousfield, a sapper, who was a craftsman at making keys. Both had been shot down by Richthofen and were hoping for a chance of another scrap with him. We spent some time in dying flannel pyjamas in coffee and ink until we got the exact shade of colour of the German working uniform. We then cut out of gilt tin the Army Corps and Divisional numbers for the collars and the Westphalian crosses for hats. Hats we managed to buy from the Germans. An Australian gave me a belt with the 'Gott mit uns' motto, which he had stolen. I made a wooden bayonet coloured with ink and gilt paint. At ten yards we were not distinguishable from the Germans. The camp was arranged thus:

No. 1. sentry's beat was between the two gates. My intention was to open the side gate while No. 1. sentry was opening the main gate, and at the same time draw off the attention of No. 2. sentry. Bousfield got a soap impression of the side gate by crossing 'no man's land' in a mist and very soon made a key from an alloy of lead and German spoons. We dressed 17 times for this, but on every occasion a sentry was looking or some soldiers appeared outside the camp. On the 17th attempt Challover stood at the corner near No. 2. sentry while we waited in the barrack opposite the side gate. A German with a wheelbarrow moved out to the main gate and No. 1. sentry walked down to open the main gate. Challover signalled and two fellows sent a hockey ball into the fence near No. 2. sentry and argued with him about it. Challover signalled again to us and we walked out to the side gate. The key fitted the lock, to my joy, and opened the gate. We were just through when No. 1. sentry had shut the main gate and looked round at us. Having a bayonet, I marched behind the other two as the N.C.O. and told them in German to go straight ahead. We went on expecting a bullet in our behinds at every minute. As we rounded the German barrack a cart drove up and a German asked us where the Commandant's house was. I told him, but saw him staring suspiciously after us. Either my accent, kit or walk was at fault. However, nothing happened and we walked down the road. I said 'Tag' to every German we passed who greeted us without any pronounced surprise, so we began to get more confident. After a while we got off the road on to the heath and moved as fast as we could. I was thrilled with excitement – the best thrill of my life, I think. I really believed we could get through now, with reasonable luck.

As soon as it was dark we pushed on across country, guiding ourselves by compass. It was all heather and bog and we fell into the bog several times. Towards dawn we struck some cross roads and, reading the sign by electric torch, we found our position. As soon as light began to break, we hid up in a wood, ate some food and slept. So we moved on night after night, avoiding villages but getting rather careless about using roads because moving across country was so slow. One day we were in a spinney, as we judged, by the Dutch frontier, sleeping. We were woken by a German patrol who came at us with fixed bayonets. On discovering that my bayonet was made of wood they concluded that we were British prisoners. It was just luck that they came to our spinney when the country was dotted with woods. We were returned to cells at Strohen – one month's solitary confinement.

This escape is recounted with some difference in Hugh Durnford's book, *The Tunnellers of Holzminden*, a later escape which included both Gray and Bousfield. It was common procedure that recaptured escapees were transferred to a new prison camp and it would seem that these two, Gray and Bousfield, were sent to Holzminden some time before Puck was transferred there in January 1918, possibly because, as leader of the escape, he languished in solitary confinement rather longer. Whatever the reason, Gray and Bousfield were able to join the tunnelling group in Holzminden which, after nine months of tunnelling, effected a highly successful escape in July 1918 when 29 officers, including the most senior of them, Colonel Rathbone, got away.

The German Camp Commandant at the time of this famous escape from Holzminden turned out to be none other than Hauptman Niemeyer, who had been Commandant at Strohen when Puck had made his escape there. Possibly, Niemeyer had been transferred to Holzminden because of that escape. To be responsible for the safe guarding of prisoners at Holzminden when 29 of them had successfully got away can have done his reputation no good. He was a notorious bully and, after his initial deflation, the sound of laughter which permeated the camp roused the devil within him. The chanting of 'Neun und Zwanzig' was like a red rag to a bull and open war was declared between himself and the senior British Officer remaining. Durnsford, in his book, devotes a whole chapter to 'Niemeyer – and Pin-pricks'. It would seem that Niemeyer's conduct at Strohen had been strongly condemned by the German War Office and on transfer to Holzminden he had become 'More truculent than hitherto'. A policy was adopted to annoy him by pinpricks, 'to goad an already maddened creature'.

Puck was in Holzminden camp while the tunnelling was proceeding. Since his accomplices in the Strohen escape, Gray and Bousfield, were clearly involved it is strange that he did not write about it in his memoirs; but they had got to Holzminden before him and possibly the tunnel was so well kept a secret that he had no knowledge of it. He had written to Tickie from Strohen in July, 1917, saying that everyone is talking about the big exchange to Holland for all those who have been prisoners of war for 18 months, but didn't want to finish the war that way and supposed that he could refuse. In that same letter he had written to thank her for four letters, all written in May, presumably awaiting his return from his escape, and saying how glad he was to hear that Martyn had returned to the Western Front and how he had always wanted to pay for her son, Dudley's education if he wasn't married himself, but would now like to do so anyway. However, he would certainly get married if he ever got back to England again, adding that he 'must do something of the sort after all this imprisonment'! Much as he would have cherished an invitation to join the tunnellers he didn't get the chance to do so because he was sent for internment in Holland in April 1918. No doubt the Germans were glad to get rid of him – he had caused them enough trouble.

Clearly his thoughts were turning to his future military career and private life. He had lost three years' experience as a soldier in the front line and those of his contemporaries, who had not been killed, had moved up the promotion ladder. During his pre-war service in India he had been much impressed by the Indian Civil Service in the field, and by the responsibilities heaped upon Political Agents in the Princedoms. He was of a mind to transfer to the ICS.

In this letter to Martyn written soon after his arrival in Holland, in which he congratulated his brother on being awarded the DSO for outstanding courage on the Western Front, he was already thinking about his post-war career.

The Faithful Soldier

Pension Persijn
Oud Wassener
Den Haag
26.6.18

Dear Old Boy,

It was topping to get your letter and to get a little idea of what you've been doing. You have had some marvellous escapes and even when you were commanding a group, it didn't seem to make any difference to the amount of risk you took. There are very few fellows, and I'm not one of them, who would walk three times through a heavy barrage in order to sketch some positions. Those are the things I like to hear of in the war. I am sure that you have deserved the D.S.O. a hundred times when you were not seen. I'm afraid I can't help hoping that they will give you a job in England for a bit. After all you relieve some one else who goes out. Let me have some more of those long letters if you can spare the time. That last one has done me the world of good.

I've just come back from five days' leave with another fellow in the I.A. We did a walking tour through the prettiest part of Holland. I can't imagine anything more peaceful than a village in this country, except that you can just hear the guns in Flanders – but I generally make a noise to drown that sound. I haven't enjoyed anything so much for years. We just did anything we wanted to and it gave one a topping feeling of freedom. I am bursting with health now.

I have a job which takes up the mornings and which I like to think is useful, and generally read or play tennis in the afternoon. I've written to the India Office to find out if there is any chance of getting into the Indian Political after the war. It's a job which I should like very much and I don't think I could stay on in the Army. I'm waiting till the Indian N.C.O.s come through to take them out on a farm. Our chances of repatriation are practically nil.

The very best of luck, old skin, if you do go out again soon. Don't forget that the Bosche are *damned* good at anything which they can prepare beforehand, but, if you can spring a surprise on them and push it all you know, you'll have them cold. But you know much more about Fritz than I do.

I see Lumsden has been killed. I suppose he was bound to be. I liked him enormously, though I spent most of the time quarrelling with him. I think that Vi was cut out to marry a blind man – she will be very happy, I think. What has happened to Squeaker Milward! His brother was afraid he was either scuppered or a prisoner of war in the March show.

Cheerioh!

Yours

Ernest

He was still there in Pension Persijn, in August 1918, from which he wrote to Tickie to say that he did not have much hope of being repatriated before the next Spring and had put in to go to Leiden University to work at Persian and Arabic when the term opened in September. His course was cut short by the Armistice and he was not to return to The Hague until thirty years later when, with his wife, he was the guest of His Majesty's Ambassador, Sir Philip Nichols, at the Embassy.

10

IMMEDIATE POST-WAR

Puck was repatriated from Holland a week after the war ended in 1918, arriving in Hull on 22 November, and was attached to the RFC. He was granted leave over Christmas and the New Year, enjoying for the first time in seven years a reunion with his family in Yorkshire. He joined 29th Squadron for a week's refresher course in February 1919 being promoted Honorary Flight Lieutenant, Royal Air Force, before being transferred back to the 3rd Brahmans, Indian Army, at the end of that month. He attended the Senior Officers' School in Aldershot and then, travelling overland to Marseilles took the HT 'Caledonia' to Alexandria and spent a brief holiday in Egypt before embarking at Suez on the HT 'Northbrook' bound for Karachi, joining the 3/23rd Sikh Infantry, Rawalpindi in July on attachment as Second in Command. Puck wrote:

> When I arrived the Colonel said to me: 'Now I can put in for leave. I've been in India the whole war without leave and you are the first regular officer I've had for a year'. Within a month he left for England and I, as a junior Captain, was left to command a regiment of Ramdasia Sikhs, most of whom were professional thieves. I had fourteen war-time British officers, twenty Indian officers and eight hundred ruffians about whom the Colonel's advice was to be ruthless.

My job was to train them for war. The British officers had little knowledge, and could hardly speak the language well enough to convey any meaning to the troops. All had an admiration for the senior Indian officer, the Subedar-Major, who was a great character, of a higher caste than the men, and held by them in great respect. But I soon discovered that he was the virtual dictator of the regiment. That was wrong and I had to show him at once that I was commanding the regiment. He did not like it and began to speak to me about his retirement and his advancement to the great dignity of 'Sirdar Bahadur' before his retirement.

Now I did not want him to retire; I knew that I could not do without him at present. Furthermore, the Sikhs were giving great trouble in the Punjab, and messages were constantly coming to me from Simla, warning me of sedition which was undermining the Sikhs. The Chief of Police in Rawalpindi came to see me and informed me of dacoits who had held up buses, carts and cars outside the cantonment, robbing the passengers at the point of a gun. These dacoits were Sikhs and my men were suspected. I told him that I could do nothing unless he caught one. The Subedar-Major said that it was better for them to sow their wild oats outside the regiment than inside, with which remark I could not help feeling in sympathy but, if it were true, it must be stopped.

Sedition, robbery, mutiny seemed to be growling, rumbling and growing. To cope with this I had a handful of young British officers who were of little use and could not speak the language, and the only man who could control them wanted to go. And how utterly inadequate I was to deal with it and make these ill-disciplined robbers into an efficient fighting unit! I had been away from India and the Indian Army for the whole of the war, knew nothing about Sikhs, and had forgotten how to express myself in Hindustani. Furthermore there was no officer in the station who had any experience of Sikhs.

In my difficulties and weakness I had learned, while a prisoner in Germany, to turn to Almighty God, and to wait for an answer. The answer was always the right one in the long run, if I approached God with humility, concealing nothing. I therefore prayed every day for the regiment and for those individuals whom I knew personally. The answer I got was very different to the advice which I had received, it was : 'love them and work them'. I started on the British officers; insisted on them learning the language properly with a Murshi, an Indian teacher, in their spare time and did it myself. I took them out on tactical schemes, and had to work hard to bring myself up to date.

Those tactical exercises with breakfast out of doors in the perfect Punjab winter climate were very happy. I got to know the officers and to like them very much. Then I drilled and drilled the regiment until we were all sick of it, including myself. But they became almost perfect in drill and the discipline and cleanliness obviously improved. Every week there were fewer defaulters, fewer punishments, and no court-martials. Above all, I went round the lines in the evening, talking to the Indian officers and men until they lost their shyness and furtiveness and spoke to me freely about their villages, and the trouble which Sikhs were giving to the Government and the reasons for it. I got to love those Sikhs.

They were men, physically beautiful, hard, turbulent and emotional, but never had I had such loyalty and never will again.

A year later we were sent to quell an insurrection in Iraq and with a temperature of 120 degrees in the shade they marched and fought with very little water but with a magnificent spirit. The Sikh religion is a fighting religion. When a Sikh is eighteen years of age he has an iron ring forged round his wrist and is given the name 'Singh' or 'Lion-hearted'. He swears never to give way in battle. They are allowed to drink alcohol, but are not allowed to smoke, in contrast to the Mohammedans, who smoke but do not drink. I sometimes attended the Sikh religious services which are very sincere. The Sikh priest or Grunthi was a friend of mine. He was a very wise old man with the face of a saint. We sometimes discussed religion. Nothing would induce him to be tolerant towards Mohammedans but he was genuinely interested in Christianity. His influence on the regiment was all for the good and we missed him when we went on active service.

Our government was always afraid and suspicious of Sikhs. There never has been any need for this. There are only three million

Sikhs, and more than seventy million Mohammedans who have Mohammedan countries outside to help them. The Sikhs therefore knew that their only hope was in loyalty to the British Government. They need to be handled very firmly, especially in peace time when they are inclined to intrigue.

The year 1919 had been an eventful one for Puck. He had enjoyed freedom from prison life and pursuit by his German captors like a hunted fox, restoration among his family again, honour from the newly formed Royal Air Force and release from it into his chosen career. Then, a return to his beloved India and temporary command of a Sikh regiment for a substantial and important training period for it, at the early age of 34 years. Before the end of it, in September, news came through that he had been mentioned in the London Gazette for gallant and distinguished services as a Prisoner of War – deserved recognition of the thorn he must have been in the flesh of his German captors.

Puck's command of the 3/23rd Sikhs for a period of seven months, overlapping into 1920 in the absence of the CO, earned him very favourable confidential reports which described him as: 'A keen and capable officer, rides well, shows organising ability, is capable of imparting instructions and is a good disciplinarian. He is temperate and tactful and takes an interest in his profession. Captain Strover is likely to make a good staff officer.' And: 'An able and efficient officer in whom I place great confidence. Efficiently commanded the Regiment for seven months at Rawalpindi during the absence on leave of the temporary commander.' And his Brigadier wrote: 'The little I have seen of this officer has impressed me favourably.'

Puck completed a course at the Mountain Warfare School in Abbotabad in April/May 1920 and this probably whetted his appetite for the Himalayas again, as he took a break away from regimental duties in July by returning to his beloved Kashmir for a month's holiday, which he wrote about in a diary. His adventure started at Srinagar which he felt was 'like meeting an old love', not having been there for ten years and, hiring a Shikari, Mahomed Baba, coolies and ponies, he made his way into the foothills, describing them as: 'Beautiful beyond description. Their beauty is so positive that it catches the least impressionable Englishman by the throat.' He camped by the side of a rushing mountain stream, near Bandipur, for three days, enjoying the abundance of flowers and apricot, mulberry and walnut trees, heavy with fruit. His goal was Astor where he might obtain shooting rights for ibex, sharpur and red bear. After four days' trek over a mountain pass at 13,000 ft he arrived at Gudhai Nullah, a valley region of over 300 sq miles, the shooting rights of which had been secured for him by his Shikari for a month. His delight knew no bounds and exploring the area they found tracks of ibex, snow leopard and red bear. Alas, after three days of searching and climbing and 'the thrills and perpetual anticipation of game', he received a telegram on 29 July, recalling him to duties as the regiment was mobilising for service in Mesopotamia. He wrote: 'It is like taking a drink from a thirsty man when he has just tasted it. Mahomed Baba frankly wept. It is eleven days to Srinagar and thirteen to Rawalpindi. Tomorrow I must walk thirty miles to Astor to settle things up and send wires.'

On the way back he met with two Scottish Riflemen who told him that there was serious trouble in Mesopotamia and troops were being sent there as soon as possible. That lifted his spirits no end as he had suspected just a 'Simla scare'; but a real war in Mesopotamia, 'there is nothing better I could wish for'. He hastened his journey, going back by the Kamri pass and into cloud at 14,100 ft getting only a brief glimpse of Nanga Parbat at 26,000 ft; and on the way down, as they broke cloud, it reminded him of flying over Hertfordshire. By speeding up his ponies and taking a boat along the river to Srinagar, and organising a car to meet him there, he was able to rejoin the regiment after only ten days, on 8 August.

11

MESOPOTAMIA

On arrival at HQ of 3/23rd Sikhs Puck learned that there had been an Arab uprising in Mesopotamia and that it had been decided to send for reinforcements to the Expeditionary Force already there. The regiment entrained at Rawalpindi on 10 August with a strength of 9 British officers, 18 Indian officers (5 Subedars and 13 Jemadars), 685 other ranks, 53 followers, 7 chargers and 20 mules under the command of Major R.N.B. Campbell, DSO, OBE with Puck as Second in Command. On 13 August the regiment embarked in RIMS Northbrook at Kiamari sailing at 1900 hrs. The voyage to the Persian Gulf was described as rough but without incident and they arrived at the mouth of the Shatt Al Arab on 17 August in 'very hot and steamy weather'. They sailed up river to Basra, disembarking the next day at Magil Wharf at 1430 hrs, and immediately entrained for Naziriey on the River Euphrates, arriving there the next day at 1300 hrs having stopped overnight at Shaiba while they waited for dawn to break, it being considered dangerous to travel at night while raiding parties were in the area, especially since this same transport had been sniped at on the previous night.

Naziriey had been a Turkish stronghold with German and Arab support in the campaign of 1915 when the Expeditionary

Force fought their way up from Basra to Baghdad, to protect the oil pipeline which ran from Persia to the gulf, and also to prevent German ambitions of reaching as far as India through Persia and Afghanistan, and to combat German influence in Turkey especially over the 'Young Turk Party'. The curious thing about the Arabs, though, was that they had no fondness for the Turks yet many would fight for them against the British seeing that they are heathen, and Turks are of the 'faithful'. However, they were just as likely to to turn against the Sultan and help an invader, as of course they did when they joined Laurence and Allenby in their campaign in Palestine and Syria.

The Expeditionary Force was composed mainly of Indian regiments because of the extreme climate, it being as hot as in India in the plains in hot weather and often enough, when the cold season came along, bitterly cold and wet. Mostly it was hot, damp and trying so that native troops were far more suitable. The 3/23rd Sikhs were one of four Indian regiments in the 74th Brigade of the 6th Indian Division, the others being the 2/123rd and 2/125th Rifles and the 2/117th Mahrattas. The Brigade was responsible for the area Samaweh – Khidr – Naziriey – Ur Junction.

The regiment went into lines at the East end of the Naziriey cantonment, on the right bank of the Euphrates and started work on building parapets. The political situation was delicate owing to the uncertain attitude of the powerful Mutafik tribe to the North in the region of Shatt al Gharaf. Work continued on the parapets and building blockhouses throughout August, and at the end of the month the regiment was involved in an expedition of Fly Boats to take rations to Samaweh, beleaguered sixty miles upstream, apart from radio contact. Reports had reached brigade headquarters of 1,500–3,000 Arabs, well armed and well led, operating between Amaweh and Ur Junction, with small parties firing at posts all the way down to Basra.

Apart from the extreme heat the cantonment in Nasiriey had to put up with severe dust storms from the North West in September, but training continued. Some sniping was reported and three Arab sheiks responsible for it were taken prisoner. There was a report of several hundred camels moving West, belonging to the friendly Suk Asn Shuyukh tribe, considered to be restless, and there was worry that if they declared for the insurgents they might influence the Mutafik tribe against the MEF with an estimated strength of 20,000 men.

Regimental War Notes reported the following:

By the end of September the regiment had acclimatised and was ready for action. On the 27th inst. they marched up to Ur Junction starting at 0600 hrs and arriving at 1015 hrs to join a stronghold of 400 men. From there two Companies (A&C) under Captain Strover proceeded to the advance rail head. There they encountered sniping and suffered some casualties. The next day they moved forward and were fired upon by about 200 Arabs from Ishan Al Hamrah. The platoons attacked with well directed fire and the enemy retreated NW – 'eight horsemen and many on foot were seen to fall.' A&C companies rejoined the regiment at Darrah on the R. Euphrates and, despite a violent sandstorm in the night, advanced the next morning on Khidr with Captain Strover leading the two front line companies. 'A' Company was commended for 'showing considerable spirit in pressing forward on the left of the railway'. The regiment occupied Khidr station.

This was Puck's first real action in Mesopotamia and no doubt was in the back of his mind when he used to speak to his sons of 'the thrill of bullets whizzing through the air' when under fire. Two days later Lieutenant- Colonel Carey arrived and took over command of the regiment. Puck therefore reverted from Second in Command to 'A' Company Commander.

The River Euphrates is, by all accounts, 'stuffed full of sand-banks and muddy islands which are always changing, especially after rains and storms and is not the sort of river that one cares to steam up at any kind of pace during the hours of darkness', yet the Royal Navy operated a flotilla of defence vessels up and down it. Drawing as little as three feet of water they were able to penetrate the marshes to seek out insurgents. One of these vessels, DV Greenfly was reported aground between Khidr and Samaweh in one foot of water and when last seen the only apparent survivor had been its commander, 'Captain Roach sitting in a chair on deck unwilling or unable to leave his ship which was riddled with bullets'. The regiment with 'A' company as advance guard crossed the river by ferry and proceeded to Jazireh where Greenfly was lying, to collect evidence of the crew. 'A' company burnt the village where snipers had been located and eventually reached Greenfly to find it stripped of everything and just one corpse aboard. The Colonel reported: 'all ranks showed considerable endurance over a distance covered of 9–10 miles'.

War Notes continued:

> From 10th–15th October the Brigade column advanced up to Samaweh encountering little opposition on the way and were able to relieve the garrison there. On the 20th Oct. the regiment formed the advance guard of the force which moved three miles up river to reconnoître the Imam Abdullah railway bridge which had been destroyed, and to burn the villages nearby. 'A' company led in the 'usual diamond formation' and were fired at from Siyagh village. By 0914 hrs the regiment was in occupation of the near bank of the Shatt Abu Shuraish. The column retired to Samaweh for five rest days.
>
> On 27th Oct. the regiment was in a column which destroyed more villages around Samaweh, Ghumaijah and Rumh – 'A' and 'D' companies under Capt. Strover forming the left flank guard. 'D' Coy dropped two strong piquets in nullahs South of Abn and the advance guard entered Rumh, finding the remains of seven enemy bodies – the village was burned. The piquets proved to be a tactical stroke of great importance for they denied the nullahs to the enemy and enabled the flank guard to withdraw with the least amount of casualties; at the same time inflicting serious casualties on the

insurgents. Ghumaijah was burnt on withdrawal. The next day the regiment formed part of a column ordered to burn villages on the left bank of the river, Darrah and Abu Quaitar. 'A' and 'C' Coys under Capt. Strover formed the advance guard but met no opposition from the enemy. More burning of villages followed over the next two days before the regiment returned to Samaweh.

On 3rd Nov. the regiment received orders to move to Khidr for a punitive operation against the Jowabir tribe. They entrained at 0530 hrs the next morning, arriving at Khidr at 0700 hrs and crossed over the river to the left bank by ferry – a string of ten bellums (local craft) fastened fore and aft and pulled across by about sixty men. On 6th Nov. the force under Brigadier Jacob moved out with the objective of reaching Farrah; 'A' Coy under Capt. Strover forming the right flank guard. They came under heavy fire from 300–400 Arabs who were holding the line at Dhuwaihrah, suffering 12 casualties, and so halted before withdrawing to Khidr. The regiment was ordered to burn as many buildings and trees as possible between Budairi and Bab before returning to Samaweh on 9th Nov. This operation earned the regiment congratulations on its fine behaviour.

On 11th Nov. 3/23rd Sikhs was in the thick of an action at Imam Abdullah bridge. The objective was to seize the crossing of the Shatt Abu Shuraish at the ford, East of the bridge, and then make good the line from Artaubari, West to Falbah as a bridgehead to be occupied pending the repair of the bridge. They moved off at 1500 hrs. and by daybreak at 0610 hrs. had encountered no opposition. 'A' and 'C' Coys crossed the ford (about 3 ft deep) and took up position on the further bank. 'A' Coy under Capt. Strover, accompanied by one section of Machine Gun Corps then advanced over open ground to the N.E. under fairly heavy fire from Nalas to the N.E. by making double platoon rushes. They reached their objective by 0900 hrs. having suffered 2 casualties wounded, and remained in position there until 1400 hrs. when they were relieved by 3/5th Gurkhas, having made good their ground at Artaubari. 'A' Coy was withdrawn and transferred to the village of Falbah. Meanwhile, 'B', 'C' and 'D' Coys had fought their way up to Falbah having encountered stiff opposition. Altogether the regiment suffered casualties of four killed and two wounded. The regiment consolidated at Falbah over the next two days and on 17th Nov. Capt. Strover took 'A' and 'B' Coys back to main camp at Samaweh, about 3 miles South of the bridge [see War Map prepared by Major Campbell on the page opposite].

By 19 November negotiations for a peace settlement with rebel Sheiks were in progress at Samaweh, the terms being signed by Rumaitha Sheiks on 20 November. Over the next week Arabs of the Abban and Ajib tribes came into Falbah through the outposts to accept terms; and on 30 November the Zayyad tribe came in to ask for terms after a punitive expedition against them. On 1 December the regiment moved to Wawiyah and bivouacked there without tents. It was bitterly cold with a biting North West wind and a third blanket was issued. The next day a supply train brought up tents. On 4 December the regiment marched to Sayidali and on to Rumaitha, 4 miles, where the Union Jack was hoisted. That marked the end of hostilities.

On 6 December the regiment received a complimentary order of the day from the Brigade Commander, Brigadier Coningham: 'The reoccupation of Rumaitha where the Arab rising commenced on 1 July, coincident with the reoccupation of Diwaniyah by the 53rd Brigade column marks the virtual termination of hostilities and the column is proceeding to break up immediately. I wish therefore to take this opportunity to thank you all for your loyal cooperation. You have borne the severe cold with the same uncomplaining spirit as you showed in the intense heat. At Imam Abdullah when the enemy attempted to put up a fight they were severely handled and sought terms immediately. May you all have the best of luck in future.'

Puck had been a leading spirit of 3/23rd Sikhs: first as acting CO in Rawalpindi when he inculcated a new discipline into the training of the regiment; then as Second-in-Command in the move to Mesopotamia and training there for warfare; finally as the Company Commander who led the regiment in all its actions.

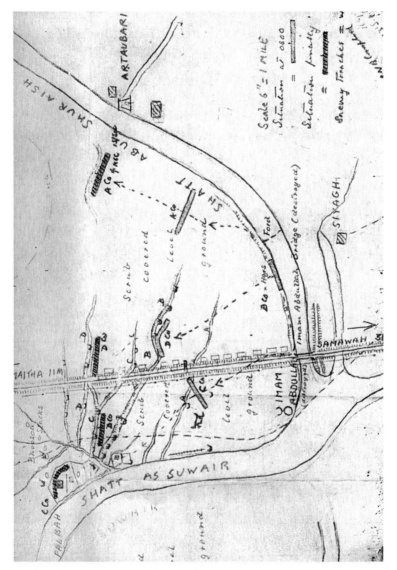

Battle plan of the action at Imam Abdullah bridge.

It could have been no surprise to his fellow officers that he was chosen to take over as officiating Brigade Major in Rumaitha, when the column broke up on 7 December, in the absence of Major Witts DSO who left for six months' home leave. As one of the few British officers who could speak some Arabic he would have been invaluable as a staff officer. By 11 December he was writing brigade reports showing that many more local Sheiks were coming in to Rumaitha to seek peace terms.

In the New Year news came through that Puck had been given the choice of a Brevet-Major or the award of a Military Cross for his 'distinguished and gallant services and devotion to duty' during the campaign to quell the Arab uprising. He chose a Brevet-Major as he was anxious to further his career as a soldier, especially as he had spent three years away from action as a prisoner of war. His was one of only 21 awards for the entire campaign (3 Brevet-Colonels, 3 Brevet Lieutenant-Colonels, 2 Brevet-Majors, 3 DSOs, 10 MCs) and the only one from his regiment. However, he and his Colonel, the Second-in-Command, one sepoy and one Naik were all mentioned in despatches, as were two officers of 3/5th Gurkhas, the honours being gazetted in the London Gazette on 9 September 1921. Another officer mentioned in despatches was his friend Jackie Smyth, VC, MC, 15th Sikhs, also on the staff at Basrah.

Puck enjoyed his time at Brigade HQ and his reports show that the Brigadier and his staff toured many of the local Sheik territories: Nasiriyeh, Butiniyeh, Sawaij, Badda, Mazaifi, Karradi, Suq Abn Hawan and Al Baddah. He often used to regale his family at the dinner table with stories of feasts in tribal tents and Arab hospitality, no doubt enjoyed in these Sheikdoms. In April 1921 he wrote to his sister-in-law Tickie: 'I have never enjoyed a job so much as this one…we said good-bye to the brigadier this week – he has been an excellent commander.' During the summer months he worked for his examinations for promotion to Major.

In September 1921 Puck was posted to 4/10th Chin Rifles. His CO of Basrah District wrote of him: 'A quiet, sound, reliable worker, specially skilled for staff employ and should be given a special mention for the Staff College', of which General Haldane wrote, 'I concur'. He took some leave in Baghdad to work for the Staff College, not holding out much hope of a place as there were only four vacancies for the entire Indian Army, and joined the regiment in Burma in May 1922 as a Company Commander, remaining with them until the end of the year when news came through that he had, indeed, been selected as one of the few I.A. officers to attend Staff College. His CO, Colonel Maymigo, wrote of him: 'A good leader with a wonderful amount of vitality. A keen polo player. He was working his Company up to good state of efficiency when he left in November to go to the Staff College, Camberley. He is an officer with a wonderful amount of tact and self-reliance.' 'I agree with the CO', wrote the Major-General Indpot District, ' A very good officer who is now at Staff College where he should do very well. He has the makings of a very good staff officer and I certainly recommend as a 2 i/c.'

12

STAFF COLLEGES
AND MARRIAGE

Puck arrived back in England in December 1922 and was able to join his family for Christmas and the New Year celebrations before starting at the Staff College Camberley in January, having been promoted Major. He used to speak of the intellectual challenge of the course and of some of his fellow officer students, among them Alan Brooke, Henry Pownall, Bernard Paget, Alan Cunningham, Bill Slim and Pug Ismay, all of whom made their names in the Second World War and two of whom, at least, reached the very top of their profession. There was time too for steeplechasing – he rode in the Staff College point-to-point – and played some polo. He took parts in Staff College drama productions and enjoyed the post-war social life of Camberley and London. Apart from one or two romantic liaisons which he formed during his two years in Camberley and on vacation with his Brown cousins in Yorkshire, his most loyal companion during this period was his cocker spaniel, Jimmy.

The Commandant was Major-General Ironside who later commanded an army in the British Expeditionary Force to France in 1940. Puck wrote of him: 'Ironside was full of thrust and ambition. I never thought him a great man, because his overweening self-confidence made him contemptuous of any failure. Consequently he never faced the possibility of the worst. Hence Dunkirk, and it was not due to him that our army was saved.' Ironside reported on Puck as he passed out of the course in December 1924: 'A thoroughly loyal officer, gallant in character and of a cheerful disposition. No one can fail to like him and he is of a type who is at his best when conditions are at their worst. He has little ability, but has worked very hard. He will always make friends wherever he goes.'

Puck had a period of leave following Staff College and in January 1925 he volunteered to take a party of young Indian Officer Cadets from Sandhurst, skiing in Switzerland. The party arrived in St Cergue to find that there was virtually no snow. Very little skiing was done so that he had to find ways of occupying and amusing his young charges off the slopes. In a neighbouring hotel there had arrived, at the same time, a family group which included in their number a young lady, Rosalind Atkinson. One evening Puck brought some of his cadets to that hotel to join in the entertainments there. Rosalind was a professional musician and both she and Puck were fond of amateur dramatics and games. There were children in the hotel who needed to be amused *après ski* and Puck soon found himself taking cadets round to that hotel every evening to organise, with Rosalind, the entertainments. They struck up a relationship together.

Before the ski holiday was over Puck told Rosalind that he had a problem over his spaniel Jimmy. He would be returning to India in April and could not take Jimmy with him and had nobody with whom he could be left. Rosalind said that she was sure that her parents would agree to her looking after Jimmy while Puck was away. So it was that on their return to England Puck took Jimmy up to Mistley Hall in Essex.

Rosalind was twenty years younger than Puck. Her father had distinguished himself in the Great War as a professional soldier in the Royal Horse Artillery and had risen to the rank of Brigadier-General. He retired from the Army after the war, commuting his pension in order to take up pig farming. Rosalind's mother was a Norman and her bachelor brother owned the two thousand acre Norman Estate which included eight farms. He lived at Mistley Lodge where Rosalind and her mother and two brothers had resided during the war years.

From that home in Essex, and after the war from Mistley Hall, Rosalind had pursued her musical career, gaining her LRAM in violin teaching and performing locally with Edmund Rubbra, then a railway clerk at Manningtree station, as piano accompanist. She had the distinction of having taught Rubbra the violin.

It was then to a rather grand house that Puck arrived in February 1925 with his dog. He and 'The General', as he was known locally, were able to swap memories of the war. After dinner there was music for entertainment and Rosalind, with her mother at the piano, played Bach and Brahms. Puck was invited to perform, and not being one to refuse an invitation, sat at the piano and gave a rendering of 'Oh my darling Clementine' accompanying his music hall voice by striking the chords with his large hands, which could span an octave and more, in a kind of 'oompah... oompah' rhythm. This amused 'The General' and Rosalind but did not endear him to her mother.

Puck invited Rosalind up to London to watch the Army v Navy rugby match at Twickenham. Afterwards they went to the 'In and Out' and it was there that she suggested to him that perhaps it would be a good thing if they got married because they got on so well. Puck was hesitant because he was so much older than her and he needed her father's permission. So back to Mistley they went and to a rather cold reception. It was decided that there should be no engagement and while Puck was in India there was to be no correspondence between them. Puck returned to India where he had been posted to his first staff appointment as Brigade Major of Ambala Brigade, while Rosalind remained at Mistley with Jimmy and her music and the social round of the 'gay twenties' which included balls in London and a trip to Cologne and Paris.

Within a year Puck was back in England again for he had been selected for the first intake at the Royal Airforce Staff College at Andover. This was a great honour for him. He had impressed his general in Ambala who described him as 'a capable, reliable and thoroughly trained staff officer, a good instructor and well suited to "G" work; has energy and character, is tactful and popular. He has done excellent work this hot weather in teaching officers for the Staff College and for promotion examinations. Has helped his temporary Brigade Commander to produce some excellent schemes in the Simla hills, fighting with and without troops.' He He was doing all the right things to gain promotion and greater responsibility in the armed services.

Major 'Puck' in 1923.

Puck and Rosalind on horseback at Mistley.

The wedding group at Mistley Hall. Martyn as best man. Barbara next but one to Puck's left.

Puck was soon back at Mistley to see Rosalind. Her parents had expected him to be away in India for two years and thought that a separation of that length would cool their ardour sufficiently. Not so, they were determined as ever and so it was agreed that the following April, 1927 they should be married. The wedding took place in Mistley Church, Martyn was best man and Barbara Hodson-Mackenzie, Rosalind's closest musical friend, was one of eight bridesmaids.

The honeymoon was spent at Lenno on Lake Como, and on return to England they packed their belongings and Jimmy into Puck's open tourer and drove down to Andover. Barbara Hodson-Mackenzie captioned her caricature of the move with the following limerick

> There once was a young man called Puck
> Who said, 'With very great luck
> My baggage, my life
> And my new wedded wife
> Will get there without getting stuck.

Puck and Rosalind set up their first home at The Cottage, Upper Clatford, close to Andover where he still had two months of the Staff College course to complete It was a delightful four bedroomed Georgian house at the end of the village and there they were able to entertain their friends and relations. Nellie Collins came with her daughter Peggy (Rosalind's Goddaughter) from Mistley to cook for them. Guests included the Brown cousins from Yorkshire; Puck's sister Nancy, now widowed; Doody Wynne, Puck's prisoner-of-war friend whom Rosalind thought 'a perfect dear' and Barbara Hodson-Mackenzie. Rosalind would have had all her Gurney, Buxton and Ruggles-Brise cousins over from East Anglia had time permitted. And, of course, the village school being next door, they were continually having children in to tea.

13

RETURN TO INDIA

The Staff College course finished in July and the Commandant, Air Commodore Ludlow-Hewitt reported on Puck:

> He has thoroughly entered into the spirit of the course, and has been most helpful both in and out of working hours. He has contributed more than his share to the operation of the atmosphere of happy good-humoured co-operation between the services. He has set an excellent example in every way, is very popular and at all times cheerful, tactful and ready to help. He has taken a real and lively interest in the course and has worked hard and conscientiously throughout. He has a broad mind directed by high ideals and unfailing geniality. Though not possessed of exceptional ability he is always sound and clear in his views, and expresses them simply and effectively both in speech and in writing. A charming and intelligent officer whose presence has been of great value to the course.

After two months' leave, some of it spent at Mistley sailing on the River Stour, Puck and Rosalind embarked on His Majesty's Troopship Dorsetshire on 20 September. The voyage to Karachi took a month and on the way there they put in at Basra – Rosalind's first taste of the East which she found 'fascinating but deplorably hot'. On board ship Puck gave her lessons in Hindustani, and they joined in all the deck games and fancy dress dances. Clearly they caused a stir as a newly married couple: at the last of the weekly race meetings in which dice were thrown to move named horses along a track their horse was named 'Honeymoon', trained by Major E.J. Strover and ridden by 'B.Liss'. On arrival in Karachi on 20 October they took an overnight train to Quetta where Puck had been appointed Deputy Assistant Adjutant General of Baluchistan District. They lived at 187 Finnis Road, a bungalow where they employed a bearer, cook, house boy and gardener. This gave them plenty of opportunity to entertain which they loved doing.

Puck found his new job to be rather dull at first, that was until he was asked by General Harrington to organise the reception for the King of Afghanistan who would be visiting India before Christmas. A few days before the King's arrival Puck and Rosalind drove their Cubitt up to Chaman on the Afghan frontier to rehearse the reception for him. There, there was assembled a Cavalry Regiment under the command of Colonel Abbay, a Norman relation, a Field Battery, a Brigade of Infantry and three squadrons of aeroplanes – a formidable array of British imperialism. Rosalind enjoyed standing in for Lady Harrington for the initial rehearsal and, after she had arrived, for the final rehearsal as one of the ladies in purdah.

The great day arrived and all went well for the reception at Chaman. Then, the King and his party boarded the specially constructed royal carriage of the train which was to take them down to Quetta. As soon as the train left Chaman station Puck and Rosalind got in their Cubitt and drove on a hair-raising journey, down all the S bends of the Khojak pass so as to be in Quetta in time for the arrival of the train. They needn't have worried for the train was held up in the tunnel through the pass because a member of the Royal party, in his fright, pulled the communication cord which, bringing the train to a grinding halt in the middle of the tunnel, broke a coupling. It arrived in Quetta three quarters of an hour late, which gave Puck time to be smart and ready to greet King Amanollah and his retinue. In his book, 'Fulness of Days', the Viceroy of India, the Earl of Halifax, confirms this story and adds: 'One or two of the Afghan Staff had been to the smartest Indian tailor to order themselves uniforms, and had asked for them to be the uniforms of Colonels in the Afghan army. Upon enquiry by the tailor as to what these were exactly like, the answer had come, "Make them like a British Field Marshal's. It is the equivalent rank!"'

General Harrington was pleased with the arrangements and wrote a special note of congratulation to Puck. Sadly for the King this trip which went on to Bombay and then England led to his demise, for on return to Afghanistan he tried to introduce reforms, alien to the wishes of his people, with the result that he lost his throne in a popular revolution and was exiled to Italy. Seventy years later his heir, Zahir, who had accompanied him on that trip, returned to Afghanistan to find a war torn country ravaged by a defeated Taliban and harbouring terrorist and Al-Qaeda forces.

The Harringtons turned out to be a great blessing. General Sir Tim was a friend of Rosalind's father, 'The General', who had written to him to say that his new DAAG was his son-in-law. Puck and Rosalind were quickly invited to dinner at the Commander-in-Chief's house and it emerged that Lady Harrington, an ebullient Irish lady, was a keen musician and invited Rosalind to join her jazz band. Rosalind described her as looking 'simply frightful, very tall and brawny, fuzz brown hair, a great pouting mouth and her cheeks made up with great patches of rouge, which are always put on unevenly – one patch just under her left eye and the other at the bottom of her right cheek – it gave her a most lopsided look. However she is the kindest thing that ever was and does so enjoy everything'; and Puck wrote: 'it does one good to hear her laugh'. General Harrington was altogether gentler in manner and Puck described him as 'a topper, just the sort of man that the army has wanted and knows what matters'.

The jazz band got going, Lady Harrington taking centre stage. Rosalind wrote: 'playing her banjalele, self on the fiddle and a very good pianist. Lady H was too funny for words – she does enjoy it so, twanging her old instrument and throwing back her head and singing the tune in a shrill high soprano, completely drowning my fiddle. When I glared at her and suggested that we should play a little softer she subsided into a shriller whistle and danced about the floor still twanging.' The band performed at many of the balls but Lady H insisted that Rosalind should have a substitute so that she too could join in the dances. Perhaps it was Lady Harrington's vocal offerings which encouraged Rosalind to take singing lessons, which she did, finding that she developed a fine contralto voice. Another great character in Quetta society was Jed Fitzgerald, a bachelor Major whose sister Frances was housekeeping for him and who became a great friend of Puck and Rosalind. Jed's group, the 'Gloom Club', organised societies, dances and wild parties, much enjoyed by all.

Puck described his day as riding out on horseback with Rosalind before breakfast; then work in the office until tea-time. Then more riding until a bath and sundowner before dining, either at home or out to a party. He was a very good horseman and was keen that Rosalind should enjoy it too. He was patient and it wasn't long before he could write to 'The General' to say that she was 'getting a very good seat'. Before long they were hunting together – 'twice a week', Puck reported, and 'Rosalind goes fullout right up to hounds'. Colonel Abbay, the Norman cousin, was Master of the Quetta Hunt and a very shrewd one too. Puck suspected him of 'artificial holes and drag lines', they had such good runs with the hounds, yet 'he hardly ever fails to put up a fox or a jackal'.

The dull beginnings of Puck's staff job became more interesting once he was fully involved in a new mobilisation scheme, so that his Colonel reported: 'an officer possessing good powers of command, his attitude towards his superior and subordinates is correct. His reliability is very fair, but he requires to improve in matters of accuracy and attention to detail. He is of energetic habits, is interested in military matters, keen on instruction work. His professional knowledge is above average...' Puck felt that he had a special aptitude for instruction and when a vacancy came up in April 1928 for an Instructor at the Staff College in Quetta he applied for, and got it.

Puck enjoyed his time as an instructor at the Staff College where he was responsible for Army/Airforce tactical warfare. Most of his teaching was conducted in the morning so that he had time off in the afternoon to prepare lectures and spend time with Rosalind. There had been earthquakes in Quetta in 1928 and by January she had become pregnant with their first child, Paul, born on 19 September. They were thrilled with their son, with their life in Quetta and with his job which kept him at the Staff College for a whole year, at the end of which the Commandant wrote of him: 'he volunteered for and was selected to fill a vacancy on the teaching staff at very short notice. He has carried out his duties entirely to my satisfaction and is a most pleasant person to work with. Having him through the course at the RAF Staff College the knowledge he has gained there has been of the greatest use.'

Puck and Rosalind with their baby son were able to take a long leave home from April 1929 and 'oh!' how Rosalind 'appreciated the primroses which were out' when they arrived back in Mistley. Much excitement as her parents saw Paul for the first time. They took a cottage in Dedham for the summer months and once again entertained their friends and relations. They returned at the end of the year, not to India but to the Federation of Malay States where Puck had been posted to a new job.

The 1920s had been a fascinating decade in which to be tied into the fortunes of India. Lord Irwin had arrived as Viceroy in 1926 when the debate over what exactly was meant by the 1917 declaration for 'progressive realisation of responsible government in British India' was still raging. It was not long before he was pushing for Dominion Status as the natural issue of India's constitutional progress. Unfortunately there were powerful voices at home, Churchill's included, who opposed any such thing and rather naturally Gandhi had latched onto the idea of 'how' and 'when', to which there was no immediate answer. So the proposal failed, to be replaced by another great opportunity, a Federation of Hindus, Muslims and Princely States. This, too, faded from the statute books in the next decade as India fought for its independence and the fatal partition.

14

SECOND IN COMMAND AND FAMILY LIFE

Puck took up his next appointment as Second-in-Command of 1/20th Burma Rifles in Taiping, Perak, Federation of Malay States in November 1929, arriving there with Rosalind and Paul. There being no house for them to live in at first they stayed with the Officer Commanding the Regiment, Lieutenant-Colonel Percy Gout, and his wife. Mrs Gout was an accomplished pianist and she and Rosalind soon struck up a good relationship playing violin and piano duets together. Colonel Gout was a very charming, light-hearted, extravagant and generous man who enjoyed racing and betting, but could be hot-tempered and selfish with his wife. Mrs Gout was very quiet, artistic and High Church, very unselfish and disapproving of her husband's interest in the turf. Rosalind was amazed by the attraction of two such opposites. After a few days with them they were able to move into their own home, 90, Museum Road, which they loved.

Puck threw himself into regimental duties and found that his CO gave him full scope to exercise his powers of command, which Lieutenant-Colonel Gout described as being 'excellent' and 'his attitude towards both his superiors and subordinates is all that can be desired; he is absolutely reliable; has unlimited initiative; good judgement and zeal and is indefatigable; his professional ability is such that I strongly recommend that he be promoted to the next higher rank by Brevet', to which the Major-General commanding troops in Malaya added: 'I have seen this officer on a few days of battalion training. He strikes me as being above average for his rank and I concur in recommending him for Brevet promotion.'

Taiping turned out to be a very pleasant station and once they had got used to the humidity Rosalind could write home after their first Christmas: 'it is such a perfectly lovely place, beautifully green with lovely flowers everywhere, heaps of birds and gorgeous butterflies. Taiping is pretty low, being only just above sea level. There are lovely green hills behind us, covered with dense tropical forest and the blue mists on the hills in the early morning are simply beautiful. The nights are always quite cold and the early morning air fresh for walking round the lakes. We are awfully lucky in having extraordinary nice people in the regiment … it was very sad that we didn't have a service on Xmas Day in the Church, so Ernest, Nanny and I had our own little service in the study here. Hardly anyone goes to Church here as they had a frightful parson who put everyone's back up. He has gone now and a new parson is coming out from home.' Evidently this lack of a priest spurred Puck on in his studies for Lay Readership for in the following March, 1930, he was licensed as an Honorary Lay Reader in the Diocese of Singapore by Bishop Basil Coleby Roberts. He was then able to hold services in North Perak which included their own Parish Church in Taiping.

Quite apart from his Church activities Puck started up a regimental Children's School for the families, using Montessori methods of teaching Arithmetic and English. This was an innovation for regimental families and ex-patriates in Taiping and proved to be a great success, recording good results within eight months of its opening. And Rosalind got involved in setting up a children's welfare unit and a women's hospital for Asiatics.

Other extra-regimental activities included a play, 'The Joker', produced by Puck and in which he played the part of the villain, described 'as the brains of a bunch of crooks' and a 'very convincing criminal'; and Rosalind, who took the 'exacting part of the heroine', being on stage for most of the play, which was received with great acclamation and a warm review in the Perak weekly.

A regular feature of their social life was a week-end up on Maxwell Hill which required transport by mule to the rest bungalows there, complete with croquet lawn – a first introduction to the game for Paul who in later years became a national champion. By the end of their first year another baby was on the way and John was born in Penang on Candlemas Day, 1931. The family returned to Taiping soon after the birth and moved into the Colonel's residence in Swettenham Road as Puck took over command of the regiment while the Colonel went home on leave. But soon after moving into that capacious residence with its large garden Rosalind took the two children with their nanny back to England for the summer months while Puck stayed on as officiating CO of the Burma Rifles.

Despite the new responsibility which had come his way Puck missed his family and soon after they had left for England he wrote two letters for his sons to read when they were old enough to appreciate them, the first one dated 23 May (his birthday) 1931:

Dear Paul and John

It is unlikely that you will appreciate, or even trouble to read this, before you are at the Public School age and, by that time, I may not be alive to explain it. You see, although I wanted to marry some twenty years ago, I could not bear the thought of marrying any girl except the best. I found her a few years ago and she is your mother, but so much younger than me that I am afraid you may have to do without a father, when you are beginning to understand things. Therefore there are many things to tell you in writing. First you've got to choose a profession. Your Grandfather told me not to go into the Army and he told me that his father told him not to go. I don't know why. Anyhow I'm not going to tell you not to, partly because I think it's a grand life but chiefly because it doesn't matter what I say, you will probably insist on going.

The following reason is obvious:

Capt. John Strover, Royal Navy, 1790–1845

Lt-General Samuel Strover, 1810–1841

Maj.-General Henry Strover, 1853–1882

Major Ernest Strover, 1907–

This is your direct line and if your instinct for soldiering is like mine was, or your Uncle Martyn's, you will enter the Army. How insignificant a mere Major looks! I wonder if I shall get any higher!

It is quite difficult to get enough officers for the Army now. I think the chief reason is that people are sick of war and consider it very much like murder. Well I think we all want peace, but the chief reason why peace exists is because of the British Army. If you read the history of the Empire for the last 200 years, i.e. since the Army existed, you will find that there is only one war which we have not fought for liberty and that is the only war that we have lost (against America). If our Army did not exist neither peace, liberty or justice would exist. Here in Malaya, Chinese and Malays would be cutting each other's throats, and both cutting the throats of English planters. In India, Hindus and Mohammedans would be massacring each other. Even in England, without the police, no one could go about unarmed.

But the Army does much more than that. The British soldier is the most civilising influence in the Empire. Wherever he goes he makes himself extraordinarily popular. He manages to make himself understood in every language and is so good-natured, friendly and cheerful with men, women and children, white, brown, black or yellow that he carries his influence to the most uncivilised parts of the world, and brings peace and good-natured humour everywhere.

In the first Burmese war when British soldiers were first encountered by the Burmese they hated the British so much that they murdered and tortured them if they found them alone. But before the last Burmese war (when, incidentally, your great-uncle was Governor of Lower Burma and your grandfather commanded the

Artillery in Burma) the Burmese protested volubly at the suggestion of withdrawing British troops from Burma.

Now to tell you the possibilities of the Army. Your life is spent in commanding men. That means that you are raising and strengthening the character of the men whom you command – or should be. There are many ways of doing this. The first is by encouraging leadership. You should make every man you command a leader. Pull him out of the ranks and tell him to command the others and you can watch his initiative growing. Leadership consists of many things but the chief are: Loyalty (to ideals and men above and below); Unselfishness; Determination; Keenness. Another way is to send them off on their own to do a job in their own way. Another way is punishment for doing wrong, but this last is a negative sort of way. It is sometimes necessary, but you will never make a good regiment if you rule by fear.

Then, as to the job itself. It is still one of the few jobs left for a gentleman. If you go into business your motive for work will be a desire to make money and its effect on you all through your life will accumulate so that outlook becomes entirely selfish. In the Army you can never have that motive. However hard you work you will never get any more money. All your life you will be poor. But your motives will be keenness on your job, loyalty to your country, the desire to serve her and interest in the men whom you command. Ambition may be another motive, but it will be a laudable ambition.

Then it is a man's job. All the time you are setting an example. Never, never for a moment must you show the slightest sign of fear, or even hesitation. If it is getting on the back of a vicious horse or into an aeroplane on a bad day, or standing up with bullets flying around, you must not be anything but cheerful and serene. You may feel very much afraid but you can never show it. The Strovers have a reputation for not feeling fear. It is not altogether true, but they never show fear. Above all you make decisions and stick to them, and you develop a mind which is clear and decisive.

One more point. It is a life in the open air. Look at any Army officer of 45 and a business man of the same age. Their figures alone will usually enable you to decide which is the fitter. If you are fond of games you get lots of them. If you are keen on shooting and fishing and hunting, you get wonderful opportunities all through your life, especially in India or Africa.

Perhaps one of the greatest, if not the greatest reward an officer can have is the loyalty of his men. In the Indian Army this is wonderful and sometimes leaves you gasping…

Puck had commanded a regiment, the Sikhs, in the absence of its Colonel, in the early twenties, but ten years on, with active service in Mesopotamia, Staff College and a substantive appointment as Second-in-Command of a regiment behind him he jumped at the

The Taiping Amateur Dramatic Society. The villain getting what he deserves.

opportunity of this increased responsibility. Before going on leave the Colonel had written of him:

> An officer of high character and strong personality; popular and respected by all ranks; a good but human disciplinarian; hard working, conscientious and capable and a brilliant instructor. An organiser of high ability, takes the greatest interest in the battalion, not only its general efficiency, but its games and welfare of the men. His powers of command, attitude towards superiors and subordinates, reliability, initiative and judgement are all that can be desired, he is a zealous and energetic officer of quiet habits, with endless professional ability. On vacating command of this battalion in the near future he would, in my opinion, be the most suitable officer to relieve me; being a p.s.c. and f.s. [Army and RAF Staff College qualifications] already, I consider him fit to command a battalion now and, as in last year's report again recommend him very strongly for accelerated promotion.

Puck was able to justify that confidence placed in him as he improved the efficiency of the battalion during those summer months.

Lt. General Samuel Rogers Strover and his third wife Harriet, grandmother of Puck.

An official visit from the Sultan of Perak and the GOC Malaya District, General Oldfield, confirmed the smartness and fine discipline of the regiment under his temporary command. General Oldfield wrote of him: 'A keen and capable officer with the experience of staff work. Tactful and easy to deal with. Should do well as a battalion commander.' The command was cut short, however, by his posting back to England to the Senior Officers' School for three months at the end of the year, which pleased him as he was able to rejoin his family which had stayed on at Mistley.

On a short continental holiday which Puck and Rosalind took before his course began in September, the two of them went to Oberammergau to see the Passion Play. They stayed with a family, one of whom played the part of Jesus. The experience had a profound effect on them.

Attendance at the Senior Officers' School was a preliminary to substantive command of a regiment, and at the end of it the Commandant, Brigadier McCulloch, wrote of Puck:

> Personality agreeable: quiet, but he has plenty of decision and
> confidence. Capability good: he can arrange his points to express

Puck taking the salute with the Sultan of Perak.

himself fluently and clearly. He requires to cultivate a more alert manner to display at best advantage his wide military knowledge and sound views. He can think things out for himself and has good judgement. A useful officer, up to average.

Puck and family stayed on in England for leave at the end of the course until his next posting – to India, to take over command of 4/2nd Punjab Regiment.

15

REGIMENTAL COMMAND

The family arrived in Secunderabad, a British cantonment in Hyderabad State, in June 1932. At first Puck was only in temporary command of the regiment and it wasn't until the following January that he was promoted Lieutenant-Colonel as permanent commander. Regimental command proved to be the fulfilment of all his training and experience in the Indian Army. He had spent more years at Staff College or in staff appointments than most of his contemporaries and, happy and fulfilling as they were, they had taken him away from the regimental life which he most enjoyed, and which appealed to his leadership and human qualities. He very soon found himself embroiled in the hurly-burly of regimental command.

He wrote:

It was a good regiment I was appointed to, consisting of Mohammedans, Sikhs and Hindus, with a happy and efficient body of British Officers; but one tribe of Mohammedans, named Khattars, who came from the North West District of the Punjab, had given a good deal of trouble. A short time after I arrived there was a murder in the regiment. It was followed of course by a Court-Martial and the murderer was given fifteen years imprisonment. But the intrigues, feuds and hatreds among these Mohammedans which came to light, opened my eyes and taught me what to expect. I had spent most of the last five years at Staff Colleges and was quite unaccustomed to regimental life. I was married, and my wife and two little boys were with me, and I was looking forward to some family life. But calamity upon calamity came upon us.

There was a large Indian village close to our barracks and near my bungalow. It developed plague and the people in the village began to die in large numbers. Then one of my men caught it and died. I gave orders for the whole regiment to be inoculated, including my family. The doctors had not sufficient anti-toxin, and we had to wait several days before it arrived. Meanwhile another man caught the plague and died. I did everything I could, and prevailed upon a Political Officer to clear the village and isolate the inhabitants in a camp. But my anxiety was intense, particularly for my family which was so close to the village, knowing that inoculation does not bring immunity. I came nearer to God than ever before because my need was so great.

It seems that we need great anxiety or great responsibility or great sorrow to bring us close to God. After three weeks it became obvious that the awful scourge had passed. I could feel something of the gratitude of the people of Oberammergau 300 years ago who swore that they would produce the Passion Play every ten years in thankfulness because the plague left their village. Murder, plague – what was the next thing? I began to hope that the worst was over. Our Brigade was marked to be the first to go overseas in case of any war, and we were therefore kept on our toes and ready for immediate mobilisation. For a year we worked hard, training for every kind of war, and I was thankful for it because the whole regiment was keen and becoming very efficient.

It had been a testing time, so much so that at the end of that first year his Brigade Commander wrote of him:

He has only very recently taken over command: it is too early to give a definite opinion as to his capabilities as a commander. He has good ability and energy and a genial personality. Keen on sport; sociable, popular and ready to take a hand at anything. In the six months that

I have known him, his character seems to be somewhat complex and contradictory, being impulsive and obstinate, yet indecisive and vacillating. He is inclined to be too soft-hearted in his handling of the battalion. His new experience of command should, however, benefit him greatly and may eradicate the above weakness.

His District Commander added: 'A very pleasant and hard-working officer who is imbued with a strong sense of duty. I feel sure that when he has found his feet and has been able, as permanent commander, to impose his will on his battalion that he will develop into a good Commanding Officer.'

If the truth be known his inclination towards soft-heartedness arose from his warmth for, and love of the men, including the rogues and villains, under his command, who in the years ahead would respond to the training and discipline which he imposed, out of respect for his leadership and humanity as their Commanding Officer. Thus at the end of the next year a new Brigade Commander could write of him: 'He has an energetic mind for, and shows great keenness at, collective training exercises – he appreciates a problem quickly and makes a decision which once made he acts upon without deviation.'

After two years in command of the regiment Puck and Rosalind took the two children back to England for eight months of well-earned leave. They enjoyed a very happy time in Mistley culminating in a production of 'Aladdin' in the village hall, produced by Rosalind and in which Puck, playing the part of Widow Twankey, was described in the local paper as being 'screamingly funny'. The pantomime was so well received by the first night's audience that it had to be extended to a whole week of performances.

Soon after they had sailed home on this leave an official inspection of the regimental armoury was held which elicited a very adverse report, in which it was said: 'The CO failed in his responsibilities for the condition of arms in the unit under his

The family on leave at Mistley Hall.

Widow Twankey taking her 'medicine' on the Mistley stage.

command.' This was followed by a directive from the Adjutant General which greeted Puck on his return to India, which stated: 'Regarding the bad state of arms on charge of 4/2nd Punjab Regiment. After careful consideration of the facts of the case (CCMA's report on the inspection of arms), His Excellency the Commander-in Chief has directed that an adverse note be filed with Lt.-Col. E.J. Strover's confidential reports.' The fact that he was home on leave while all this took place did not absolve him of responsibility and it was a major setback for his command which he determined to put right. Puck wrote about a further incident:

> Two revolvers were reported missing from the armoury. It was obvious that they had been stolen by men in the regiment and the suspicion fell on the Khattar tribe who had probably done it to get an Indian Officer into trouble. It is a disgrace for a regiment in India to lose one of its weapons, and I determined to get them back. My senior Indian Officer advised me to punish the whole regiment until pressure was brought on the thieves to restore the revolvers. It was the hot weather and I sent them daily after work on long marches with packs on their backs under the command of a British officer, and then turned them out at night. But still no sign of the weapons being restored. My British officers said that the regiment was becoming restive and that, if I continued, it might become mutinous. A mutiny would finish me and my family. Yet, if I gave way, I would never break this Khattar intrigue. Prayer gave me the answer to go on at all costs.
>
> There was a large pond near the parade ground, and I gave orders that this was to be emptied by buckets – a long and arduous job. It was possible that the revolvers had been thrown into it. However, before the pond was emptied, a notice was put up stating that the revolvers could be found in the Mohammedan Mosque. It was a tremendous relief to all in the regiment except the Khattars, but I never had any more trouble from them. It certainly was a direct answer to prayer.

No doubt the long disciplinary marches and the clear resolution of the missing revolvers had a beneficiary effect on the battalion for at the end of the next year his Brigade Commander wrote: ' I consider that he should be given credit for the fact that his battalion is now showing a very fine spirit in its standard of turn-out and drill, and individual training is high, whilst its spirit of endurance during the months of marching to and from manoeuvres was excellent, its record being no men falling out and no mule sores.' And his District Commander added: 'I agree. Lt.-Col. Strover is proving himself a good C.O. who is impressing his mark on his battalion. He is keen and fair-minded. A good leader in the field. Fit for promotion to the rank of Colonel. His administration of his battalion and care of arms has greatly improved during the last year and are now excellent.'

As a keen sportsman Puck encouraged his battalion on the sports field and running track. Recreation after the day's work gave him the opportunity to indulge his own great interest in polo where he led the regimental team to many victories. Club facilities with its swimming pool, much enjoyed by the children, and tennis courts on which Rosalind won several tournaments occupied many of their evenings. Rosalind was much involved with the Kindergarten School which she set up for officer and ex-patriate families, and with her music. And then there were the dinner parties both as hosts and guests. One of their hosts had been the Nizam of Hyderabad whom they got to know well through their friendship with Jeremy Fisher, the Political Officer.

At Christmas 1935 they were invited to a tiger shooting camp by Sir Terence Keyes, the British Resident of Hyderabad, organised by Jeremy Fisher in the Nizam's forest. Rosalind was struck by the luxury of the camp facilities, having bedroom, sitting room and their own bathroom in tented accommodation and expected to dress formally for dinner each evening. The two of them needed to take a break from it to be with their sons on Christmas Day, and returned to the camp on Boxing Day when lots were drawn with other guests for position. This entailed climbing a rope ladder to a platform and waiting for the village beaters to drive in their direction. Suddenly, out of the bush beneath them a beautiful tigress appeared and with a single shot Puck felled it after it had risen in the air with a great roar. They were lucky in their draw for they had the only 'kill' of the shoot. Later, when the tigress was skinned, there were found to be three baby cubs inside her which were also skinned and became part of the trophy which adorned their bungalow and subsequent drawing rooms. For a short time after this Puck became known as 'Tiger'.

Summer months on the plains of India were insufferably hot and most families made for the hills. Puck and Rosalind chose to go to Kotagiri in the Nilgiri Hills close to the well-known hill station of Ootacamund (Ooty). In May of each year Rosalind would set off with the children and Ayah taking the Nilgiri express to Coonoor. From there they took the miniature railway train up to Ooty. This had a toothed central rail onto which the locomotive locked on the steeper slopes, passengers in the quaint yellow and blue carriages enjoying spectacular views of the rainforest covered Nilgiris. From Ooty a local bus took them along the level some 20 miles to Kotagiri. There they rented a bungalow and Puck would join them later on a short local leave, enjoying some family life and the local golf course.

It was there in Kotagiri, in the tiny Anglican Church that Puck had his vision of Christ: Jesus standing in front of him, with his arms extended in a welcoming way, inviting him to join him. It had a profound effect and was to lead to a momentous change in his life.

After three years on the plains of India the regiment would be moving to a new station and Puck decided that his children should go back to England, for their health and education. Accordingly they were packed off with a nanny back to Essex where, eventually, they were installed in a rented house in Frinton-on-Sea in the charge of a Governess. Rosalind stayed on with Puck as the battalion was moved up to Shagai Fort on the North West frontier to guard the Khyber Pass. There were various skirmishes with the Pathans during his final three months with the regiment which were often retold with vigour at the dinner table in later years. At the end of his command of the regiment he received the following farewell address from the Subedar-Major of the battalion:

Respected Sir,

In view of your impending transfer to Quetta, on your appointment as Assistant Quarter Master General Reconstruction Quetta, we have assembled here to-day to express our overwhelming feelings of gratitude and love to you, our most worthy and popular Commandant, who held command of the battalion from February 1933.

Although time does not permit us to enumerate in detail the various advantages the Battalion gained during your period of command, Sir, we can not refrain from making mention below of some of the various ways in which the Battalion has distinguished itself through your judicious management and able guidance.

It is no exaggeration to say that your sympathy with officers and other ranks, has won for you, our undying fidelity and gratitude. Above all your special interest evinced in the soldiers have evoked the affection and love of us all here. In short we were singularly fortunate in having so noble and able a Commandant as you are.

On parade and on manoeuvres our capabilities are well known. Under your guidance and shrewd control we secured the foremost position and earned a very good name at Secunderabad.

In games, your goodself has inspired a keen interest, and it was through your warm support that we won the Secunderabad Area Sports Cup, for three years in succession. We dare say, that the standard of efficiency of the Battalion as regards musketry and training is now far better than it was in the past, and it is unnecessary to point out that the sole cause of this improvement is to be found in your most efficient supervision.

During your tenure of office you have granted many privileges for the well being and prosperity of those under your care, which are extremely valuable and advantageous and for which we are deeply

grateful. The introduction of various Funds i.e. I.O.'s Provident
Fund, I.O. Rs. Provident Fund, Family Provident Fund and Family
Hospital Fund, bears a sufficient testimony to this fact.

Your noble work in the cause of Child Welfare, while the Battalion
was at Secuderabad, is fresh in our minds. The keen interest taken
by Mrs. Strover, in this connection, will ever be remembered by
those ladies who had the privilege to reside with their husbands in
the married quarters at Secunderabad. Your activities in the Rural
Reconstruction are notable too.

You have similarly taken interest in the welfare of ex-soldiers and
their dependents in that you very kindly took the onerous duty of
touring villages in a trying weather when the rain had set in, meeting
pensioners and ex-soldiers, hearing their complaints and helping
those who were in need of it.

We sincerely pray that the Almighty God may grant you long
life and prosperity, and grant you still higher rank which you so
well deserve.

We beg to remain, Sir, your most obedient servants,
Sub. Major Amir Ali, I.O.s & other ranks, 4/2nd
Punjab Regiment, Shagai Fort.
30th August, 1936.

It was a touching address, spoken from the heart of the men he had
commanded for over three years, and followed by three excellent
confidential reports from his seniors: his Brigade Commander
wrote: 'He has a particularly attractive personality, cheerful and
imperturbable. A strong character who develops the esprit de corps
of his unit by great attention to the well being of his men and
their families. His military qualities are most excellent and he is
above average for his rank.' The Commander of Peshawar District
wrote: 'An excellent battalion commander possessing ability and
character. Loyal and easy to work with. I consider him well above
the average and fit for a first good staff appointment. After that
he should be found qualified to command a Brigade.' And the
GOC-in-Chief of Northern Command, General Sir Kenneth

March past of the 4/2nd Punjabis. The Resident of Hyderabad, Sir Terence Keyes, taking the salute, with Puck at the head of his regiment.

Puck at the end of his command at the Khyber Pass.

Wigram, wrote: 'He impressed me most favourably and I put him well above the average. Fit for a first grade staff appointment and for command of a Brigade. He is old for his service and merits early advancement.'

Thus Puck and Rosalind were once again in Quetta in the aftermath of the earthquakes. The job of AQMG Reconstruction was very specialised and did not really suit his talents, his District Commander commenting that although he had worked very hard and loyally he was somewhat handicapped by lack of previous experience of such work. Nevertheless the two of them were able to enjoy the social life.

On his last leave home Puck had consulted the Bishop of Chelmsford about going into the Church and had not received a very encouraging response, the Bishop considering that he was too unorthodox in his views to take Holy Orders. Even so he felt that he had been called to be a priest and his young family beckoned from England. Added to which, Rosalind had had a bad riding accident while out with the Quetta Hunt and had gone home to recover and to be with the boys. So in March 1937, despite an encouraging report from his general on his suitability for higher command, he took leave home to decide on his future.

16

RETURN TO ENGLAND

Puck was clearly in a mood to seek a future life which would keep him in close touch with people, as had been his experience of commanding a regiment, rather than sitting behind a desk in a staff job or even commanding a brigade. On his way home on the SS Mongolia, as he approached the Suez Canal on 18 June 1937, he wrote the following poem:

> The Sinai hills through evening mist
> are dressed in gold and amethyst;
> and Red Sea waves on either side
> the two great continents divide.
> Here an enslaved down trodden race
> fearful of Pharoah who ground their face.
> No hope for deliverance, no purpose or plan,
> contemptible cowards were saved by a MAN.
> A man among men, Moses his name,
> strong in his faith, unswerving in aim.
> In the years of the future whatever their length,
> determined to give them both courage and strength.
> Let them who despise the folly and greed
> and the cringing of those of the Eastern breed,
> take courage from Moses who triumphed o'er fate
> and from such material made Israelites great.

No doubt, as the month's voyage passed by his thoughts were concentrated on the vision he had received in Kotagiri and how he could best respond to Jesus's call. But first, on landing, he must make his way up to Frinton and join his family. There he would find two wayward sons brought to heel by their mother (they had had almost a year without their parents) after she had quenched a beach gang, led by their eldest son, in opposition to an enemy gang, both of which had tormented beach hut dwellers by their antics and fierce battles. A beach pony, Peggy, was purchased, for Puck was determined that his sons should learn to ride, and Peggy later turned out to be an excellent cub hunter. No doubt, too, he wanted to play a full part in the bringing up of his two sons. His second letter to them of May 1931, dated the 31st, shows how much that meant to him:

Dear Paul and John,

This is a letter on how to enjoy life. For heaven's sake realise quite soon that you are put into the world to enjoy it. Why not? Thank God that nightmare of the Puritan age which could see no goodness which was not allied to misery, has gone. Today people are enjoying life all through the country as they never did before.

The standard of life has risen and far more people are able to enjoy themselves than before. It is often looked down on with contempt as 'the pursuit of pleasure'. Well pleasure, if it is of the right kind, is a very good thing to pursue. The wrong kind of pleasure is a silly thing to pursue, because it ends in pain. For instance if you drink a lot of alcohol, you may see the world in a very pleasant rosy light for an hour or two, but you will soon cease to see or feel anything; and next morning you will find the world a dull and unpleasant place. If you do that often you will get such a liver and such a dull brain that life will not be worth living. Similarly with gambling, you may win a lot of money on a horse, but, if you go on betting, you will eventually lose. I have never known a man who betted a lot and who gained money in the long run. That is the point of all vices. They are attractive at first but are stupid things to indulge in because they lead to misery in the long run. But the worst part of them is that they make you a slave. Those who are slaves to gambling are no longer men. Those who are slaves to the pursuit of women, just to indulge their physical passion, are no longer men.

It may take you a long time to realise it, but the best and most lasting pleasure is to do things for other people. Try it and see. It is really a form of selfishness. It gives you so much pleasure that you will want to go on doing it. The worst of it is that, if everybody did this, there would be nobody left to be kind to. Fortunately for yourself very few people have discovered this secret of life and so your opportunities are enormous. This is the magic thread which will be woven through all your pleasures and your work. It will make your work into your pleasure and your pleasure into your supreme pleasure.

The real pleasures of this life are many. The first I put down is talking. To talk well is an art. Very few Englishmen possess it but many Englishmen have it. To talk well it is necessary to interest your audience. Directly your audience begins to feel bored you must stop. It is therefore necessary to have that subtle sense to know, at once, the moment when your audience is losing interest ...

That is where the letter ended, perhaps he thought that he had gone on long enough!

Bishop Ernest Barnes of Birmingham was well known for his outspoken views and unorthodox religious beliefs. Puck wrote to him and was duly invited to talk over his vocation. The bishop was encouraging and arranged for him to go and see Dr Major at Ripon Hall, Oxford. It was suggested to him by Dr Major that he should take over two parishes near Oxford as Lay Reader, while they were having an interregnum, to see if the life of a parish priest would suit him. So it was that the family moved to Barford St Michael, near Deddington, Oxon and resided in the Rectory for six months.

Puck soon found his feet as a vicarious country parson, took the services at St Michael and at St James, got himself a horse and visited the parishioners. Peggy came over with the family from Frinton and was stabled at the Rectory, and another pony, Jimmy was purchased so that father and sons were able to hunt with the Heythrop, over the open country where stone walls rather than barbed wire separated the fields. It was an idyllic life and it wasn't long before he begged Dr Major to take him into his Theological College for the training of clergy and wrote to the India Office to resign his commission. He had done thirty years in India, on and off, and it was time to start a new life.

Puck took up residence in Ripon Hall in January 1938, and the family moved into lodgings in North Oxford, the boys being sent to the Dragon School. Having a degree from Cambridge and already licensed, and having practised for seven years as a Lay Reader it was necessary only to do a short course of theology and in the following June he was ordained Deacon by Bishop Barnes in Birmingham. The family then moved up to Sutton Coldfield where Puck became curate and looked after the parish of St Chad's. His dream of being a country parson came to end. No visiting on horseback so a car was bought although the two ponies could still be stabled nearby; and he found himself very much involved in a suburban parish.

The boys had to board at the Dragon but when they came home for the holidays they found good companions among the choirboys of St Chads. Puck set about educating them in the real life of the Industrial Midlands and arranged for them a visit to a Nottinghamshire coal mine where they crawled on their bellies to the coal face and fed the pit ponies, and to Bourneville where he held up for them the example of the Cadbury family in looking after their employees and where a free sample of chocolate was their reward. And there were opportunities for holidays in Wales, Cornwall and Devonshire now the family had a car. On one such holiday in Looe, Puck wrote of the following adventure:

April on the South Coast of Cornwall is always delightful if the weather is fine, but in the midst of our enjoyment my wife was called away because of the sudden illness of her father, and I was left with our two rampageous boys Paul and Johnny, aged 9 and 7. In our own house I would have felt no qualms but in the hotel, mostly occupied by elderly ladies, I feared the worst, nor was my foreboding unjustified. On the first night I was woken up by a thumping on my door. Switching on the light, I called out: 'Come in'. The hotel proprietor's red and agitated face looked in and said: 'Miss Fitzroy Hume, whose bedroom is below, complains that water is dripping through her ceiling'. I rushed into the boys' bedroom next door and found, to my horror, that the tap over their basin had not been turned off. I apologised profusely and offered to pay for the damage. The boys, of course, went on sleeping. Next morning as we came down to breakfast I made them go across to the lady and apologise. Whether it was their sincere penitence or their golden curls or her pity for a harassed father she not only forgave them but even offered to wash and darn their socks. She also, unwisely, informed them that there was a smugglers' cave about two miles to the West. The hotel manager, who was again his bland and helpful self, corroborated the evidence although he had never been there. He warned me, however, that there was a dangerous approach along a footpath with a precipitous drop to the rocks and sand below. The prospect of an adventure naturally whetted the appetites of my boys, but filled father with anxiety. However, it would at least keep them away all day from the hotel and I knew that they would never rest until they had explored it.

So we made our preparations. The hotel manager gave us a packed lunch and we repaired to the village shop to fit up the expedition. According to all stories about smugglers' caves a ball of string was essential to be sure that we did not get lost by taking wrong turnings and were always able to return to the entrance. Other necessities were a candle and matches, a torch and ginger beer. Then, having pin-pointed the cave on a large scale map we set off. The coast became wilder and wilder, the path narrower and narrower and the rocks below more and more jagged. At last we reached the point where path ended and was continued only by a narrow goat track. It was here that the cave should have been seen. But there was no sign of even a rabbit hole. I argued that a smuggler's cave was more likely to be at the foot of the cliff and that our best hope was to go back to the more civilised bit of land where steps led down to the shore. But Paul's sharp eyes saw a dark spot on the face of the cliff about two hundred yards ahead and at once he was flying along the goat track courting instant death. I grabbed Johnny refusing to let him follow. A shout from Paul: 'Here it is', and I knew that we were for it. Grasping Johnny's hand I gingerly edged along the goat track, avoiding every temptation to look below until we reached our goal.

The mouth of the cave was damp and dark and forbidding in its prospects, but it was a sanctuary from the precipitous cliff and precarious footholds of the path outside. The eagerness of the boys was so infectious that I volunteered to lead the exploration after agreeing to divide equally any gold or other treasure which we might discover. First the end of the string was tied securely round a boulder. Then candles were lit, torches flashed and I led the way. The cave was low and I had to walk with bent head, water dripping from the roof on my neck. Such inconveniences did not affect my sons who urged me on with cries of 'Go on Daddy' whenever I paused to look ahead with the torch. Suddenly the cave opened out and a boulder obscured the view beyond. I struggled over the boulder on hands and knees and was just pausing to flash the torch when the boys, pressing on me in their eagerness, pushed me over and I fell into a foot of water. To the eager followers behind me this was a minor incident. The exciting fact was that the cave grew bigger and might go on for miles. Wading through the pond and flashing our torches in all directions we continued more cautiously. Then the cave began to narrow and the roof to get lower until even the boys were on their hands and knees. At last, to their bitter disappointment and my secret relief, we found ourselves in a cul-de-sac. Slowly we retraced our steps to the entrance.

It was here that the most dangerous venture began. The distance to the top of the cliff was only about 100 feet and, although almost precipitous it was covered with vegetation and looked easier and less nerve-racking than a return along the goat track. So I submitted to their entreaties and off they went up the cliff while I remained below with a vague hope of catching them if they fell. They climbed steadily and surely but suddenly there was a yell from Paul. He said that the tufts of grass came out in his hands when he pulled himself up by them. Johnny was further up and being so very light he did not pull out the grass as he climbed. Paul was really frightened and I did not blame him. He said that he could not move up or down without falling. The prospect of rescuing him was appalling and there was no time to lose. So, somehow, with the help of the Almighty, I got up to him and, together, we slowly and with immense care climbed down to the cave. Telling him to go slowly along the goat track, which now seemed a comparatively light danger, until he reached the safe path, I then began the still more arduous and dangerous task of climbing to Johnny. Very slowly I climbed, using only my feet, and leaning against the cliff, inspecting every foothold before I trusted it and never daring to look below. Johnny, who did not comprehend the danger stayed quite happily in his position and could, I felt, have climbed to the top much better than me. But if he had fallen because I was not with him remorse would have clouded my life. Terrified as I was, then, I edged up to him foot by foot. Then, bidding him climb ahead of me we slowly and with immense caution reached the top. The sense of relief was so great that I seized Johnny and threw him over the top. Almost immediately he gave a cry of anguish – I had thrown him into a bed of nettles!

Sermons which Puck gave from the beginning of his ministry at Barford in 1937 and during his curacy at St Chad's covered a number of themes relating to his own experiences of war, command of men and family life. Preaching to the Mothers' Union on the first Sunday of 1938 he spoke of the importance of religion being caught and not taught; of the influence which the home, good or bad, has upon a child; and he went on to urge mothers to train their children to handle their independence positively and for the good, and to set for them an example of the power of prayer by praying together at home.

In a sermon on the conquest of fear he spoke about fear being an elemental alarm system and that our business is not to get rid of it but to harness it. Quoting from Psalm 111 v10: 'the fear of the Lord is the beginning of wisdom' he differentiated between being frightened of the Lord and holding Him in reverent awe, confirming that no good life is possible without a healthy presence of fear. With the prospect of war already on the agenda, he linked fear of it as being its chief cause and the reason for rearmament. He looked forward to the day when nations would agree to disarm – a theme to which he would return many times in his post-war sermons. He had himself faced up to fear in war as a pilot in the RFC, as an escaping POW, and as a Company Commander in Mesopotamia, and could speak at first hand about the tragedy and unpleasantness of war. He said that he had met only one man who liked being shot at – 'clearly he had not been shot at enough!' The secret of the conquest of fear, he said, lay in faith of the kind held by St Paul who could say: 'I can do all things in Him who strengthens me'.

There was nothing pretentious about Puck's character: he was very much his own man; he dared where others would not dare, both in action and in word. Taking as his text St Matthew 16 v18: 'Simon thou art Peter', he encouraged his congregation to be themselves, saying that no one can import qualities from outside, for qualities are already in us, undeveloped, imprisoned 'as seeds which have not been watered', and need to be nurtured, just as Jesus recognised rock-like qualities in Peter, for all his impetuosity and vacillation, and developed them. 'Never mind if someone else is wiser, cleverer...that is not your affair,' he said. He encouraged self-expression, and self-denial not as an end in itself but as a means to disciplined service, and so by losing oneself may find oneself and, as Jesus said, 'have life and have it more abundantly'.

In the summer of 1938 the family took a camping holiday in Morthoe, near Woolacombe on the North coast of Devonshire.

There they found, for sale, a small house, with barn and path from the garden down to an uninhabited beach, and with Rosalind inheriting from her Uncle Ebbe, they bought it for £1,000, complete with furnishing, linen and crockery. The only problem was that there was a tramp who lived on the first floor of the barn and try as they would, the boys, pretending to be policeman, could not remove him. Instead he gave chase and frightened them out of their lives.

Back in Sutton Coldfield Puck was enjoying his curacy, especially the contact with parishioners whom he visited regularly, it being quite natural for him to do so after his many years as an Army officer. Clearly he made a good impact on the congregation with his sermons and it was only six months after being ordained Deacon that the Bishop of Birmingham thought fit to ordain him Priest. By that time the clouds of war were gathering and in a sermon preached to the British Legion in June 1939 he reminded the congregation that in the Great War the British soldier was always at his most cheerful and amusing when conditions are at their worst. This was not the time for gloom. The happiest and most cheerful men whom you meet, he maintained, are religious men. 'Religion is like a tunnel through the Alps,' he said, 'go into it a little way and you are plunged in gloom; but if you go on you come out into the sunlit stretches of the Italian hills. Jesus was cheerful and joyful right to the end and the source of all his power was his communion with God and his knowledge that he was doing His will. England was at its greatest when spiritually fulfilled, as in the Elizabethan age when men went out to colonise the world believing that they were doing God's will.' He urged these old comrades to cultivate the habit of prayer, which, he said, 'will lift up your spirits and give you the power and ability to meet any difficulty with cheerfulness'.

The family were once again down in the Morthoe house for their summer holiday, Puck joining them at the end of it. On 3 September they were with others, sitting on the stairs of the local hotel, to hear the Prime Minister speak on the radio that Britain was now at war with Germany. Puck's immediate response, much to the alarm of his family, was to say that he would join up immediately. What he had in mind was to become a pilot again but to his chagrin, when he applied to the Air Ministry, he was told that at 55 years of age he was too old for Spitfires and he could join the RAF only as a padre. But first he must return to his parish.

On 26 September he preached in St Chad's about the right attitude to war: 'War', he said,

> debases human thought. We rightly look upon Hitlerism as an evil thing but once we become vindictive we lower ourselves to his level. Spiritual exertion is called for in order to maintain our humanity. Without it we shall dictate a peace which will inevitably sow the seeds of another war. The moral and spiritual fact which bears upon war is the relationship of the strong to the weak.

He spoke from his experience on the North West frontier of not just guarding the Khyber Pass but of protecting the Indian villagers from invading Pathan tribes from across the border. Quoting from Romans 15.1, 'We that are strong ought to bear the infirmities of the weak and not please ourselves,' he professed that the central pillar of the Gospel is that the highest strength should be put at the service of the lowliest and weakest, and again from 2 Corinthians v 8-9: 'For ye know the grace of the Lord Jesus Christ that, though he was rich, yet for your sakes he became poor, that ye through his poverty might become rich.' 'At last,' he said, 'this principle of the strong helping the weak has become a principle of sane government,' and quoting Lord Asquith: 'The test of every civilisation is the point below which the weakest and most unfortunate are allowed to fall.'

Following up at Harvest Thanksgiving that Autumn his mind was still on war, for as he spoke about how necessary it is to toil on the land, to have faith in nature to convert seed into grain and to have patience for the harvest to mature, so it is important to prosecute war with the utmost vigour, to have faith that it is a just war that we are fighting, 'and there can be no doubt about that,' he said, 'and to be patient that in the end good will overcome evil and we shall be victorious.'

17

PADRE

Puck's Commission in the RAF as a Padre with the rank of Squadron Leader did not come through until June 1940, and in that month he was posted to RAF Kirkham in Lancashire. It was a large training camp for fitters and riggers and he, as the only Anglican Priest, was the senior chaplain on the station. He lived in the Officers' Mess until he could find accommodation for his family. Meanwhile, Rosalind stayed on in Sutton Coldfield to pack up the house, continued playing with the Birmingham Chamber Orchestra, became an ambulance driver and witnessed the destruction of New Street station in the Birmingham blitz.

By the time school holidays started Puck had found lodgings for the family in a farmhouse, on the fringe of the RAF camp, its fields actually bordering the fence which enclosed the station. It was no more than a cattle fence with a way through to the camp so that it was possible for him to walk over the fields to work each day. The farmer and his wife, Mr and Mrs Whiteside had three sons and three daughters, and during that summer they took in two evacuees from London quite apart from the Strover family. The problem was, where would everybody sleep? It was solved by making over two of the four bedrooms to the Strover family, Mr and Mrs Whiteside remaining in the principal bedroom through which everyone had to go to get to the only bathroom, and the three girls and two evacuees sharing the large double bed in the fourth bedroom. The farmer's sons slept in the hay loft. The Whiteside family ate and lived in the kitchen during the day, the parlour being made over to the Strovers. No doubt the two older sons and daughters found greater comfort in barrack room accommodation when they were called up later in the war.

Puck soon found that he had a real job on his hands: regular Sunday services, monthly Church parades and pastoral work for several thousand officers and men who had been separated from their families. Visiting barrack rooms and talking with the airmen off duty was second nature to him, and he could outgun any officer in the mess with his stories of flying with the RFC, prisoner-of-war escapes and campaigns in Mesopotamia and on the North West frontier. There were few RAF padres who could sport wings and campaign medals on their uniforms, and who could speak with first-hand experience of war and of a faith which had carried him through many ventures. In that first year of the

Paul and John on cart horses with Bill and Dorothy (Dot), the youngest Whiteside son and daughter, and evacuees Harry and Beth in front.

war he gave five sermons on the subject of faith which he dedicated 'To the RAF whom I have known, loved and admired since their birth when I was flying with RFC.' In many ways they sum up his philosophy of a purposeful and happy life, based on an adventurous spirit and a solid foundation of communion with God, of answer to prayer and of God's protecting embrace.

In 'Faith I' he spoke of Faith as holding reasonable convictions about something that we cannot prove. He said,

> no one can live without vision to see as true what, as yet, we cannot prove, or without courage to act on the basis of our insight, quoting Oliver Wendell Holmes, 'It is faith in something that makes life worth living'. Scientific knowledge has grown, but like Paul who faced his journey to Rome, 'not knowing the things that shall befall me', you cannot tell what strange situations you may find yourself in tomorrow...A life of faith is like building a cantilever bridge: part of the structure is solidly bolted but beyond that we audaciously thrust out new beginnings in eager expectation that from the other side something will come to meet them...There are plenty of people to do the possible; the prizes are for those who do the impossible...The first necessity for adventure is courage and it is Faith in God which sustains courage.

In 'Faith II' he spoke about the road to truth. He posed the question: 'What is it that prejudices man against religion?' And in answer he suggested:

1. Upbringing – when too strict, religion brings rebellion against its teaching, but this is only an excuse, not a reason for rejecting it.
2. Those who have never felt any great need for God, who don't know the deep experiences of serious souls with responsibility for great causes, experiences which throw them back on God as their only refuge and hope because, quoting Abraham Lincoln, 'there was nowhere else to go.' If we want faith we must humble ourselves before God and follow those great men of history all through the ages who have found their strength and power and

happiness in the companionship of God … Like a Labrador dog which bounds across the field and comes back to you, be like that with God and find his companionship … Most of you will be going into battle. I have been shot at many times and it was faith in God which enabled me to carry on as if there were no bullets around. Cultivate the companionship of God before you go into battle. Jesus said: 'go into thy room and shut thy door and pray to thy father in secret'. In the barrack room get under the bedclothes and pray to God before you go to sleep.

In 'Faith III' he took as his text Hebrews 11 v1 'Faith is the substance of things hoped for, the evidence of things unseen'. He said,

We begin as children with unlimited ability to believe what we are told'. He said, 'One prescription is enough: ask our parents … then we discover the fallibility of parents … the enlarging intellect requires reason, not dogma … there is a transition from hearsay to reality … hitherto faith has meant the acceptance of another's say-so, so faith and credulity appear to be the same … what we need to see is that faith is one of the chief ways to reality – a road to truth without which truth cannot be reached at all … Faith is not a substitute for truth, it is a pathway to truth … There are realities which without faith can never be known, e.g. you can never know persons without faith; entrance into another life with insight and understanding is a venture of trust … We cannot penetrate the secrets of a human personality without sympathy and faith … We do not know first and then supply gaps in our knowledge by faith. We believe first, as did Columbus … If faith is the pioneer that leads us to a knowledge of persons, of moral possibilities and scientific facts why should we be surprised if faith is the road to God? Of course God is a matter of faith. Faith is always the great discoverer … finding God is like finding a friend – we do not consider the logical rationality of friendship until intellectually convinced … faith engages in an adventure where logic plays a minor part.

In 'Faith IV' he spoke about 'Faith in a personal God'.
'God in the Bible is personal,' he said,

He knows, loves, purposes, warns, rebukes and punishes as only persons can. If He is not personal then He has no concern for human life, and if He has no concern then He is of no consequence. Quoting Joubert, 'It is not hard to know God provided one will not force oneself to define Him', he went on to speak of his experience of Eastern religion: 'Every wayside shrine of Hinduism incarnates the old faith in gods conceived as friends, not things, and Buddha who taught impersonal deity is now adored as the personal 'Lord of Love and Blessedness' ... Whenever religion is vital God is no dry impersonal abstraction but man's friend ... does this idea of a personal God conflict with the God who created the universe, reducing Him to the similitude of human life? ... only if we think of a person as inseparable from the flesh. Remember John Adams, former President of U.S.A. He was met in the street and asked how he was that day. 'John Adams is well, quite well', he said, 'but the house in which he lives is becoming dilapidated, tottering on its foundations. Its roof is nearly worn out: the old tenement is becoming almost uninhabitable and John Adams will soon have to move out. But he himself is quite well thank you.' ... such a conception of man as being a permanent personality is the most unlimited reality with which we have to deal. In comparison a solar system is a little thing. Consider memory – only persons can remember; or imagination by which sitting still in body we can project ourselves round the world; or love by which we live; or creative power by which human beings project themselves into the future ... our supreme good is personality ... We must not be upset by the modern knowledge of the vastness of the Universe ... Our Lord taught us that God is personal – He is our friend, our Father.

In 'Faith V' he spoke about 'Belief and Trust'.
'Some people's faith,' he said,

is little more than an opinion about God. The Christian says, 'I believe in God'. The atheist says, 'I believe in the physical universe without spiritual origin or moral purpose'. The Christian says, 'I believe in the immortality of the soul', to which the atheist replies, 'I believe that the spirit dies with the body' etc ... The atheist can match the Christian on almost every point but he cannot match him on Trust. The Christian says, 'when misfortune comes upon you or you have to face the last mystery of all you have no one to trust but, 'the Lord is my shepherd, I shall not want.' 'Father, into Thy hands I commend my spirit' – you cannot match that...Many of our intellectual troubles are caused by the bankruptcy of our spiritual lives...communion with God has got crowded out...I beg of you to keep your companionship with God, your private inward trust, by daily meeting with Him in spirit. With that I can promise you a happy life.

In the Autumn of 1940 Rosalind became pregnant with another child and it was essential that the family should move into greater privacy. Puck had made friends with George Duckworth, a millionaire and the local landowner, who was reputed to have made his money by inventing Venos cough cure. One of the cottages on his estate, Woodside Cottage, had become vacant and Duckworth leased it to Puck for the duration of the war. It was ideally placed, being in the lane leading up to the Whiteside farm, so that a liberal supply of milk and eggs were always available, and it had a large kitchen garden for fruit and vegetables. Dick was born in the following summer and Puck Christened him in the RAF camp when the two elder boys were home for their holidays, standing as Godfather in the absence of other Godparents.

Woodside Cottage became the family home for four years and was a centre for much hospitality. Puck had a nose for seeking out interesting airmen on his evening visits to their barrack rooms. One such man was Leading Aircraftsman Michael whom he found practising his violin. Michael became a frequent visitor to the cottage joining Rosalind in string quartets along with Corporal John Pardell and his wife Daphne who were permanently based on the camp. Another was Squadron Leader John Graham, an artist currently serving as a camouflage specialist, who painted the boys' portraits and who, after the war, with his wife Dorothy and family came to live in a half of Lawford Rectory for a period.

Social life in the camp was inhibited by rationing yet there were memorable occasions such as New Year's Eve dances and guest nights, which included on one evening George Formby who had entertained the troops with song and his ukulele earlier in the day. But Puck's time at RAF Kirkham was best remembered for the number of airmen whom he prepared for Confirmation, running into several hundred. Increasing numbers came forward to the altar for Communion at the Sunday services and Puck used to say that he had to fill the Chalice to the brim, several times, when the Fleet Air Arm were on parade.

By the summer of 1944 the Allies had made great inroads into the German defences and the end of the war was in sight. Puck planned to return to a parish when the war was over and he had applied earlier in the year for the vacant incumbency at Lawford, next door parish to Mistley and Manningtree where Granny Atkinson still lived in Mistley Hall. Interviews had taken place that year and Puck was installed as its Rector that summer, the living to be taken up as soon as he could be released by the RAF, and permission being given for Rosalind and the children to camp in the Queen Anne Rectory for a part of the holidays. They moved in temporarily for the month of August and began preparing for the permanent move later on. In that month they came closer to the realities of war as the doodlebugs flew overhead on their way to London, often dropping nearby as they ran out of fuel, one of the flying bombs landing so close that it blew out the East window of Lawford Church. The family slept under the Anderson shelter most nights, a large iron framed table and the only piece of furniture left by the previous incumbent. It served its purpose during the day as well, not only for eating meals and playing board games but also as a platform on which Rosalind rehearsed her speech for opening the village fete, much to the amusement of the children.

Puck stayed on at RAF Kirkham until hostilities with Germany had ceased. On the eve of victory he preached:

Never, I suppose, in the history of the world has there been so sweeping and complete a conquest. We should have to go back to the ancient world to find a defeat in anyway comparable to that which confronts the German people. Their country occupied by the Allies, their state utterly destroyed, the social and economic structure of the country shattered and their culture in ruins. They are completely in the power of the victors, dependent on them for the necessities of life. Truly we are in the presence of the terrible judgement of God. But don't let us think that it is only the German State which is under God's judgement.

In our legitimate rejoicing and thanksgiving we must remember that the victorious nations now have the responsibility of making decisions for the future of millions of human beings. In that responsibility, and opportunity, lies our test…Never before were conquerors so powerful. For all practical purposes the three great powers are masters of the world. The question at San Francisco is how they will use that power. St Paul provides us with the phrase that sums up what we should pray for the representatives of the great powers: 'to be more than conquerors'.

The temptation will be great to remain in the role of conquerors. It will mask itself plausibly enough under the guise of 'realism'. It will be easy to exploit the conquest to the utmost and to impose a conqueror's peace not only on the enemy but on the whole world. That is the temptation which faces us. The alternative is to go beyond conquest and to plan and work for a future in which all nations can cooperate. It is obvious that the peace of the world depends on ourselves, the United States and Russia. I put ourselves first because the whole world is looking to us for leadership.

The systems of the U.S.A. and Russia are so different that in some things they cannot see eye to eye. It is we on whom the responsibility chiefly rests to maintain the cooperation. In this war we have learnt the meaning and value of cooperation. As a nation we are tolerant people and are able to see the other man's point of view. Above all we have a long Christian tradition of which the peculiar British expression is a sense of fair play. That is the reason why the world looks to us for leadership. We each have a great responsibility in this.

Every word which is spoken against Russia or against the United States strikes at the peace of the world.

The five British representatives at San Francisco are not only very able men and men of strong personality, but also, all of them, men of strong religious faith. I ask you to pray for them. They need your prayers.

Millions of people in all nations are hoping that the result of the Conference will show a real prospect of a lasting peace. It would be difficult to exaggerate the depression and despair which would sweep through the world if the Conference should fail.

The war years were a learning period for Puck as Priest and Pastor. Within two years of being ordained and of being a Parish Curate he was launched into being Senior Chaplain of an RAF Station of several thousand men. Having been a man-at-arms for thirty years he had become a carer of souls of men who would be posted into war zones. With his experience of being shot at in the air and of leading men into the front line of battle he immediately won the respect and trust of both officers and men in the camp. But caring of souls in those difficult times when the men were separated from their families and were uncertain about their futures was a considerable challenge for him. That he could rise to it was due to his deep faith in an Almighty God who had rescued him from life-threatening ventures.

Unlike those to whom he ministered Puck was fortunate in having his own family around him during those years. He was overwhelmed by the generosity and hospitality of the Lancashire people he got to know. However the climate did not suit him, and after thirty years of heat in the plains of India, the damp and cold affected his health. Fortunately, being only just 60 years old when the war ended, he still had plenty of energy to take on a new role of parish priest.

18

RECTOR

Puck was released from the RAF soon after VJ Day, in the Autumn of 1945, and the family moved into Lawford Rectory, being united with the furniture which had remained in storage throughout the war. The house had been empty for most of the war and was more than large enough to accommodate one family. Having a long corridor both on the ground and first floors, joining servants quarters to the main part of the Rectory, it was easy enough to divide the house in two and provide a home for another family. Previous Rectors had private means and could afford living in servants. Puck had only his Indian Army pension and his Rector's stipend (generously increased by Sir Philip Nichols, the local squire) and needed the rent from another family, if only to pay the wages of Ted who maintained the large garden. John Graham, an artist who had been in the camouflage branch of the RAF at Kirkham and his wife Dorothy and their two children were the first tenants and they occupied the servants' quarters end of the house.

Being a man for all people Puck immediately made an impact on the parish. He was out visiting most afternoons and kept an open house to all comers. The key to the Rectory had got lost in the transfer of the freehold and was never replaced so access was easy, and in all the thirteen years he was in residence it was never abused. He very soon got to know the village people and within the first month many of the children came up to play with Paul, John and Dick. Games of French and English were popular on the lawn, if you could call it that. It had clearly been a well kept tennis court before the war but by 1945 the grass was so high that Puck had to take a scythe to it.

Even with the Rectory divided in two there was plenty of room in the Strover half for visitors, especially for returning prisoners of war. One of the first guests was Puck's nephew, Chev Wilmot who had been captured in Crete and who came with his mother Nancy for Christmas 1945, and regaled the boys with stories of tunnelling and of his own attempts at escape. Chev brought his accordion, which he had learned to play as a POW and went out carol singing with the boys. When they got to the local, 'The Kings Arms', they got everyone to join in and one old fellow found it too emotional and had a heart attack. Puck was called to give the last rites but all was well, he survived. Another Christmas guest was Ben, Rosalind's brother, also an ex-POW, captured at Tobruk, who was living for a short while with Granny Atkinson in Mistley Hall before he got married.

One of the first jobs was to see to the repair of the stained glass East window in the church which had been boarded up after its shattering by a doodlebug. Puck set about getting a grant from the Church Commissioners and St John's College, Cambridge, in whose gift was the living. An expert in stained glass drew up designs based on Puck's vision of Jesus opening out his arms to him in welcome, which he had experienced in the Anglican Church of Kotagiri in the Nilgiri Hills, South India. The background chosen for it was the Dedham Vale and the Stour Estuary which can be seen from outside the East end of the church. Once installed, the new window let in a blaze of light, for so much of it was clear glass, contrasting incongruously with the Victorian butterfly adornments at its top, which had not received war damage and which for economic reasons were retained. Puck had insisted on this arrangement despite the protestations of the traditionalists who preferred a match with the butterfly windows and it remains today, a reminder of the war years and, for those who question its non-uniformity, that Christ welcomes us into His Church, not just in the beauty of the Dedham Vale or of the Nilgiri Hills, not only as traditional Churchgoers of the nineteenth century, but also as liberated Christians of post-war twentieth century. It was not long before the Church began to fill up again.

Puck, in many ways, was an unorthodox clergyman – he did not agree with all of the 39 articles of faith, the reason, no doubt, why the Bishop of Chelmsford would not ordain him before the war – ironic, though, that he should have ended up in his successor's Diocese. For example, he never preached against Rome (Article XIX). He was an old soldier and airman who had faced up to the dangers of his profession and inspired a regiment of thieves and robbers to a disciplined life of service. One of his greatest adherents was his Church Clerk, Ray Smith, another POW captured at Tobruk, and awarded the Military Medal for gallantry. Another was Len Parrington, one of the two Church wardens, ex-Brigadier, captured by the Germans in Crete. Len, married to Pat, a Catholic, never failed him and Pat ardently supported the social functions in the parish even though she and their daughters worshipped in the Church of Rome. The other Church warden, Robert Kirk, was a local apple farmer and keen clarinettist who joined with Rosalind in making music. The older members of the pre-war choir came back into the fold and Puck soon got to work in the village school to recruit youngsters, and in the village to swell the numbers with some of the young women.

Puck's faith was a simple one, drawn from his experience of life and on examples of answers to prayer, already touched upon in this biography (also see Appendix I). He never spoke openly about these life experiences although he preached frequently on the subject, taking as his main theme that prayer, like religion, is caught and not taught. He liked to quote H.M. Stanley who wrote, 'On all my expeditions prayer made me stronger, morally and mentally, than any of my non-praying companions. It did not blind my eyes, or dull my mind or close my ears; but on the contrary gave me confidence. It did more, it gave me joy and pride in my work, and lifted me hopefully over the 1500 miles of forest tracks, eager to face the day's perils and fatigues.'

Puck was a man of prayer. He had had experiences of life which proved to him that prayer is powerful, so it is not surprising that he preached more sermons on the need to pray than on any other subject. His experience of commanding a regiment of Muslim soldiers, who were obliged by their religion to pray several times a day, taught him the value of regular prayer. He often quoted in his sermons how the first Apostles 'continued with one accord in prayer'

The choir in action. Puck standing in front of the East Window.

and spoke of how Jesus had trained them to receive the power of the Holy Spirit, and how their prayer became deeper and stronger so that 'they did not withdraw from life in idle meditation, but invaded life armed with new creative powers'. He advocated the habit of prayer so that at any time of the day you can turn to God for direction. Prayer, he said, is giving God an opportunity to bestow what he is more willing to give than we to receive; that it is not to ask what we wish of God, but what he wishes for us. The essence of prayer, he said is in the Lord's Prayer: 'Thy will be done'.

One of his favourite prayers was R.L. Stevenson's prayer for Joy: 'Grant us O Lord the royalty of inward happiness and the serenity which comes from living close to thee. Daily renew in us the sense of joy...' He found joy in every aspect of his life, his early years in a family whose relative poverty was liberated by a talented mother with a zest for living, his champagne years at Cambridge, the friendships he made throughout his life, the handling of the joy stick as one of the first aviators, the difficulties he encountered in commanding a regiment of Punjabis, his work as a priest, and as a family man when not everything was a bed of roses, but which turned out well for him as he put himself in the hands of God. He drew inspiration from the prayer of St Francis: 'Lord make me an instrument of thy peace; where there is hatred let me sow love; where there is sadness joy... For it is in giving that we receive and it is in forgiving that we are pardoned.' Giving and forgiving were the hallmarks of his professional and married life and in his personal relationships.

Puck was fortunate in having a prayer companion, Rosalind. Both had been brought up in a tradition of family prayer, meeting with parents and the household for prayer before breakfast. It was formal of course and Rosalind admitted that as a child she had tried to catch a servant's eye and make her laugh; so they never inflicted that formality on their own children. Times had changed and Puck was not the kind of Victorian father figure who expected his own children to accept his discipline without demur. Instead he gave them good advice: 'go to the lavatory after breakfast and say your prayers'. Either he or Rosalind heard their own children's prayers before bed time. However, they had both caught the habit of prayer from their early experiences and together it became a regular speaking with God as the day began, and not something resorted to in an emergency. In a sermon preached to parents (Ref. British Legion Service, 1939, p. 166) he spoke of the example they should set for their children in bringing them up to be spiritually fit citizens. He said it can only be done by prayer and in these days of having to rush off to work he begged them to cultivate the habit of getting up ten minutes earlier and, spending if only five minutes, listening to God. It will make all the difference to your day, he said.

Rosalind really came into her own as a Rector's wife. Her music was a great asset in the parish and in the neighbourhood. Not only could she fill in for the organist when he was away but she took on the WI choir which proved to be a huge success over the years. Principally, she was a viola player and quartets met frequently in the Rectory. One of the regulars was Barbara Carr (*née* Hodson-Mackenzie), her cellist friend and bridesmaid who, having been widowed, came to live with her three children in Abbots Manor, Lawford, a stone's throw from the Rectory; but Rosalind's great forte was teaching the violin and viola. That is what she was trained to do, graduating as LRAM when in her teens, and in her Rectory years she went on to gain ARCM in teaching, as pupils continued to roll into the Rectory for lessons. Puck's years as an Instructor at the Staff College and in training a Regiment to come up to scratch for frontier duties proved him to be a born teacher. Many of the confidential reports on his military service point to that strength. It was another interest and accomplishment which they had in common.

Puck held Education to be of vital importance in the training of mind and the development of spirituality and personality. The years between 18 and 22 when young men and women begin to be their own master he considered to be the most important, the years when a person notes peculiarities in him or herself and which distinguishes that person from others, noting strengths and weaknesses and to be his or her own tutor and physician, 'Not without the thought of the Great Physician,' he said, 'through whom the trials of the body may be likened to blessings upon the soul.'

Before he was married and had children of his own Puck had wanted to contribute to the education of his brother Harry's son, Dudley, who was his Godson; and when his sister Nancy was widowed with two young sons he and Martyn, Puck's brother, both of them bachelors, clubbed together to see to the education of the two boys. Then, when he had three sons of his own, he managed to send them all to the Dragon School in Oxford and onto Public School up to the age of 18. And when John went on to Oxford he gave him his last £600 of savings to see him through. All this was at a sacrifice of personal pleasure. In the post-war years when the older boys were being educated he and Rosalind never took a holiday or had a car until they were freed from paying school fees. In one of his Sermons he said: 'It is one thing to have a motor-car – that is part of our civilization. It is another to be carried by it on a summer's day into the loveliness of the countryside and to use that experience, not to go dashing through it all at 50 mph (this was preached in the 50s!), but to absorb the loveliness so that one returns saying: 'He maketh me to lie down in green pastures; He leadeth me beside still waters; He restoreth my soul.' Puck had neither the means nor the desire to accumulate wealth or possessions. Indeed on several occasions he warned about the inherent dangers of wealth. In that same sermon he said:

> Most people are now richer than they have ever been and I am glad that you are able to enjoy it, but please think a little: the words of Jesus have an even greater application today: 'How hardly shall they that have riches enter into the Kingdom of Heaven'. A strange

paradox is man's search for happiness. St Francis of Assisi was the gay and wealthy son of a prosperous merchant, with ample means to live by, and he was not happy. Then he stripped his gay robes from himself and deliberately made himself one of the hungry poor and washed the sores of lepers. And then what happened? That same Francis preached joyously to his brothers, the birds, sang the 'Canticle of the Sun' and, incidentally, shook Christendom to its foundations. He found happiness not by the means by which he lived but by the object for which he lived.

Don't misunderstand me: I am not recommending literal copying of St Francis. To each generation its own way. But this is clear! If a man seeks happiness directly as his first objective he fails to find it. Our experience teaches us plainly that happiness is obtained as a by-product. A person who spends his life in what is called 'pleasure seeking' is not nearly so happy as the person who is doing a useful job of work. Indeed the selfish person who is always thinking about his own happiness ends up by becoming thoroughly miserable. Happiness is not the ultimate truth. What people are really seeking for – although most people do not know it – is God. And when they find God they find happiness. As St Augustine said 'Thou hast made us for Thyself, and our hearts are restless until they rest in Thee.'

It will be asked, 'how can we know if we are really seeking God?' There are two tests: We can judge this by noticing if we are jealous of other people when they seem to be more successful than we are. If we are jealous it is clear that our primary motive is selfish; that is why we cannot rejoice in the success of others. But, if it is God's work about which we are concerned we will rejoice when we see others prospering and we will not be over concerned through whom it prospers. Moreover, we will be content if we are able to do the work even if we get little or no recognition. As has been said: 'you can do much good in the world provided that you do not mind who gets the credit for it.'

Secondly, we can apply the test our Lord Himself has given us: 'by their fruits ye shall know them'. If we are really seeking, above all else, to do God's will we shall have an inner satisfaction and peace which is quite independent of outward circumstances. This is the peace of Christ; the peace and contentment which comes to the man or woman who is not seeking great things for him or herself, but simply the will of God.

Puck was a happy man. He had learned the secret of happiness in a long life of service. In 1931 he wrote to Paul and John on the subject when they were infants, in a letter to be read when they were old enough to understand (see Chapter 16). Twenty years later, with the experience of commanding a regiment, ministering as a priest to thousands of wartime airman, educating three sons on a paltry salary and bringing hope and love into a community recovering from the ravages of war, he had enlarged on that simple but important message.

The immediate post-war life was a great blessing: the Rectory was a beautiful and substantial home with a large garden, a big walled kitchen garden, an orchard with abundant fruit and thirty acres of glebe land and a tithe barn. No way could Puck employ a farm hand, so the glebe was leased to James Harter, one of many local retired generals who had taken up fruit farming, to grow blackcurrants. With plenty of vegetables grown by Ted, a pig fattened on scraps from the table, a goat providing milk and chickens fed from gleaning the cornfields the family were able to supplement the meagre rations available from the village stores. The stores were run by Cecil Cookson and his wife Dorothy as a side line to Cookson's Garage, his brother's business, which not only sold petrol, repaired vehicles and dealt in cars, but also ran coach and taxi services in the district. Bicycles were the main form of transport for the family, but there were good bus services into Colchester.

Granny Atkinson, who still lived in Mistley Hall, had kept her Austin locked up in her garage during the war and her licence to drive (for which, of course she had never been required to pass a test!), and had it brought back onto the road with her at the wheel. The exit from the long drive out from the Hall onto the main road was known to be a local danger spot, for she considered that traffic should give way to her as she emerged! Things did not improve greatly when her 'man', Biscoe, took over the driving. He had the same attitude, that oncoming cars should slow down when he decided to overtake. She was generous with her petrol allowance, transporting her family into Colchester on occasions, but it was a nightmare of a journey.

Granny had been a keen sportswoman in her youth, riding to the Essex and Suffolk hounds, and had played tennis, hockey and croquet at county level. As her children and grandchildren grew up she became a keen follower of cricket being a regular spectator at Mistley Cricket Club of which she was its President. The cricket ground, with its club house emblazoned with MCC, was situated adjacent to Mistley Church and Sunday matches never started until Matins was over and always had to finish before Evensong – the club captain, Lionel Goldsmith, sometimes having to retire early in order to robe for the choir – so Puck was often there too, especially when his sons were playing. He was a frequent visitor, too, at the Frinton-on-Sea lawn tennis tournament which his sons entered when they were at home during the summer holidays. The tournament, held a fortnight after Wimbledon was over, attracted some of its players and on one occasion when an umpire was required for the centre court he volunteered his services, not perturbed by a pair of Wimbledon Doubles finalists playing, sitting in the high chair and calling the score without recourse to the marksheet – never one to refuse a challenge!

Although Mistley Church which her grandfather, Canon Norman, had built was her regular place of worship, Granny was a frequent attender at Lawford Church, sitting in the front pew and was renowned for going fast asleep during the sermon. On one occasion when Puck wished to demonstrate the betrayal of Judas Iscariot he poured out thirty pieces of silver onto a tray with a resounding clatter. Granny awoke with a sharp jolt which added to the consternation and merriment of the congregation. In the early days of his incumbency the organ had to be pumped by hand from the balcony above and on Good Friday for the three-hour service Paul and John were commissioned for the duty. In order to while away the hours, they took with them a pack of playing cards and got so absorbed in their game that Puck had to call out the next hymn number several times before the organ came to life. Later on, after money had been raised in the parish, not only did the organ get an electric pump but heating also was installed.

Family life was important to Puck. His own marriage had held together through difficult times. Rosalind was twenty years younger than himself and it was inevitable that she might be attracted by much younger men than himself. Passions ran high during the war years and they slept in separate rooms despite the cramped conditions of Woodside Cottage. That had become a habit when they moved into the spacious accommodation of the Rectory, and for some years the older boys sensed a certain coolness between their parents. As the peaceful years rolled on and their common life in the parish drew them more and more together Puck and

Lawford Rectory facing South over the garden.

Rosalind developed a lasting affection for each other. They had both made sacrifices for their children, giving them the best education possible with their limited resources; they had shared their good fortune of a beautiful Rectory with other families and had entertained their own and their children's friends generously throughout the years of rationing. Added to which their prayer life was a regular feature over the early morning cup of tea.

It was from his own experience then that Puck was able to preach the Christian ideal of marriage and family. He condemned the so-called 'new morality' whereby the personality should have full liberty of expression and neither husband nor wife should expect from each other any restraint upon the passions which might cause complexes and repressions, so that free romantic adventures should not be checked. He contrasted what he called that shoddy, selfish life and sensual style of living, with the Christian ideal of marriage

St Mary's Church, Lawford; its East end overlooking the Stour Estuary.

and family which comes to fruition from a man and a girl pledging themselves in the presence of God by a vow of life-long fidelity and loyalty. 'No fair-weather friendship', he called it. 'The cynic may sneer at the ideal of standing together through thick and thin but he cannot deny that it is a great and noble ideal. If it is a folly, then it is a grand folly.'

'The marriage vow in the Prayer Book,' he said,

> is primarily a matter of affections – affections first and passions afterwards, of self-sacrificing friendship, friendship at its highest point, sanctified by the blessing of God. If the first, friendship, is rightly understood, the second, passions, will take their proper place. Divorce arises primarily out of the reverse, being concerned with passions and not at all with affections.

Puck did not go along with the commonly held view of the 'innocent party' in a divorce. 'When the promise of sexual fidelity is broken by the so-called guilty party it is most often the case', he said, 'that the moral lapse has come about because the other party had broken the first part of the marriage vow of self-sacrificing friendship.'

Drama had always been a major factor in Puck's life, from his earliest years in Bath when his mother produced an annual play in the family home involving all his brothers and sister in the cast; in Pantomime and in the 'Andover Aeronauts' Revue at the RAF Staff College, as production manager of the Theatre Company in Taiping, and performing as Widow Twanky in the Mistley pantomime, Aladdin. Rosalind, too, had always participated, being the producer of Aladdin and acting in the plays in Taiping. For several years she produced the annual Nativity Play at the Ogilvie Hall in Lawford, involving her family when they were home for the Christmas holidays. One year when Paul played the part of the Angel Gabriel she arranged for him, in the darkness of the stage, to be transfigured by a light shining on him from behind. This involved John and

Simon Carr shining a powerful torch from below the stage through an open trap door. Just as Paul was annunciating to the Virgin Mary his attendant angel, six-year-old Ian Smith, took a step backwards and fell, screaming, into John's arms. That brought up lights on the stage and the sight of Ian's father, Ray, the stage manager, rushing on to rescue his son. It brought the house down!

Christmas in the Rectory was packed with merriment. The church was always full for Matins and those who did not have to rush home to rescue their turkeys from the oven repaired to the Rectory for sherry. A hearty lunch was followed by hockey on the lawn when all comers were invited to bring their sticks, hockey or otherwise, and join in until the light faded. Then tea and Christmas cake. It became the tradition for family friends in the

Puck, Rosalind and
the three boys on the
Rectory lawn, 1950.

village to assemble in the drawing room for charades after supper. Each family had to produce its own charade. The Moynaghs, who lived in the other half, were well regimented by Digby, a Colonel in the RAMC who had won an MC in the Italian campaign. The Minneys were very professional under the guidance of R.J. who was a film producer. The Parringtons, with Pat and Len and their two lovely daughters were well rehearsed. The Carrs were innovative and difficult to pin down with their catch words. The Nichols's and the Shones from Lawford Hall were sometimes hilarious. The Strovers often acted with a script written by Puck. One such script (see Appendix IV) had a very political flavour, the red herring being 'Sputenik', a misspelling and mispronunciation of 'Sputnik' – the Russian earth satellite which had just been launched – made up from parts of 'dispute' and 'Nixon'; the charade word being 'upstairs', with the first two scenes taking place in the Kremlin and the Whitehouse and the final scene being in the Earl of Rutlandshire's stately home. He was an imaginative writer with a good sense of drama and a puckish sense of humour.

No doubt the script was influenced by Peter Tapsell who was staying with the Strover household over the Christmas holidays. Peter boarded at Tonbridge School, Puck's old school, and usually spent the Christmas holidays at the Rectory as his parents lived in Tanganyika, his father being in Government Service. As he was in between Paul and John in age the three were always invited together to parties. Peter had ambitions to be Prime Minister and at that time was very left wing in his politics. He and Puck enjoyed their political dialogue and later in life when Peter became Chairman of the Coningsby Club he invited Puck to be his guest of honour, along with R.A. Butler. Suffice it to say that when Peter left Oxford with his First in History he had changed his party allegiance and sat for over fifty years on the Tory benches, becoming Father of the House in 2010, always a thorn in a Labour PM's side.

Puck embraced Politics and Current Affairs and was not shy of expressing his opinions from the pulpit. In a paper written in the late 1950s when there was acute discussion over the arms race he spoke about Christianity and the H-bomb. He acknowledged the view taken by many who were not pacifists in the Second World War that with inter-continental H-bomb rockets anything is better than a world war today, but he believed that the majority of Christians had not yet made up their minds for fear of embarrassing the Government who had a far-reaching responsibility. He had formed his views from a recent Reith lecture on the arms race, leaders in *The Times*, broadcasts, House of Commons and Lords debates and private conversations with MPs (Julian Ridsdale, the member for Colchester, who was a friend, and R.A. Butler), and Sir Philip Nichols, a frequent dinner companion. He considered that the Soviet threat was more political than military and that we should get over the obsession that Russia is yearning to attack and occupy Western Europe. Historically, a build up of arms combined with hostility had led to war. A nuclear war was a threat so terrible that even our dislike of Communism becomes comparatively unimportant. If none of the other great powers agrees to abandon the insane nuclear arms race then the unilateralists will say that we should do so anyway. The Kremlin would not wish or be able to take over a defenceless Western World. Even if they did, that would be better than the mass murder of millions of innocent people. If that is a defeatist attitude his reply would be that it is a grosser form of defeatism to accept the possibility of nuclear war, blind optimism being a more cowardly way out than submission.

The Government's case, he thought, would be that the existing power to retaliate had undoubtedly kept the Communists outside the stockade for the past ten years, and would not accept the inevitability of nuclear war although bound to accept its possibility. The US feel themselves technically able to match any horror inflicted on themselves and a British move to leave the alliance would be regarded as an act of treachery. In peace time it would have terrible consequences on our economy and in war time we would suffer the penalties of defencelessness and humiliation because the US would have no scruples about occupying us as an outpost to prevent the Russians getting here first. We would become a prime target from both sides. As an experienced soldier who had been involved in several campaigns he knew that you do not embark on a war unless you have reasonable confidence that you can win outright. It must be the opposite of immoral, therefore, to make clear to an aggressor that a nuclear war is a war that he cannot win, but he must not be allowed to feel that, in the last resort, his enemy will not carry out his threat. If that doubt lingers there would be some justification for the charge of immorality: it would be abetting a crime through negligence. The Christian viewpoint must be, he said, to get a political and economic policy with potential aggressors but that would mean some sacrifice of sovereignty – difficult for statesmen to achieve because of the immense opposition to it but, nevertheless, it is a Christian virtue to overcome national prejudice. However, if Russia and the West could establish a joint economic agency for help to the Middle East, that could be an answer to a real threat to mankind which has the potential for boiling over throughout the world. His military and political experience in Mesopotamia and on the borders of Afghanistan was good justification for that view – how prophetic and perspicacious that was for events which took place half a century later! But human relationships must dominate the Christian viewpoint and he considered that we should be convinced that the Russian people are, at heart, peace loving and that the existing tension would disappear quickly if people really got to know each other. Therefore he proposed that we should present plans to Russia for a large scale and far-reaching programme of a get-together character at the level of the ordinary citizen; a vast exchange of young people backed with economic resource and drive. If the Kremlin refused to collaborate we would need to take political warfare seriously and make a determined effort to outflank its leaders and reach the masses and their intelligentsia on whose support the Politburo depends for its power.

Not surprisingly, many of his most telling sermons were preached on Remembrance and Empire Day Sundays, for his experience of two world wars and the suppression of the Arab Revolt in Mesopotamia had taught him the cruelty and misdirected glory of war. He would say that his own generation entered the First World War convinced of the glorification of fighting and even dying for one's country but had learned, during its duration, of its obscenity. He liked to quote from Wilfrid Owen: 'My friend, you would not tell with such high Zest to children ardent for some desperate glory, the old Lie: Dulce et Decorum est pro patria mori' (what a glorious thing it is to die for one's country). As a padre on an RAF station in the Second World War he could be more dispassionate about the reasons for going to war with Nazi Germany, as he liked to call the enemy, and knew young pilots who had risked their lives in the cause of freedom. These young men were realistic about war, knew that they faced death but could see no alternative.

In his congregation were those like Len Parrington, Digby Moynagh, Cecil Cookson and Ray Smith who had been at the sharp end of that most recent conflict, and Sir Philip Nichols, a veteran of the First World War trenches, also awarded the MC for gallantry, whose elder brother Robert Nichols, the poet, had been killed in action. Soldiers returning from the Western Front came expecting a land fit for heroes but found, instead, that you had to be a hero to live in it with all the unemployment which resulted from the economic crash. To them, war was no longer glorious, but cruel and sordid.

The leaders of the nations, he said, were unprepared for the Second World War and were saved by a power outside themselves. Churchill, Alanbrooke, Dowding, all good Christian men, were sustained by their faith which like so many others brought out the best in them. His experience of being a prisoner of war with

Russian officers in 1917, and his years protecting the British Empire in India, made him realise that the British have a genius for evolution rather than revolution. Christian men and women went out to serve in the Empire with fair play, justice and freedom, gaining the good will, even the affection of the ruled, all of which sprang from their faith. He liked to speak of the comradeship generated by regimental attachments and recalled how as a POW he had received two food parcels from a Naik (Corporal in the Indian Army) one of his NCOs in the Second Brahmans. He had huge respect for the soldier, whether British or Indian and their great sense of loyalty and sacrifice in time of war. Of course there were exceptions, he said, but in general the Empire was ruled with the spirit of duty which took over from the spirit of acquisition.

Much of his preaching in the aftermath of the Second World War was directed at bringing everlasting peace, and living with the power to split the atom. He sensed its dangers in its use for either good or evil. The League of Nations failed after the First World War but he saw more hope for the United Nations especially under the Christian leadership of Dag Hammarksjold, though he could wish that it was bound together by Christian principles as was the Commonwealth of Nations, at that time emerging from the independence given to Dominions, Colonies and Protectorates.

Puck was in no way a conventional clergyman. When the Deanery Chapter assembled in Lawford for one of their monthly meetings and came to breakfast after Communion, and the sons were home and commissioned to serve at table, they were only too aware of the differences. His real friends were not clerics but more likely Indian Army 'Wallahs', many of whom had retired to East Anglia as fruit farmers. Major-General James Harter was one; Colonel Freeland, whose sons Paul and John were contemporaries of his own sons Paul and John at Cheltenham College, was another. Major-General Freddie Birch, who lived in Dedham always brought his family to Church in Lawford because only there could he find harmony with the sermon. Lady Munnings, wife of Sir Alfred, controversial President of the Royal Academy, also preferred to attend Matins at Lawford rather than in her own Parish of Dedham and brought her Pekingese dog with her (when the dog died she had it stuffed so that it could still accompany her). Sir Alfred was a friend in the Dedham Vale Book Club, to which both he and Puck belonged and was a frequent visitor, on horseback, to Lawford and its environs, but never at Church!

Puck had great rapport with Phil Nichols who frequently invited him up to Lawford Hall for dinner where he met some interesting guests, among whom were Joyce Grenfell, Nancy Astor, Field Marshall Lord Alexander of Tunis and his family, and Stephen Potter. It is said that Potter's books on Oneupmanship and Golfmanship were hatched in Lawford Hall. Sir Philip was a keen golfer. In Puck's early years at Lawford, Sir Philip was the British Ambassador at the Hague and Puck and Rosalind with Dick, were invited to the embassy there for a short holiday. Field Marshall Lord Montgomery of Alamein was also a guest and Dick, same age as Martin, Phil's son, were befriended by 'Monty' who played games with them. When Phil died, Puck gave a most moving address.

Parties at the Rectory were always enjoyed. With the free run of the house we could dance through from the large drawing room into the equally large dining room with a band in the corridor in between. Fancy dress was often 'de rigeur' and in the summer we would spill out onto the lawn for Scottish reels. Puck and Rosalind were great hosts, enjoying the youthful exuberance of their childrens' friends.

Far more of Puck's time was spent visiting his parishioners. He had visited men in their barrack rooms throughout his service career and found no awkwardness in breaking in on home ground. He liked to visit when the men were at home and in the days before television he was generally welcomed. The dog collar was a good passport for entry and gave his hosts an opportunity to bare their souls to him. It also gave him an opportunity to invite them to Church and many of his congregation were made up from these home visits. He always ended his visit with prayer and such was his profound belief in it, it would not have caused embarrassment. His means of transport on these occasions was often 'Snowball', Dick's pony, who could be seen tethered to a front garden gate, giving notice that the Rector was in attendance. Snowball's increasing girth from the lush grass in the Rectory paddock rendered him an impossible mount as the years rolled on and Puck took to his bicycle instead. In the evening he could often be found in the village pub yarning with the men.

The annual fete and flower show was always a great success. It took place on the field behind the Ogilvie Hall, now alas totally built over. Ray Smith was in charge of proceedings in so much that all stall holders reported to him; the marquee was erected by him and his helpers and its layout supervised by him. Puck's role was as chairman of the fete committee and Rosalind took its minutes. The parish rallied round for the event of the year and funds were raised for Church, School and Hall. A well-known personality was invited to open the fete and great interest in the event was taken when the film actress Margaret Lockwood was guest of honour. She had been the star in 'The Wicked Lady', a film produced by R.J. Minney who lived in Lawford House. Another personality invited to open the fete was Percy Edwards, the BBC bird-man. Had they but known that a future Prime Minister was working in the village they might have asked her to open the fete. Margaret Thatcher was a research chemist for BX Plastics, working in Lawford Place.

The parish included the Foxash settlement of small-holders where Puck took services in their community hall. He was much loved there, as much by the example he set as by the word which he preached, encouraging the Sunday School, led by Kath Baalham.

The Church and Rectory, situated on the brow of the Dedham Vale afforded wonderful views over the River Stour and the Estuary.

They were no more than three miles across fields and along a tow-path to Flatford Mill, famous for Constable's 'Haywain'. Indeed you could stand exactly on the spot, facing Willie Lott's cottage where the artist painted his picture, and nothing much had changed in over one hundred years. It was always a good walk there and back with plenty of bird life on the river and on the marshes. Dr Ennion, who ran the bird sanctuary from Flatford and lived in the converted mill with his family, was a good friend and his beautiful daughters were an added attraction for Paul and John. Many visits were paid, and on the way there or back the boys would often stop for a swim in the river at Judas Gap, the weir where the River Stour divided into the Suffolk and Essex sides of the Vale before joining again at Cattawade bridge into the estuary. Judas Gap was a good meeting place with friends, on a hot day, for a swim.

Family holidays were at a premium. A sailing holiday in Bosham, Sussex, when Puck stayed with an old Indian Army friend and his wife in their retirement home on the quay, and the rest of the family camped on the tennis court, was a new experience and led to the purchase of 'Aza', a clinker built dinghy, which later became a source of adventure on the River Stour, and racing with the Manningtree Sailing Club.

Then in 1953 Puck, Rosalind, Paul and Dick set off in the 'White Van' for France. This was a new acquisition, their first car since the war, and not eligible for purchase tax since it had no rear side windows. It was an uncomfortable ride for the two boys in the back. They drove down through Chartres, stopping to view the cathedral, to Tours and stayed with Monsieur and Madame Boyer in their beautiful home, 'Grand Beau Regard', at St Symphorien, on the River Loire. M. Boyer had been a fellow prisoner of war with Puck and was a distinguished architect, extremely cultured and well acquainted with 'Les Châteaux' in the area, which the family enjoyed visiting. A visit to 'Les Caves de Vouvray', nearby, led to its wine becoming a favourite over the years.

The years spent as Rector of Lawford proved to be the culmination of a life of service in the cause of humanity. Puck's forbears had served the British Empire with distinction and it was with that background he had sought a life which would be of service to his fellow men and women. His mother saw in him the potential for Priesthood and sent him to Selwyn College with that in mind but he did not consider himself worthy of that calling at the time. He, therefore, set off on a life of adventure which would bring him into contact with people from different parts of the world and from a variety of social groupings. It was only when he got to India as a young subaltern that his eyes were opened to the conditions of real poverty in the world and he made it his business to get to know the language and lifestyles of the men whom he commanded, and to help them with family problems.

Puck's POW years brought him into contact with the Russian aristocracy and with the German soldier. He also mixed with French officers and was perceptive of the differences between the European nations and of the cause of turmoil on that continent between the two world wars. He was also in sympathy with those who sought the independence of the sub-continent even though that would mean the end of a military career which he loved.

Although trained for staff appointments his three years of Regimental Command were the highlight of his military career for not only did he bring his regiment to a high degree of efficiency but enabled him to reach out into the welfare of the rural community. In this he was greatly assisted by Rosalind.

It would have been no surprise to Puck's mother that after thirty years' experience of the Indian way of life and its spirituality he should have felt ready to be ordained. His time as a Curate in the Industrial Midlands and as a Padre on a large RAF Station in Lancashire, surrounded by a farming community, afforded him then opportunity to get to know a variety of different people and he made the most of that opportunity by visiting them in their homes and barrack rooms.

Lawford, then, was an ideal parish in which to make his mark as a priest. It embraced a large farming community as well as workers in the BX plastics factory across the river. There was a good Primary School in the village where he taught each week and a large Secondary School within the parish boundary where he was a governor. The military garrison at Colchester was nearby and family contacts through Rosalind's relatives and friends and his own 'Indian Army Wallahs' who had taken up apple farming, brought new blood into his congregation. Added to which his own personality and experience was widely respected among his parishioners.

He worked hard to swell his congregation and on the pastoral care of the surrounding community and enjoyed every minute of it. He didn't have the cash to enjoy many holidays and found relaxation in reading and writing and with good conversation, and with his family and friends in his beautiful home which he and Rosalind shared with all comers. However the cold East Winds had only accentuated his health problem which had been provoked by the damp climate of Lancashire.

19

RHODESIA

Puck was an ill man when he set off for Rhodesia at the end of January 1955. He had been invited there by his nephew Dr Minto Strover and his wife Ethelwyn who lived in Bindura, about 60 miles from the capital, Salisbury (now Harare), where Minto had a large medical practice involving general surgery. This was at the end of the Rhodesian summer when the youngest two boys, Angus and Paddy, of their three children had returned to school at Plumtree, the eldest, Roger, remaining at home prior to going to Cape Town University to read medicine.

The family lived in a largish bungalow with a certain amount of land and stabling for nine horses. Ethelwyn had help in the house with two African servants, in addition to a garden boy and a groom. However, she liked to supervise the cooking and cleaning and did all the accounts and administration of Minto's practice.

Bindura, being situated in a granite bowl, had wonderful riding country and the family were out on their horses every morning before breakfast. Puck was soon into the saddle on a thoroughbred stallion called 'Newlite' who was a real gentleman. He was one of those rare stallions who was a wonderful hack as well as being fast and very easy to control. The routine was, wake up at 6a.m. with a cup of coffee, ride out for an hour before breakfast at 8a.m., and then off to work. Minto would be out at his practice all day until about 7p.m. and Puck would retire to the garden most mornings with table and chair and do his writing or else go out visiting. Then rest after lunch and more riding. All met up for the sundowner before dinner and then bed at 9p.m. It was a routine that entirely suited his condition and interests: rest in a warm climate, time for his writing, growing strength from exercising himself on horseback, which he loved and which took him back to his polo playing days.

Puck soon felt the need for less indulgence and to make a contribution locally. The Church in Bindura had no parson, only a priest who would come out from Salisbury once a month. Needing to be useful he persuaded Ethelwyn to drive him into Salisbury to meet the Bishop of Mashonaland, who turned out to be the brother of his old Army friend, General Sir Bernard Paget, and son of the Bishop of Oxford in the diocese where Puck had studied for his ordination at Ripon Hall, Boars Hill. So the two had much in common and it was no surprise that the Bishop appointed him temporary Rector of Bindura, hoping that he would be able to stay for six months. That, he would not be able to do, as he had refused payment on the grounds that Minto would not accept payment for his upkeep and he couldn't afford to pay Reverend Manthorpe, his locum at Lawford, for that long. In any case he felt that he would be outstaying his welcome after May when the boys returned from school for their holidays.

Bindura was a huge parish, half the size of Wales, and he would not be able to give it his full-time attention. As it was, he committed himself to taking a Communion Service every Sunday, teaching in the school, running a Confirmation class and visiting in the village and local hospital. Within a fortnight of arrival he had amassed a congregation of 25 people for Communion, presumably using his well-tried tactic of visiting homes and encouraging attendance at Church on Sundays. This congregation was to grow and grow as time went on, with large numbers coming to the Easter Service of Confirmation and Holy Communion presided over by the Bishop. It is amazing that in the short period between arrival in late January and Easter in mid-April he should have persuaded the Bishop to come to this outlying parish on the most important day in the Church's calendar and to have brought together five adults to the point of Confirmation, when he had arrived in Rhodesia in such poor health.

It spoke much for his quick recovery of health in the warmth and sunshine. He had suffered from bronchitis more or less ever since he had retired from the Indian Army to the English climate, especially during the war years in Lancashire and the cold winds of East Anglia. In a letter to Rosalind only a fortnight after Puck's arrival in Rhodesia Ethelwyn wrote: 'He was so pale when he arrived but we have had a dry spell with lots of sunshine...his colour has improved miraculously; he is sleeping well and seems to have only very short spells of wheeziness, if any at all.' Sophie Shone and her husband Sir Terence, diplomatic friends of Phil Nichols, living in the converted stable block at Lawford Hall, spent a day with the Strovers at Bindura while on holiday in Rhodesia, also wrote to Rosalind: 'Puck looking wonderful – has that puckish look about him which makes me wonder what he is really up to! You would like their house but may take exception to the snakes of various kinds which are regarded as house pets! This only when the children are there which, mercifully they weren't !'

All three sons were keen naturalists. They were on their horses for half the day, with their dogs, capturing animals and insects and even making pets of them. They would look these up in their books, draw and catalogue them. Angus, in particular had a fascination for reptiles and had discovered a new breed of snake which had been sent to America. He was soon to join an expedition with the Rhodesian Biological Department. His method of capturing them was with a loop of wire hanging from the end of a stick. Directly the head of the snake went through the loop he gave the stick a jerk upwards and the wire loop tightened behind the snake's head. He then ran his hand up the snake from the tail and held it behind the head so that it could not bite him. He thus caught the most venomous snakes without harm, and as a precaution carried a strong anti-toxin in a hypodermic syringe.

One day he had come back in triumph with a puff-adder which he had safely bestowed in a box. His father had been horrified, realising that one bite would kill him in ten minutes. But Angus was not to be deterred; he had dug a square pit four feet deep and covered it with doors which stopped every possible egress. The puff-adder had been lowered in beside a saucer of egg and milk. It moved very slowly and relished its meal. Angus said it looked at him with an affectionate eye. Although accustomed to Angus's curious tastes, the whole family regarded his latest adventure with apprehension. After a few days Angus, who had gone out before breakfast to feed his pet, had come running back to the house in wild excitement. There were thirty baby snakes in the pit. There was a rush from the house led by Angus. There they were, 30 tiny puff-adders, each one, as they knew, a harbinger of death from its birth. Angus's days were spent in feeding and watching his progeny and reading up everything he could find in the Salisbury library on the subject. And he discovered things which no book had shown him, that the babies mewed like kittens.

By the time Puck arrived in the household Angus had returned to school, and the puff-adders were safely secured. He left his pets with sad regret and begged everybody to look after them properly, leaving full notes on their diet and times of feeding. His instructions were carried out with great care but, as a precaution, Puck donned his riding boots when opening the horizontal folding doors above the pit, which were made of wood and wire mosquito-proof gauze. The youngsters grew apace and did their best to get out. But Angus had done his work well and there was no possible exit.

At Easter there was a small house party. The guests came to church on Easter Sunday, and then went off to play their games, coming back for lunch. Then all went to see the puff-adders of which the visitors had heard so much. On arrival at the pit they saw a gaping hole in one of the doors. One of the horses had broken loose during the night for a short time and must have put his foot through the door. On opening the pit and counting, one snake was missing. It was essential to find it and the party looked around very cautiously. Suddenly one of the ladies shrieked to her husband: 'look behind you!' He leaped forward and there, within a yard of where his foot had been was the missing puff-adder. It was too much. By unanimous consent guns were brought and a massacre ensued. Puck wrote up this experience in an article for *The Times* which was published a year later under the heading: 'GREAT SNAKES! HOW THE YOUNG HERPETOLOGIST LOST HIS FAVOURITES' (see Appendix IV).

Puck immediately fell into colonial society. What he most appreciated was its lack of class distinction when he found himself drinking at the bar with the local garage man and butcher. Club membership was not the least bit exclusive and he enjoyed the company of all comers, especially at the dances where he found a new lease of life. When he could spare the time at week-ends Minto would take him up country, over the dusty tracks, into native reserves where they often painted together.

One such trip was to the Mount Darwin area, 80 miles North of Bindura where Minto had a clinic; there they met up with farming friends, varied in background from Lords to ex-tradesmen. These were self-reliant, most of them had built their own farmhouses, doing their own plumbing, electric wiring and joinery. The further the land from Salisbury the cheaper it was to buy. Puck made enquiries with a view to Dick coming out to

Rhodesia to farm and found that it would be necessary for him to get a diploma from an Agricultural College, then be an Assistant Manager and learn the native language, then Manager and save enough to buy his own parcel of land to start on his own. That was how most of the farmers had won their own hard-earned living. They worked hard and played hard.

Polo was the game of the farmers and rich businessmen. In the areas where tobacco, maize and sugar were being farmed and exported from Rhodesia, the farmers were very prosperous and on the week-ends they used to load up their horses and grooms (of which there were plenty) in their horseboxes and travel sometimes hundreds of miles for a week-end of polo and socialising. Some came from as far distant as South Africa, particularly Natal, the Orange Free State and the farming areas of Transvaal, even Kenya before the Mau Mau put a dampener on those activities.

As his health continued to improve Puck's thoughts turned to bringing his family out to Rhodesia permanently. Minto arranged for him to have a chest X-ray which showed that he had fibrosis of the lungs as a consequence of many years in the heat of India followed by the cold and damp climate of Lancashire. He told him that if he stayed in Rhodesia he would not get any worse and might even get better, but if he went back to England he would get worse and worse and have two more years at most in Lawford, and then he would have to retire. If he stayed in Rhodesia he could go on working for years.

Minto and Ethelwyn were so keen for him to stay that they found a 75 acre piece of land with a pre-fabricated house only 13 miles outside Salisbury going for only £5,000 which they wanted to buy for him. Ethelwyn took him there but it would mean him working with African missions up country and he didn't think himself suited to that kind of life at his age, nor would the opportunity for Rosalind's musical talents be easy, and in any case he was not one for accepting that kind of charity even though it was offered with such grace and enthusiasm. Nevertheless he pursued opportunities for working in a Salisbury parish and music teaching for Rosalind, who had written to say that although she would be heartbroken to leave Lawford she was equally sure of being happy in Rhodesia.

There being no vacant incumbencies in Salisbury all the Bishop had to offer was as assistant to a High Church Vicar, and Puck's response was an emphatic NO! However, he had heard that Plumtree was short of a Chaplain and his hopes now lay with a visit to that school with Minto and Ethelwyn for the end of term ceremonies. He much enjoyed the visit and the Strover contingent's hearts swelled with pride when the Headmaster spoke of the great honour accorded to Plumtree by the award of one of the only two medical scholarships available at Cape Town University to none other than Roger Strover. However, he was disappointed to hear on arrival that the Chaplaincy had recently been filled by a younger man who would probably stay for years. He stayed in the Chaplain's house where he met the Bishop of Matabeleland whom he described as being clever but not his cup of tea personality wise so did not ask for a job. He also met there Frank Cary who had taught Paul and John at the Dragon School in the war years, and had now set up a prep school, Eagle House, on Dragon lines.

The boys coming home for the holidays, and there not being room for him at the Strover home in Bindura, Puck went on to stay with Mary and Johnny Broster at Que Que, which he described as the ugliest place in the world with its rich gold mines and no decent scenery. The only good thing about it were his hosts and the sunsets, one of which he chose to paint as a storm was brewing. But a visit to an African Mission greatly impressed him with its school and chapel built with their own hands; firm discipline among staff and pupils and great opportunities for boys to learn building, plumbing, wiring, carpentry etc.; and for girls to learn dressmaking and cooking. He much enjoyed the African songs performed for him by the pupils in great harmony with rising and falling in tempo. However, it confirmed for him that he was not suited for mission work and that he 'was best with cultured English people and polo players'.

Back in Bindura after the school holidays the polo season was starting and Puck played his first chukka of polocrosse. Thereafter he turned to umpiring and for the rest of his stay in Rhodesia he turned out, mounted on 'Newlite' every Saturday. The farmers came in from miles around every week-end for their sport and he made friends among them finding himself dining out almost every night of the week. He was urged by them to stay on in Rhodesia, so too did the Bishop of Mashonoland saying, 'there is no doubt you are wanted out here: the need for priests such as yourself is very great, in order to take temporary jobs to relieve parsons due for home leave.' However, there was a difficulty over diocesan finance and he was asked to take less than the usual salary. Puck thought this to be unfair on his family and, having spent the last of his savings on sending John to Oxford, decided that he had to face facts and go back to England permanently. He left Rhodesia at the end of May, pleased that he had been able to recompense Minto and Ethelwyn for their wonderful hospitality by handing over to them the entire collection from the Easter day service, for over 100 people, which had been given to him.

Puck enjoyed his time among the African and ex-patriate community, but it was an unrealistic, colonial, life which could not and did not last into the second half of the twentieth century. African nationalism took hold in Rhodesia from its surrounding countries; Mount Darwin became a centre for terrorist activities and devoid of its white farmers; Minto and Ethelwyn eventually retired to England; their sons left the country to work and raise their own families; and Puck soon came to realise that, tempted as he had been to bring out his own family to such an idyllic existence, like the British Raj in India, it held no future for younger generations.

20

RETIREMENT

Puck retired from the Lawford Parish in 1958 and, having no house of their own, Granny Atkinson made space for them to move into the top floor of Mistley Hall. It had already been converted into a family flat for tenants some years before and there was plenty of space for all their furniture. Living there, in some part of which had been the servants' quarters, must have seemed incongruous to both of them who, in the early days of their marriage when on leave from India, had stayed in the private side of the house, servants' rooms being strictly out of bounds. But neither of them had ever stood on ceremony and they lived harmoniously with Granny, on the floor below, for a couple of years before they could move into their own home.

Puck managed to get planning permission to build a bungalow at the entrance to the drive up to Mistley Hall. It was on a piece of land which had originally been part of the main drive, a broad avenue between superb beech trees, many of which still remained. Not having very much capital at their disposal he and Rosalind hired Rose the Manningtree builders to design and build within their limited budget. After much discussion with the family they decided on an open plan layout, which was all the rage at that time, so that dining and drawing rooms merged into one large space – good for entertaining and the parties they had in mind – and three bedrooms. Central heating was, for them, a great luxury, never having had it before and with sun pouring into its front for most of the day, the bungalow was warm and cosy. It faced South, overlooking the large meadow in front of Mistley Hall and noise from the traffic running alongside the plot was muffled by a thick and tall hedge. They named their retirement home, Mistley Wood.

Rosalind set about creating a garden in the half acre of wooded land at the back of the house and a good sized croquet lawn was laid at its front, bordered by a sea of daffodils. Puck was not well enough to do much gardening, his main project being a plantation of rhododendrons which he had always hankered after.

The sons had by that time fled the nest but returned for holidays and festivals, using the guest bedroom. Granny was a frequent visitor, especially for Sunday lunch. Often there would be games of scrabble after lunch and Granny was famed for her remark: 'Oh dear, I can only think of four letter words!'

Retirement gave Puck an opportunity to write. His success with the publication of 'Great Snakes' in *The Times* led him to write a short story on staying behind in India after Independence'. The story (Appendix VI) is written from the heart of one who had a great love for the sub-continent, its people and its traditions, with an understanding of those who had served in the Empire. It was turned down by *The Times* for being too long and it's a pity that he didn't seek wider publication for it. Other writings poured out of him, ranging from world affairs to morals and religion and, of course, he was in demand to fill vacancies in the pulpit.

Over the years he had often preached on 'the Mind of Christ' and the Divine Authority of Jesus – a theme which he developed in his retirement, saying that Christ's appeal was to reality – 'this is what I say and you will see that this is what ought to be'. It was, he said, an appeal to truth which circumvented tradition but had too often been judged by tradition. He spoke to his listeners about the development of Christianity from Jesus's own religious faith and practice, through the stages of the founding of the Church, dogmatism, Papal monarchy, reformation and revolution to the age of modern science, and liked to quote Francis Bacon: 'It is true that a little science inclineth man's mind to atheism; but depth in science bringeth men's minds about to true religion.'

'The doctrines of Jesus,' he said, 'rest on the Gospels, are reasonable and living and, unlike the doctrines of Christians which are not lasting, they are eternal.' He took as an example the abolition of slavery which came about through Jesus's teaching on the brotherhood of man. In this respect he spoke of the Saints and that to follow them is not to imitate their particular practices but to follow what they followed, namely the seeking of the knowledge of God (in Christ), and to see that there is a spiritual qualification for every experience and that without that experience nothing fine and beautiful can ever be real to anyone. He liked to share the story of the man who said to the artist Turner: 'Mr. Turner I never see sunsets like yours,' to which the artist replied: 'No sir, but don't you wish you could' – perhaps it was that story which inspired Puck to paint a vivid sunset in Rhodesia when he was there in Que Que! 'The sense of God's reality,' he said, 'is a progressive experience of the Spirit. We cannot all be Saints but we can at least bring our hearts and minds into the presence of God every day, and the more we concentrate on that the stronger the reality of God will grow.'

Despite poor health Puck remained active during his retirement and it wasn't long after leaving Lawford that he was invited to fill the interregnum at Myland in Colchester. That he took on with full commitment, driving over for early morning Communion every Sunday, being given breakfast by the very hospitable Churchwarden and his wife, who lived opposite to the church, and staying for Matins. He was invited to make their home his base when in Myland, as he often was when visiting families on week-days and when chairing the PCC. He was very aware of the rather ancient congregation so he started up a youth club which met in the Church Hall. It was a slow process building it up and he needed help from a younger person, especially with some of the energetic games which they played; but he got a good response from one of the more sceptical teenagers when he made him the leader of the group. He always ended the session with prayers which, at first, they found rather quirky, but soon responded to, as he persisted. He was much loved and respected in the parish, as was evident from letters of condolence which Rosalind received on his death.

Puck had held an annual service for cyclists in Lawford Church during his incumbency and some of the visitors made a round journey of over 100 miles to attend the service, coming from as far afield as Chelmsford and Bury St Edmunds, the church being filled to capacity.

He was intrigued by the variety of racing bicycles with their dropped handle bars, so very different from his own classical machine and upright posture, and in his sermon liked to drink to their good health and 'bottoms up'! Before his retirement he had secured an interest from the BBC for a broadcast of the service in 'Christian Outlook'. These services continued with his successor and he was often invited to preach at them. Indeed, only a fortnight before he died he had to call off such an invitation through ill health.

Puck was in demand in many other capacities during his retirement and in the County he was well known for his range of experience. He had sat on the Governing body of the Manningtree Secondary Modern School and was invited to give away prizes; and his service in both world wars brought him an invitation to one of the many RAF stations in East Anglia, with Rosalind accompanying him.

His last appearance in the pulpit was in his beloved St Mary's Church of Lawford, when he gave the address at the funeral of his great friend Sir Philip Nichols who died only a month before his own death. It was a very moving tribute to a man whom he had come to know as an eminent diplomat, a decorated veteran of the First World War, wise counsellor, fully involved in national and local affairs, respected local squire, generous with his wealth and with his friendship – at ease with all kinds, young and old. It could be said those were many of his own virtues.

On the evening before Christmas Eve, 1962, Puck and Rosalind had arranged a drinks party in their home for their returning sons and their friends. Puck had to retire to bed and was not well enough to mix in the hurly burly of the party so he received guests, one by one, in his room. The next morning he had deteriorated significantly and the doctor was sent for. John was sitting with him when he spoke his last words – typical that they should have been on topical issues and his concern for the future of the world.

Christmas Day and Boxing Day were full of gloom but suddenly there was joy among the family – they all felt it. A memorial service in Lawford Church followed his cremation four days later, and the congregation was packed.

The Lawford parish magazine reported that

> The Church was filled to overflowing. Many were there from the boundaries of our parish, indicating how widely Mr Strover was known and respected. But to those of us who worshipped at Lawford while he was Rector the service had much deeper significance. The hymns he loved, the familiar prayers, brought back so many memories. And they are happy memories, for although a Memorial Service is inevitably a sad occasion, at this one there was a note of joy as well as of thanksgiving for the life of one who meant so much to so many. As each Sunday we rise to sing the Jubilate, all of us, especially the older members of the choir, will specially remember him:

> O be joyful in the Lord, all ye lands: serve the Lord
> with gladness, and come before his presence with a song

And,

'A FOXASH APPRECIATION'
'Since Strover strives to make us good,
Let Lawford live as Lawford should'

Those words on vegetable marrows at Harvest Festivals were from
his old friend Thomas Westmacott – very apt in illustrating the real
character of the lovable man who was as much Rector of Foxash as
of Lawford.

His ministry was by example, perhaps, more than by words, and
by enthusiasm for the small as well as the greater things, as was shown
when, approaching three score and ten years, he ran a rounder at our
Sunday School games.

In less prosperous days, when cars were few and Church seemed
distant, we much appreciated his kindly attention to those 'other
sheep' on the parish outskirts.'

Puck's ashes were buried outside the East end of the Church and
his gravestone bore the inscription.'

IN LOVING MEMORY OF
ERNEST JAMES STROVER
'PUCK'
1885–1962
RECTOR OF THIS PARISH
1944–1958
HE SERVED THE LORD WITH GLADNESS
AS
PRIEST SOLDIER AND AIRMAN
O BE JOYFUL IN THE LORD

Rosalind received many letters of condolence, a number of which
spoke of Puck's saintliness, a virtue which he had tried to live up to
but which certainly he would not have acknowledged for himself.

Appendices
A selection of Puck's writings

Appendix I

Personal experiences of answer to prayer

Puck wrote a short pamphlet on his life and career saving experiences of answers to prayer, and excerpts from these have been included in previous pages in order to illuminate his story. This appendix sets out the main thrust of those experiences. No doubt there were many more experiences of answers to prayer, associated with his personal life which he did not care to write about.

Appendix I.1

December 1915: Flying back from an encounter with a German Taube

My aeroplane was a Vickers Gun Bus – the first to be armed with a machine gun. My engine was behind and my observer, Holden, with his gun, in front. The wind was so strong that our full speed of 45 m.p.h. made very little progress. However we had height, and had climbed up to our full ceiling of 7,000 ft and, although we must have been a sitting target, our height made it improbable that we should be hit by anti-aircraft fire. The country below was water-logged. On the right was Lille. Ahead, as far as I could judge, only a dozen miles were the long wavy lines of our trenches.

Suddenly, shells began to burst all around me, below and above. I threw the aeroplane to the left and seemed to have escaped from the bombardment. Then a crash all round and a tremendous crash just behind me. The aeroplane dived down and to the left, while the whole machine jerked up and down as half the propeller still slowly revolved. By putting on full right rudder and joy-stick full to the right, I steadied the spin. I then switched off, which stopped the risk of fire. 'Facile descensus a verno' (easy is the descent to earth) came into my mind. Holden looked round in terror. It is always worse for the observer than the pilot. He did not appear to be hit. Nor was I. The aeroplane was not disintegrated, and under some little control. But a crash seemed imminent. The left wing seemed to be hit and the controls could not stop the dive. We plunged towards the ground, spinning to the left.

Then I prayed as I never prayed before. Of course it was fear which made me pray. Was it unmanly? I didn't know and I didn't care. But I suddenly felt that my heavenly father had answered my prayer and told me not to be frightened. The ground rushed up towards us, but I felt serenely confident – not confident in anything which I could do, because I could do nothing, but confident in Almighty God. Just before we crashed to earth the whole machine seemed to lift itself up and straighten out. Then we touched the ground. There was no undercarriage, and I fell forward against the cockpit and hit my head.

The next thing which I remember was being pulled out of the aeroplane by German soldiers and an officer saying, 'Êtes-vous blessé?' I got up and walked. I was quite unharmed. So was Holden. But my engine propeller and chassis were a tangled mass of wreckage.

Appendix I.2

January 1916: The prison camp at Gutersloh

The prison camp for officers at Gutersloh consisted of large barracks for Russian officers, smaller barracks for French officers and the smallest for British officers, all surrounded by high barbed wire and sentries. There were only two other officers of the Royal Flying Corps. In those days the Corps was small and I knew them both, and was delighted to see them because they had both been reported as missing and believed to be killed. Porter, of the Royal Artillery, a very keen early pilot, and Humphreys, a scientist and explorer, who had been with Shackelton on a North Polar expedition and had taken up flying before the war in order to use it for exploration. They got me into their room of four, and were very lively and entertaining.

Now, before British officers came to the camp, this barrack had been occupied by Russian officers. Some of these had taken up bricks from the floor of the cellar, fitted them into a tray which fitted into the floor, and started a tunnel under this tray. They let our room into the secret and proposed that we should all continue to dig at night, two of them concealing themselves in our barrack each night.

It was exciting work. Sometimes at night a patrol of German soldiers came through the cellar at an unpredictable time. We had an entrance and exit, and posted sentries to give warning of approaching danger. When the patrol was sighted or heard, the sentry, who wore socks over his shoes, swiftly and noiselessly ran to give warning. The excavators were pulled out, the tray let down, and all traces of yellow sand swept up. Then we fled by the other exit to return to our task when all was clear. But as the tunnel grew the lack of air became unbearable. (It was only later that we realised that the foul air must be withdrawn by pumping, in order to let fresh air in.)

The Russians were anxious to get back to Russia before their spring offensive began. They were very keen and enthusiastic and appeared to be quite indifferent to the fact that, as we got further, we might die of suffocation. We British, were more calculating and insisted that the digger only went in for a few minutes at a time. One night I was digging at the face of the tunnel when a Russian's voice called down, 'Come out, the Germans are coming'. I started to wriggle back but it was some way to the entrance. Then I heard a hoarse whisper, 'Stay still, we will shut down'. I heard the tray let in and then silence. The air was very bad and after a few minutes I began to gasp. I felt that I must get out or die. I was close to the tray and could lift it. Then I knew that, if I did, I should betray everyone, British and Russian. I was terrified and gasped, choking to death. Would the Germans never come? In my terror I prayed very hard and suddenly felt relaxed. Soon after I heard heavy feet above. Then I lost consciousness.

When I woke up I was lying on the floor of the cellar. My friends had opened up the tunnel just in time and pulled me out unconscious. I think that this was the most horrible experience of my life and I can imagine nothing worse than to be buried alive. There is no doubt that I was saved by prayer. If I had struggled for breath, I would have fainted soon and died before they reached me.

Appendix I.3

Germany 1917: In solitary confinement at Strohen

My cell is 8ft by 4ft with one small window. The only person with whom I can talk is my gaoler, who brings me my black bread twice a day and soup once a day. Sometimes he brings me a German newspaper with resounding accounts of German victories. Then we have arguments in which I tell him that Germans are all slaves and could never win a war against us, and he tells me that America will never help us because it would cost them too much money. He generally finishes by losing his temper and banging and locking the door. Fortunately I have books which have been sent to me by kind friends. For half an hour a day I am led outside into an enclosure surrounded by a palisade in order to get some exercise. I take off my coat and run round the enclosure as I feel that I must keep fit at all costs. But my diet does not give me enough strength to continue very long.

Three of us had escaped from the camp disguised as German soldiers. It was a long practised plot. We made the clothes by dying our flannel pyjamas and trousers in coffee and ink, making the hats and badges of red cloth, tin and wood, until at ten yards' distances we looked like German soldiers in their working clothes. We then made a key to fit a gate which was situated between two sentries. Friends made arrangements to draw off the attention of both sentries and we walked out of the camp, expecting a bullet at any moment. Outside were the barracks, fortunately with few soldiers about, and we marched through them with Prussian rigidness. As a German cyclist passed, I called out 'Tag' and to my delight he answered 'Tag', apparently taking us for granted. Feeling bolder, we legged along the road meeting German soldiers without any self-conscious feeling that they were examining our pseudo-uniforms. But, as soon as possible, we struck out across country over heath-land and through woods.

Writing this, thirty years later, I remember the extraordinary feeling of elation during that time when we were free after a year's imprisonment. In addition, we had the exhilaration of being hunted. One of the excuses made for the uneconomical sport of hunting is that the fox 'enjoys it'. When the fox is very tired, I cannot believe that he enjoys the approach of death, but he probably enjoys the earlier stages of the hunt when he is fresh, exerting all his faculties and pitting his wits against his pursuers. He must also enjoy the exhilaration of escape from death when he has put the hounds off his scent. On the whole, escaping in Germany was the most exciting thing I have ever done, because there is the perpetual risk, day and night, and the instinct of fear sharpened one's wits, especially the sense of eyesight and hearing. It is more exciting than war which is cruel and sordid, and which, at the best of times, means long periods of great boredom, punctuated by moments of intense fright.

Again, our adventure finished in acute disappointment. We were lying up in a wood when a German patrol bore down on us with fixed bayonets. They thought we were deserters from their Army. All our great hopes were suddenly reduced to the depths of despair.

All the chances of escape were in our favour, and when the countryside was dotted with spinneys, it seemed like the hand of some malignant fate that the patrol should go through this particular copse. My disappointment was so acute that I was driven to prayer. Looking back on it now, perhaps it was the hand of God. If we had escaped I should have rejoined the Royal Flying Corps and probably would have been killed.

Appendix I.4

Formation of the P.T. Club

When we had digested our experiences we were unanimous that any future tunnel must be made without the participation of the Russians. We carefully selected twelve British Officers and asked one Rogers, who in civil life was a mining engineer to organise this secret society. Someone suggested that it should be called the Red Hand, which afterwards was deprecatingly named the Pink Toe-nail (which might also stand for Private Tunnel).

Roger's plan was to cut away the bottom step of the stone stairs going down to the cellar, remove the masonry on both sides at the back so that the step could be pulled back when required. We made saws out of dinner knives and did our work, as before, at night. After six weeks sawing the step finally gave way and we wedged it with wood. Then we cut away the bricks at the back so that the step could slide back. Then we cut out a chamber from the sand below, a cubic four feet. The next difficulty was to store the sand ...

Meanwhile Rogers was constructing a fan. When the tunnel was working a gang of four went down immediately after roll call at 8 a.m. One man lay at the face of the tunnel digging ahead and filling a narrow box with sand. When full, he pushed it behind him to a second man who gave him an empty box. The second man placed the full box on a trolley. The third man, at the mouth of the tunnel pulled back the trolley by a rope and emptied the box into a sack. The fourth man turned the wheel of the fan which kept the air pure.

In the winter we had big falls of snow and the water level came half way up our tunnel. We had to close down for a month. At the end of February 1917 we opened up our tunnel and found that the water had caused the sides of our chamber to slip. Thanks to shoring up the timber the tunnel was little damaged. We went merrily along and about the middle of March we calculated that we were outside the wire, so that everything should be ready for our Spring Offensive. All of us were in high spirits collecting food for our journey, copying maps and memorising them.

When we were at our highest point of delight news came of the Russian Revolution. A week later we were told that the English were to be removed from the camp within three days in order not to influence the Russians. From the face of the tunnel a stick was pushed up through the earth into the air and waved when the sentry's back was turned and it was disappointing to find that we had reached only the line of sentries just outside the wire. In fact, the stick waved close to the sentry's box. Rogers agreed to take the risk of two breaking through provided that the sentry was not in his box.

It was decided that Owen and I were to do it. As soon as it was dark we got down into the tunnel and crawled to the face with our bags of food. There we waited for the signal with suppressed excitement. Word came down that it was raining and the sentry in his box. Hour after hour we waited and I prayed hard that we might get out. At about 2 a.m. word came that it was raining again and the sentry was back in his box. So again we waited a long time for our chance until the voice of Rogers came booming down the tunnel: 'It's no good, it's getting light, you must come out.' My heart sank in despair. So that was the answer to my prayer. All the hopes we had lived on for eight months, destroyed. It was a risk well worth taking. But looking back on it now, I am grateful for an overruling providence.

Appendix I.5

March 1919: Rawalpindi, India

Back in the Indian Army after the war, I was sent to 3/23rd Sikh Infantry. When I arrived, the Colonel said to me, 'Now I can put in for leave. I've been in India the whole war without leave, and you are the first regular officer I've had for a year.' Within a month he left for England and I, as a Junior Captain, was left to command a regiment of Ramdasia Sikhs, most of whom were professional thieves. I had fourteen British officers, Captains and Subalterns, twenty Indian officers and eight hundred ruffians about whom the Colonel's advice was, 'Be ruthless'.

My job was to train them for war. The young British officers had little knowledge and could hardly speak the language well enough to convey any meaning to the troops. All had an admiration for the senior Indian officer, the Subedar-Major, who was a great character, of a higher caste than the men, and held by them in great respect. But I soon discovered that he was the virtual dictator of the regiment. That was wrong and I had to show him at once that I was commanding the regiment. He did not like it, and began to speak about his retirement and his advancement to the great dignity of 'Sirdar Bahadur' before his retirement. Now I did not want him to retire; I knew that I could not do without him at present. Furthermore, the Sikhs were giving great trouble in the Punjab and messages were constantly coming to me from Simla, warning me of sedition, which was undermining the Sikhs. Sedition, robbery, mutiny seemed to be growling, rumbling and growing. To cope with this I had a handful of young British officers who were of little use and could not speak their language, and the only man who could control it wanting to go. And how utterly inadequate I was to deal with it and to make these ill-disciplined robbers into an efficient fighting unit. I had been away from India and the Indian Army for the whole of the war, knew nothing about Sikhs, and forgotten how to express myself in Hindustani.

In my difficulties and in my weakness I had learned, while prisoner in Germany, to turn to Almighty God and to wait for an answer. The answer was always the right one in the long run, if I approached God with humility, concealing nothing. I therefore prayed every day for the regiment and for those individuals whom I knew personally. The answer I got was very different from the advice which I had received. The answer I got was, 'Love them and work them'.

I started on the British officers, insisted on them learning the language properly with a 'Munshi', or Indian teacher, in their spare time, and did it myself. I took them out on tactical schemes, and had to work hard to bring myself up to date. These tactical exercises with breakfast out of doors in the perfect Punjab winter climate were very happy. I got to know them and to like them very much. Then I drilled and drilled the regiment until we were all sick of it, including myself. But they became almost perfect in drill and the discipline and cleanliness obviously improved. Every week there were fewer defaulters, fewer punishments and no court-martials. Above all, I went round the lines in the evening, talking to the Indian officers and men until they lost their shyness and furtiveness and spoke to me freely about their villages and the trouble which Sikhs were giving to the government and the reasons for it. I got to love those Sikhs. They were men, physically beautiful, hard, turbulent and emotional, but never have I had such loyalty, and never will again.

Appendix I.6

1932: Regimental command in Secunderabad, India

Late in 1932 I was appointed to command the 4th/2nd Punjab Regiment in Secunderabad, a British Cantonment in Hyderabad State. It was a good regiment with a happy and efficient body of British officers; but one tribe of Mohammedans named Khattars who came from the North West district of the Punjab had given a good deal of trouble. I walked straight into it.

A short time after I arrived there was a murder in the regiment. It was followed, of course, by a court-martial and the murderer was given fifteen years imprisonment. But the intrigues, feuds and hatreds among these Mohammedans which came to light opened my eyes and taught me what to expect. I was married and my wife and two little boys were with me and I was looking forward to some family life; but calamity after calamity came upon us.

There was a large Indian village close to our barracks and near my bungalow. It developed plague and the people in the village began to die in large numbers. Then one of my men caught it and died. I gave orders for the whole regiment to be inoculated, including my family. The doctors had not sufficient anti-toxin and we had to wait several days before it arrived. Meanwhile another man caught the plague and died. I did everything I could, and prevailed upon the Political Officer to clear the village and isolate the inhabitants in a camp. But my anxiety was intense, particularly for my family which was so close to the village, and knowing that inoculation does not bring immunity. I came nearer to God than ever before because my need was so great.

It seems that we need great anxiety or great responsibility or great sorrow to bring us close to God. After three weeks it became obvious that the awful scourge had passed. I could feel something of the gratitude of Oberammergau, 300 years ago, who swore that they would produce a Passion Play every ten years in thankfulness because the plague left their village.

Murder, plague; what was the next thing? I began to hope that the worst was over. Our Brigade was marked to be the first to go overseas in case of war, and we were therefore kept on our toes and ready for immediate mobilisation. For a year we worked hard, training for every kind of war, and I was thankful for it because the whole regiment was keen and becoming very efficient.

Then the third blow fell. Two revolvers were reported missing from the armoury. It was obvious that they had been stolen by men in the regiment, and the suspicion fell on this same tribe of Khattars who probably had done it to get an Indian officer into trouble. It is a disgrace for a regiment in India to lose one of its weapons and I determined to get them back. My senior Indian officer advised me to punish the whole regiment until pressure was brought on the thieves to restore the revolvers. It was the hot weather and I sent them daily after work on long marches with packs on their backs under the command of a British officer and then turned them out at night. But still no sign of the stolen weapons being restored. My British officers said that the regiment was becoming restive and that, if I continued, it might become mutinous. A mutiny would finish me and my family. Yet, if I gave way, I would never break this Khattar intrigue. Prayer gave me the answer to go on at all costs.

There was a large pond near the parade ground, and I gave orders that this was to be emptied by buckets – a long and arduous job. It was possible that the revolvers had been thrown into it. Before the pond was emptied a notice was put up stating that the revolvers could be discovered in the Mohammedan Mosque. It was a tremendous relief to all in the regiment except the Khattars, but I never had any more trouble from them.

It certainly was a direct answer to prayer.

Appendix II

Sermons

Puck's sermons could be said to have been spoken from his experience of a life of faith rather than from a purely doctrinal point of view. This selection of seven sermons from those which he preached over the twenty years of his ordained ministry, reflect the development of his faith over the period before, during and post-Second World War.

Appendix II.1

Facing life with Christ

Preached, pre-war, as the horrors of Nazi Germany, were being revealed.

The true business of life is living. No one will dispute this obvious fact. To know how to live is the objective of all knowledge. But it is just this matter of making a success of living that most people think least about. To make a success of living is not the same thing as the popular idea of being a success in life. Being a success in life is generally judged in terms of concrete results in money, position, or reputation, or eminence in one particular branch of one's business.

Success in living is a very difficult matter. Many people drift through life without much concern about it at all. They are content enough if life brings them a fair amount of happiness, and exempts them from its chief ills. They easily slip into grooves of routine which make thought unnecessary and protect themselves as best they can by some escape mechanism. Frustration and futility beset the minds of many people. Their days are full of struggle for little aims and small satisfactions.

But one has often heard people say: 'how does one live?' It may be said to be the question which Christ came to answer. The word, 'life', was often on his lips. He said, indeed, that he had come that we may have life and that we may have it more abundantly.

Ever since the last war I have often heard it said that, if a man is decent, it doesn't matter about going to Church, or what he believes. It is argued that if a man is honest and hard working and ready to do a good turn, what difference does it make what faith he adheres to. Let us be quite clear about this. If men can be decent without worshipping in any Church or believing any Creed, then obviously the day of Creeds and Churches is over. That is why, I believe, the masses of men in England to-day are outside the Church. The modern Englishman respects the moral life without understanding its nature. Valuing goodness, he is far from seeing that goodness in character or in conduct is a flower whose root strikes deep into existence and that, if he continues to disregard the roots, the flower will one day wither and die. Religion is the root of virtue, despite all appearances to the contrary, and some understanding of this has become the urgent necessity of our time. We must try to understand what it is that religion does for men and why they neglect it at their peril.

Society has become and is becoming steadily more secular. Religion plays a less and less important part in life. The rulers of this country need not be Christians. The Trades Unions have no Patron Saints as the Guilds once had. We have forgotten that the Universities were originally religious foundations. Education, in all its lower branches, becomes steadily more secular. Certain religious forms are maintained. The Coronation of King George VI reminded us that England was once a professedly Christian country, and marks the contrast between past and present. The State has drifted from the Church and become more and more secular. As yet the effect of this has not been acutely felt in England which is, in some ways, still the most Christian country in the world. But England is part of a larger European Society and we have suffered, are suffering, and will suffer still more terribly from the secularisation of Europe.

Europe no longer goes to Church. The common spiritual heritage of the Christian religion is disregarded. But you cannot say that, despite this, Europe has remained decent, or clean or just. The silent spiritual collapse has, inevitably, been followed by an open and thunderous moral collapse which exhibits itself in campaigns of lying, treachery, violence, injustice and brutality, on an unimagined scale. These things have caused many people to search their hearts and to ask themselves whether religion, after all, is so important as they had supposed. It is leading us to a deeper examination of the foundations upon which the moral life of man is built.

Jesus expressly warned us against the divorce of creed from action. A noble creed will make for noble living. Low thoughts on the meaning of life will tend to produce low actions. Then what about the decent fellow who lives up to a good moral standard and yet has no religion. Does that not prove that a man can be good without faith in God or religious worship? It would prove it if he had been born and brought up on a desert island. But he was not. We are not individuals cut off from society. We have all been born into a society which has, for centuries, been moulded and influenced by Christian faith. The man who lives up to a good moral standard and yet has no creed or religion owes his moral standard to early influence, to the influence of his parents, or the influence of his Church, or the influence of his school teaching. 'Give me a child until he is seven', say the Jesuits, 'and you can do what you like with him afterwards'. That is probably the only point on which we are in agreement with the Nazis. Man is, to a large extent the product of the society into which he was born and brought up.

The man who is good, but irreligious, ought to face up to two simple questions. First, 'would I be the man I am without the faith of my parents and teachers?' Second, 'am I giving to the next generation what I received from the last?' The great Christian heritage is being squandered by millions of individuals who live on the traditions of the past and have, in themselves, no sort of faith.

The scorn of Jesus was for those men who had no sense of moral need, because Jesus knew that we all have sin in us. During the twentieth century it has not been popular to speak about sin; but, surely, it must be obvious to any intelligent man looking at Europe that man is sinful and that dictators who have material power, without religious faith, can lead whole nations down the slippery path to destruction, because nations without religious faith will follow them.

The main object of going to Church is that it brings us face to face with God. If we honestly worship God we become conscious of sin in ourselves. We honestly confess our sins and receive forgiveness. A man is not good because he goes to Church. A man goes to Church because he knows his own shortcomings and goes to Church for spiritual strength. The modern Pharisee is the man who feels that he has no need for forgiveness. It is here that religion is realistic, with a realism undreamt of by the practical mind. It brings us face to face with the truth and purity of God, in the light of which our pride and self-assurance melt away.

In the 'Republic', Plato tells of the crew of a ship who decided that their pilot was mad because they noticed that he took observations of the stars. They argued, as practical men will, that the ship sails on the sea and is influenced by the waves and tides and currents, and that star gazing was a foolish and unpractical affair. They therefore confined the pilot to the hold and sailed on to shipwreck. They did not realise the necessity in navigation, of a fixed point beyond the relativities of wind and wave, without which a true course cannot be set.

In our generation we have failed because, like Plato's sailors, we have refused to look beyond this earth. We have sought the moral standard within the individual. We have tried to find it within society at large. We find our standards in the tides and winds of human life. But neither wind or tide is constant. They veer and shift and fling us into confusion. A moral standard will not be found in history. It is found in the worship of God. The Christian religion is very practical; it is as practical as the Pole Star since we cannot check our position without it.

Appendix II.2

Divine love

Brief summaries of five sermons which Puck preached on the subject of Faith in the first years of the Second World War are included in Chapter 17. This sermon on Divine Love was preached towards the end of the Second World War, when peace was looming.

It is well worth while, occasionally, to examine English words which, in the course of time, have become commonplaces in the Christian vocabulary. Some will be found to have lost their significance and others to have acquired a sense remote from the original meaning. The phrase, 'God's Love', seems to have suffered a change. Our Lord's teaching is that divine love is an individual and personal love for every man or woman who tries, however imperfectly, to claim it by obedience to the Divine Will. Obviously that is a truth of high value. But it does not answer a question of first-rate importance which lies behind it. What do we mean by 'God's Love'?

By many people the love of God is thought of as little more than a supernatural influence, widely diffused and benignant, intended to bring peace of mind and comfort to the disciple, protecting his soul and body against unseen dangers. Such a sentimentalised idea has been encouraged by a certain type of preaching and by some favourite hymns. Although it contains elements of truth it is lamentably defective and misleading. Often it leads to deep disappointment because the tranquillity of mind which God's Love is said to grant is not attained.

If our Lord's teaching is studied carefully this widespread idea of what God's Love means will be found to be erroneous. So far from being a gentle influence, the direction of Divine Love towards man's soul is the releasing of a tremendous force. Its first effect should be to make man restless and dissatisfied, because the intense energy of God's Love is set in motion with a single definite aim, which is to transform character. Love is to change man so that he becomes what St Paul calls, 'a new creature'. His whole outlook, his entire set of values must be altered, until he is brought into intimate relationship with God. And the first stage of the process is to fill him, not with peace, but with discontent as he realises the gulf between what he is and what he ought to be. Only when the Divine Love has done its work of transformation will the Peace of God possess his heart and mind. But the primary aim and purpose of God's Love is not to make him comfortable, it is to make him good. In religion as in every other department of life, the inexorable law holds good that, only in proportion as a man sows can he hope to reap.

I must say that I sometimes wish we could invent a new word for 'Love'. Like other hard-worked words, 'love' has to carry too many meanings. You can make it mean almost anything from degraded passion to ecclesiastical politeness, from high romance to charity. But love, in the highest sense, in the Christian sense, is the most wonderful thing in the world, and many of us have hardly yet begun to discover what happens when love predominates in our lives. It is quite clear that Jesus, Himself, made Love the supreme test of discipleship: 'By this shall all men know that ye are my disciples, that ye love one towards another'. In one of his most vivid parables he insisted that, at the final judgement men will be tested, not by their orthodox belief, but by whether or not they have set selfishness aside and taken the trouble to care for those who need their help.

Let us look freshly at this challenge to men to live by the law of love and ask whether, in the world ruled by fear and selfishness and by hatred and violence, to talk of love is NOT unpractical realism. To begin with, it is indisputable that Jesus did actually show the world a new way of living. He had to die to make men understand it – and they did understand it. He told them and they grasped it, that if in sober fact, 'God so loved the world that he gave...', that if God is like that, well then, men ought to treat one another in similar fashion – they cannot do otherwise. What such a way of living was, Jesus showed them again and again. In the inner group of His disciples, to take just one instance of His magic influence, He made Simon the Zealot, the ardent nationalist, and Matthew the publican, the hated tax-gatherer, sit down at the same table as brothers and friends. In all the rubs of daily life, in a world of divisions and hostilities and hatreds, He showed the way of triumphant friendliness, and they learnt it.

Those first Christians made tremendous claims and tremendous assertions, but claims and assertions were justified by facts. 'We know', so they asserted, 'that we have passed from death unto life because we love the brotherhood. We know what love is by this, that Jesus laid down His life for us; so we ought to lay down our lives for the brotherhood'. This ringing confidence about the way of brotherhood belongs to the very core of the Christian message; and if Jesus is right about God and life and love, it is in harmony with the very stuff of the Universe. It goes with, and not against the grain of Reality – Ultimate Reality.

Appendix II.3

Football service

Though not a keen follower of football Puck associated himself with local teams in post-war years and presented 'The Strover Cup' each year to the winners of the league. Sport, generally, appealed to him and, played in its best spirit, he felt, was a good lesson for life. This annual Service was an opportunity to open the doors of Lawford Church to complete newcomers.

Our Service this evening is particularly for football and for other kinds of sport. I do not wish to curry favour by saying that all sportsmen are the salt of the earth. I think, in fact, I am quite sure that Christians are the salt of the earth, and I simply cannot agree that you can be just as good a Christian outside the Church as you can inside it. That is not to say that all of us who come to Church are Christians. But Christianity is being kept alive by the Church – the organised Church – and organised Christianity is maintained by regular Church people. I wonder if it is realised how much Christianity owes to regular Church goers, so much that Christianity in England would fade away and die without the regular Church people? I don't want to discuss that now but only to say that all men need the Church and the Church needs all men.

With deep reverence I assert that the greatest sportsman who ever lived was Jesus Christ. If anyone ever played the true game of life, He did. I think that pictures of Jesus, especially in stained glass windows, have given a wrong impression of Him. Jesus was young, strong, athletic and hardy. If he had not been physically fit he could not possibly have lived the arduous, strenuous life he did. He plunged into life with zest. He fought against terrible odds. He never once fouled and at the end of his apparent defeat he gained the greatest moral victory the world has ever known. It is perfectly true, in a sense, that life is a sport – a sport in which all of us are players – and I am certain that if men did so regard life they would gain a very different conception both of life and of Christianity.

You will agree, I am sure, that you cannot play any game satisfactorily unless you have for that game, enthusiasm. If you see your game as an adventure, look forward to playing it, do not moan about the difficulties, you will love playing the game. Well, that's the way to look on life; that is the way Jesus looked on life. He loved life. He never cried out, as some of us do, that it was a vale of tears. He never became in the least bit cynical. He never shrank from it and, although nobody ever had a harder life than He, yet He threw Himself into it, cheerfully and confidently. No man will ever do much at a game unless he loves it. No man will ever make a success of life unless he loves life.

It is equally true that every kind of sport demands training and preparation. You can't put a 'rabbit' into a football team. You must learn the game. You must be prepared for discipline and strict training. Exactly the same applies to life, and in the life of Christ you have it demonstrated. Jesus prepared for his active ministry by thirty years spent at home. He went into the wilderness to train himself. He knew that he had to beat the temptations of self – of selfishness, of self-indulgence, of pride and of cynicism. He kept to his prayers.

I sometimes wish when I see games being played that men would be just as keen about the game of life, that they would discipline themselves and strengthen their will power. The Church, with its seasons, trains men for the sport of life. The world would be a better place if men would go into spiritual training.

One excellent method of mastering a game is to watch an expert at that game. You can learn a lot from a master player. The sport of life has had its master player – Jesus Christ – and to watch Him playing the game would help us greatly. Christ played the game of life with honesty and love and purity. His methods do not come naturally to us, but the more we practise right thinking and right acting the more expert in the game of life we become until, finally, we become experts ourselves.

Need I add that all sportsmen must take defeat gamely? The University Boat Race is always an example of this because it does not matter how great a distance separates the two boats the crew of the losing boat never gives up. It never gets demoralised. It goes on rowing hard until the finishing post is reached. Jesus never gave up. The odds against him were terrific, right from the beginning. For the carpenter's son to set out to win the world must have seemed hopeless. It was even more difficult later, when religious and secular powers joined forces against him. On the Cross the failure seemed dismal and final; yet you and I know that, in reality, the victory was his.

In the game of life victory is often with the apparent losers, because our achievements matter less than the spirit in which life is played. It is better to have played and lost than to have played with underground tactics and to have won. It is the way you play the game of life which matters. You can't really do much good in life unless you have some spiritual training. The Church with its seasons and its sacraments trains men for the sport of life. It gets a man out of selfishness and cynicism. It gives him faith in God and everything which that stands for, and gives him an enjoyment of life which he cannot get by any other means.

Appendix II.4

Christian faith – truth or fantasy

Preached in the early years of Peace when families were being reunited after the traumas of war. Puck was only too aware of the dangers of falling into a comfort zone which did not really exist.

For many reasons these are difficult days in which to hold the Christian faith. The chief events of our time are so essentially anti-Christian that against their terrific background, Christian faith seems to many to be 'wishful thinking – a pleasant fairyland'. Indeed its very desirableness is used as an argument against it. Granted, men say, that the Christian faith is comforting to people in trouble. That is the reason, they say, why it has developed, creating a world of make-belief, spoofing and bluffing on a large scale.

Against this prevalent view we put to-day the testament of the N.T. The fourth Gospel, written about A.D. 100, when the Christian Church had had time to take the measure of Christ's meaning and to see His Gospel against the background of one of the most difficult periods of human history. At the heart of this Gospel, repeated again and again, is the conviction expressed in the words of Jesus: 'I am the Truth'. Not an ideal, but the realistic truth. Pretty much everything in our Christianity to-day depends on the issue we are thus faced with: 'What is our Christian faith: comforting fantasy, or the Truth?'

Of course Christian faith can be caricatured. It is often perverted into a religion for comfort only, but the main tradition of Christian thought and life has never been primarily comfortable. The religion of Christ was not comfort. He had no light view of life which let him stay, pleasantly drugged, at Nazareth, but a very serious view of life which caused him to walk the road to Golgotha, saying to his disciples: 'If any man would come after me let him deny himself and take up his cross and follow me'. That does not sound like a pleasant drug.

To another area of evidence I ask your thought. It is this present world itself, this terrible, catastrophic world, trying to manage its affairs on anti-Christian principles. Many people are thinking to-day that Christianity is delusive because the present hideous and diabolical world shows up Christianity as impractical.

To which I answer: the Christian way of life, impractical? Do you think, then, that what is going on in the world to-day is practical? This miserable regime of anti-Christianity, would you call it economically practical? In terms of human happiness, is it practical? In terms of hope for the kind of world our children will have to live in, practical? Rather this world disaster cries out that, unless we can achieve the hard-headed realism of Christianity, we are sunk, personally and socially sunk.

Great religion has been the source of the most creative ideas in human history. And to-day the Christian faith, with its central principles: the sacredness of personality; the inescapable membership of all mankind in one body; the absolute necessity, therefore, of good will, not as an ideal but as a working principle; the call to seek first the Kingdom of God on earth – that is the welfare of all, if there is to be any welfare for each; and the reality of God above nations, races and classes, calling for the human family – that religion is no fantasy.

Rather look at the mad world to-day, trying to live on the opposite principles and see if the closing words of Jesus in the Sermon on the Mount, as Moffat translates it, do not ring true.

'Every one who listens to these words of mine and acts upon them is like a sensible man who built his house on rock.'

In the N.T. the words 'ideal' and 'idealism' are not to be found. They are not there. But the word 'truth' is there again and again. The Christian Gospel was not idealism but realism, not a message about what ought to be, but about what is. God is. Christ is the revealer. Man is the child of God. There is an eternal purpose and Love is the law of life. Such are basic realities.

Appendix II.5

Saving the life

Puck's own life had been full of interest, an interest which he ascribed to his deep Christian faith, a faith which he shared with his parishioners in this sermon preached on 9 December 1956.

'Whosoever will save his life shall lose it; but whosoever will lose his life for my sake, the same shall save it.' These words of our Lord seem at first not a little strange. How can we save our life by being willing to lose it? All this wants thinking about.

St Paul distinguishes three different kinds of life: life of the body; life of the mind (he calls it the psychic life); and the life of the spirit – that part which is most like God. It is the life of the mind which our Lord refers to. It covers all our thinking, our desires and affections, all our earthly hopes and fears and, in fact, all our ordinary life except our spirit. The life of our spirit is that part of us which is concerned with right and wrong, with God and prayer and self-discipline and with all those things which have to do with the eternal and the divine, as opposed to human life.

Now a great many people are not in the least concerned about their spiritual life. They think that their natural, earthly, life is the only thing that really matters. They want to make the best of it, to get out of it all that it has to offer in the way of comfort and pleasure. They grudge the expenditure of time and money which interferes, in any way, with what they hope and intend to get out of life and, yet, as our Lord says, in their very efforts to save, and gain, and preserve what life has to offer, they lose not only the higher things but also the very value and essence of the earthly for which they are prepared to sacrifice the spiritual.

Men are constantly trying to organise society, and their own lives too, apart from God, missing God out and thinking that by so doing they will be able to get more out of life But, as a matter of fact, they constantly fail. For instance, Love is a great and good gift of God, but unless God and God's laws are behind human love, what a dangerous thing it is. All modern novels are full of the peril, the sorrow, the suffering of love which thinks only of its own gratification and nothing of the purpose for which God gave it.

Pleasure, also, is a good gift of life. God means us to be happy, but when we pursue pleasure as a main end and purpose in life we find, to our surprise, that the happiness we expected eludes us – just as we are sure to miss health if we make health the chief object of our lives. Knowledge, again, is a great and good thing, but knowledge by itself does not bring happiness. A man may be learned and ready to echo the words of Ecclesiastes: 'of making many books there is no end and much study is a weariness of the flesh'.

All literature is testimony to the fact that life, mere life, untouched by something higher, does not satisfy man, and the more he seeks happiness the less he finds it. As a well known writer put it: 'Pleasure satiates, Knowledge wearies, love wounds until man cries: 'Vanity of vanities – all is vanity under the sun'.

Now we must notice that Christ does not say that earthly things are bad in themselves and are not to be rejected – not things to be rejected but things to be saved. But he tells us that they cannot be saved by making them the first object of our lives. The way to save them is not to become enslaved to them, but to be willing to love them and to give them up for the sake of something higher and better – for the sake of Christ and his way of living – and in doing this we shall unconsciously save and preserve all that is best worth having in the natural and earthly life. His is a hard saying, but it is profoundly true. It is hard to act upon but, when we do, we discover how absolutely true it is.

Always we must see the stars against the night. Nor is there any other way in which a Christian can keep alive a vital understanding of our Lord. The subject of sin seems to be by many an ecclesiastical subject fit for preaching on Sundays, but otherwise not emerging in ordinary thought. But now, if we go outside Churches and seriously think about human life as we know it actually to be; if we think of the hopeless miseries of the human race, its ruined childhoods, its devastated continents, its dissevered families, he will soon see that a major cause can be spelt in three letters – SIN.

Many a youth plays cheerfully with sin, supposing that he can do so or refrain from it as he pleases. Sooner or later he discovers that he is dealing with moral laws – laws which he did not create and whose operation he cannot control. By them, with terrific certainty, thoughts grow into deeds, deeds to habits, habits to character, character to destiny. Sin always comes disguised as liberty, but it soon puts man in chains. Our sins are mightier than we are in the power to make us tempt our fellows.

Sin is no bogey erected by theologians. Sin, to every seeing eye is the most real and practical problem of mankind. When a sensitive man repents he repents of his influence on others. He repents of the time when he made wrong doing easy for his family or his friends. When he looks on the lamentable evils of the world, its sad inequalities, its furious wars, he sees no need to deal delicately with sin or speak of it in apologetic tones. Jesus of Nazareth made no direct contribution to science or art or government or law. With none of these things did he concern himself. One thing he did. He made the indispensable contribution to man's fight for greater character against sin.

Christ did not judge men so much by what they were or by what they did, as by the possibilities in them being what they might become. So all good parents judge their children. They forgive and welcome back with love always. That's what we mean by 'saved by Faith'. When the prodigal son came to himself, the direction of his life was changed by Faith. And Jesus announced and showed in his life that God so deals with men. That has been a boon to mankind which puts all men under an immeasurable debt to Christ.

G.K. Chesterton once said: 'I am a Christian because it is such fun to be a Christian'. There is a profound truth in this. To the ordinary man or woman, who is careless of religion, life is, as a rule, extraordinarily dull and uninteresting. It is an almost universal complaint. It is because they find life so dull that men fly to drink and women to flirtation – in both cases often going far beyond what they originally intended. It is because they find life dull and uninteresting that people flock to cinemas, dog races and anything which they think will provide a change from their monotony and weariness. Now this very fact is itself a proof that they have lost their life – lost, that is to say, all the value and purpose and vital interest in it.

To a Christian, life is full of interest. When you see people all round you growing, expanding, blossoming into love and self-sacrifice – or withering, shrinking into selfishness, becoming critical of other people but never critical of themselves, and becoming dull, it is impossible to look on unmoved. When you believe that your life is a great spiritual drama, the issue of which is uncertain, but which is steadily drawing to a close; when you know that God is deeply interested in you; when you know that the consequences of all your actions do not end with yourself, that they affect others for good or evil, far beyond the immediate circle of your own friends and family; when you know that you are making or marring your future life, and not only your future life, but your actual present life here – then you cannot feel that your life is dull.

Appendix II

The very interest that you take in life will transform it for you. If you are interested in life simply for the pleasure or profit that you get out of it, you will soon become tired of it; but just in proportion as you realise its higher meaning it will become full of reality and purpose and of great interest to you.

Appendix II.6

Faith and science

Puck read widely and gave thought to what he had read. There was nothing he loved more than a good dialectic This sermon arose, no doubt, from discussions round the dinner table which he was in the habit of initiating. As in most of his sermons it was another lesson on living.

The conflict between Science and Theology is one of the saddest stories ever written. It is a record of mutual misunderstanding, of bitterness, bigotry and persecution, and to this day one is likely to find the devotees of religion suspicious of science and scientists impatient with the Church.

If we are to understand the reason for this controversy between science and theology we must look far back into man's history. Stephen Leacock remarks that wherever a professor discusses anything he has to retreat at least 2000 years to get a running start. Our retreat must be further back than that; it carries us to the earliest stage in which we are able to describe the thoughts of men. At the beginning, men attributed to superhuman spirits all activities in the world which they did not perform. If the wind blew, a spirit did it; if the sun rose a spirit moved it; if a storm came a spirit drove it. Natural law was non-existent to primitive man.

To primitive man, religious answer and a scientific answer were identical. Sunrise was explained, not by planetary movements which were unknown, but by the direct activity of a god, and the

Dawn then was worshipped in the same terms in which it was explained. The historic reason for the confusion between Science and Religion at once grows evident. At the beginning they were fused into one. The story of their relationship is the record of their gradual and difficult disentanglement.

Whenever peace has come between science and religion one finds a realm where the boundaries between the two are acknowledged and respected. Ask now the question: 'what makes it rain?' There is the scientific answer in terms of natural laws concerning atmosphere, pressure and condensation. There is also the religious answer because behind all laws and through them runs the will of God. These two answers are distinct. They move in different realms and are held together without inconsistency. As Sabatier put it: 'Because God is the final cause of all things, he is not the scientific explanation of any one thing.'

In how many realms where confusion once reigned between believers in gods and seekers after natural laws is peace now established. Rain and Sunrise, the tides and the eclipses, the coming of the seasons and the growing of crops – for all such events we have our scientific explanations and, at the same time, through them all, the men of religion feel the creative power of God. Peace reigns in these realms because, here no longer do we force religious answers on scientific questions, or scientific answers on religious questions. Evidently the old Deuteronomic Law is the solution of the conflict between science and religion: 'Cursed be he that removeth his neighbour's landmark'.

Of course, Science and Religion do tremendously affect each other. Life has many aspects: science, art, religion, approach it from different angles, with different interests, and while they do influence each other, each has solid standing in its own right. A Chemist might come to a spring to analyse it; a painter to enjoy its beauties and reproduce it on canvas; a man who is thirsty might come to drink and live. Shall they quarrel because they do not come alike? Let them rather see how partial is the experience of each without the others.

Religion has had her guilty share in mutual trespassing, because when the Hebrews wrote the Bible their thoughts and experience of God were interwoven with their early science. Christians, throughout the centuries have thought that faith in God stood or fell with early Hebrew science. In the seventeenth century, Dr. John Lightfoot, Vice-Chancellor of Cambridge University, said: Heaven and earth were created together in the same instant and clouds full of water. This work took place and man was created on 23 October, 4004 B.C. at nine o'clock in the morning'. Of what tragedy has this identification of science with religion been the cause. Now, when Evolution became accepted many men of religion thought the Faith destroyed. They identified the Christian Gospel with Hebrew Science. The Gospel is not bound to any science, ancient or modern, because science and religion have separate domains.

When we have frankly confessed religion's sins in trespassing on scientific territory we must note that Science has her guilty share in the needless conflict. To-day one suspects that the Church's vain endeavour to force religious solutions on scientific problems is almost over. But the attempt of many scientists to claim the whole field of reality as theirs and to force their solutions on every sort of problem is not yet finished. This, too, is a vain endeavour: to suppose that scientific observation can exhaust the truth of life, is like supposing that there is no more meaning in Westminster Abbey than is expressed in Baedeker.

Scientists, for example, sometimes claim domains which are not theirs by spelling abstract nouns with capitals, by positing Law or Evolution as the makers of the world. But law never did anything. Law is only man's statement of the way in which things are done. To explain the Universe as the creation of Law is on a par with explaining homes as the creation of matrimony. So, too, Evolution does nothing to the world: it is a way in which whoever makes the world, is making it. One might as well explain the difference between an acorn and an oak by saying that Growth did it with a capital G. So to explain the progress of Creation from Stardust to civilisation by changing the little e of evolution to a capital E. Science may describe the process as evolutionary, but its source, its moving power and its destiny are utterly beyond her ken.

Could Religion find a voice, therefore, she would wish to speak, not in terms of apology but of challenge when Science, assuming all of reality its field, grows arrogant. Describe the aspect of the world that belongs to you, she would say. I have learned my lesson: your field is yours and no interference at my hands shall trouble you again. But remember the limitations of your domain, to observe and describe phenomena and to plot their laws. This is an immense task and inexpressibly useful. But when you have said your last word on facts observed and laws deduced, man rises up and asks imperious questions with which you cannot deal, to present urgent problems for which no solution has ever been found except Augustine's 'I seek for God in order that my soul shall live'.

Without the insight and hope which faith alone can bring, we learn, the whole Universe is purposeless, engaged with blind hands that have no mind behind them, on tasks that mean nothing. Science and Religion should not be antagonists. They are indisputable to each other in the understanding and mastery of life.

Appendix II.7

Easter

Easter was always a joyful festival in Puck's life, not because the collection, by tradition, was given to the Rector, but because it occurred in the Spring – a season which he loved above all seasons – brought the family home, and filled the Church and Rectory with friends. Above all, the festival was a unique opportunity to explore the meaning of life and death.

We all have a personal concern with the Easter message. We all have friends who have disappeared into the invisible. We, ourselves, face that same experience – we have a rendezvous with death, when we shall disappear into the unseen. Probably, if we think about it, we have passed through many moods about it. We have shrugged our shoulders and said what lies on the other side, if there be any, will take care of itself without our bothering. Then death touched someone whose companionship we felt as an irreplaceable loss, and we wondered about the unseen world.

Our difficulty is that we cannot picture immortal life. We live in a world of things where reality consists in the fact that they are visible. 'Seeing is believing', we say, and then out of this world of the seen, our friends disappear into the unseen. No wonder that life beyond death is not real to us. We cannot picture it. How can we make it real to ourselves? There is probably only one answer: we must see that now, not after death alone, but now while we live in an invisible world.

In the Epistle to the Hebrews it is said of Moses that 'he endured as seeing the invisible'. When did he do that? After death? On the contrary, here in a very difficult, earthly life. Surely, Moses lived efficiently in this visible world. He saw Pharoah. He saw the Hebrew slaves. For years he saw the tyranny. He was no mystical recluse, but the New Testament says that the strength of the man and the resources of his power came from the unseen. The real world in which he lived, even here, was invisible. 'He endured as being the invisible'. And that is what we can all do. As Jesus said: 'if ye, being evil, know how to give gifts to your children, how much more shall your heavenly Father give the Holy Spirit to those who ask Him'. Even apart from religion every one of us has to do something like that.

Consider the reality of the invisible. Our bodies can be seen, but not our personalities. Personality is self-conscious being, with powers of intellect, purpose and good will. We cannot see that. Self-conscious being – mind, purpose, love – their effects are visible, and their results. Their embodiments our eyes can see, but they, themselves – the creative realities behind the invisible, are invisible for ever. Everywhere we look creative forces spring from the unseen. This Church building is visible but not the forces which produced it. The inner spiritual needs which wanted it, the faiths expressed in it, the ability of the architects, the skill of the stonemasons and builders, all the creative forces behind it are invisible.

Ideas, we have never seen, but we have seen a man transformed by an idea taking hold of him. Or love, we have never seen but what a powerful force it is. Or hope. Or faith. We can see David Livingstone going to Africa but not the faith which impelled him. We can see Darwin in his garden, but not the faith which continually pushed him on. Sometimes we see people who are suffering with a long illness, but we can't see faith which gives them a happy, cheerful outlook. One thing is certain for all of us.

If we have risen at all into those higher attitudes of life which are the distinction of humanity, the sources of our deepest power are in an unseen realm. We endure; we must endure, if we endure at all, as seeing the invisible.

Everywhere we look we see the visible created by the invisible. Jeans, the physicist, says: 'The universe seems to be nearer a great thought than a great machine'. Haldane, the biologist, says: 'the only real world is the spiritual world'. Balfour, the philosopher, says: 'We now know too much about matter to be materialists'. Once in a while the most modern scientists say things that sound extraordinarily like the New Testament. Here is one case: 'By faith we understand that the worlds have been framed by the word of God, so that what is seen hath not been made out of things which appear'.

If such is the reality of the invisible everywhere, not after death alone but here and now, does that not support the surmise about our friends who disappear into the unseen? What is the difference between life and death? Yesterday, my friend was alive. To-day, the doctors say that he is dead. What has happened: the visible is still here; something invisible has gone. Life, itself, is invisible. All the real forces in the world are invisible. 'The things which are seen are temporal. The things which are not seen are eternal.' (2 Cor. 4. 18)

If we talk about this to people who are cynical they tell us that it is all wishful thinking. We don't want to die and remain dead, so we concoct reasons for believing that we don't. Be realistic, they say. To which I answer. Being realistic is precisely what we are driving at and realistically we are not simply our bodies. Men saw apples fall for ages and perceived no important truth at all, until a man looked at an apple fall, not with his eyes alone, but with his mind, and lo! An invisible force which holds the stars together. When we look at the body alone we are not being realistic. The creative forces of personality are invisible.

I think it would be a mystery if the invisible world in which we live should have arisen by accident, with no external reality to call it forth. Nothing like that could be found anywhere. If we have eyes, it is because there first was light. If we have lungs it is because there first was air. Always what is in us was called into being by some reality. And now to say that personality, the invisible being which we really are, came by chance, corresponding to nothing; would not that be an incredible mystery? No, the invisible world is the real world.

This Easter should lift up our hearts with the knowledge that the invisible is real. If, in this Church, we get closer to God, that is reality. This is the root of all great religion. We endure as seeing the invisible.

Appendix III

A Lecture on India

In Queen Victoria's proclamation, 100 years ago, it was announced, and all parties agreed, that we were trustees in India. But that was interpreted in two different ways. To one it seemed inevitable that the wards should come of age, and right that the trustees should train them for responsibilities by giving to them in small and increasing doses. The other party believed that the White Man's Burden would go on for a very long time. They would bring protection and guidance but not liberty until some distant future when the whole vast sub-continent of India was educated.

Intellectually, the Englishmen in the Indian Civil Service (I.C.S.) were among the pick of Oxford and Cambridge. In the upper posts in India they were men of intellect; they had a strong sense of public duty and were very hard working; but they seemed to be rather lacking in imagination and sympathy, less inspired by the extraordinary and unprecedented phenomena of the country than might have been expected. They were too conventionally English. Fire and imagination, burning zeal, anything at all un-English, are qualities which it was polite to suppress if the Under-Secretary is to have a career. And by the time he was a Member of Council, the fires may have been banked down for ever. But not so in the District.

The young District Magistrate was monarch of all he surveyed, and could be as un-English as he liked, provided that he had sense enough to keep most of his ebullience out of his reports.

And, in fact, the system did produce plenty of men who had that warmth which the centre lacked – men with very great patriarchal power due to their independent position and their own personality. Almost from the day he arrived in India a member of the I.C.S. was given authority which, anywhere else, he could not have achieved in twenty years. He felt confident that he would be supported and that what he did would be understood. And he must learn to delegate if he was to get through the day's work. It was despotism, tempered by the despot's liberal upbringing and by the knowledge of Parliament's unusually liberal attitude. But despotism it was all the same, as any system must be in which people are given what is good for them instead of what they want.

The people of India were poor, but they were content. By irrigation they were able to produce food where, before, there was famine. They had peace and protection where, before, there were marauding gangs and civil war and raids from Pathans across the frontier. They had sound finance when, before, the budget was never balanced, and they had justice where, before, there was bribery, corruption and nepotism. But there grew up a generation of Indians who had not known the chaos before British rule and whose leaders, educated in the British ideas of democracy, began to agitate for self-government. There were only a few. Nearly all the four hundred million were content – poor, but content. Poor, because as soon as their standard of living was raised they bred up to the poverty line.

In handing over the administration to Indians in 1947 the changes were not great because Indians had been trained to administrate and had taken part in the government of India for so long a time. In 1947 more than half of the Indian Civil Service were Indian. It was the same in the Indian Army, the Indian Police, the Engineering Service and in the irrigation works, transport, education, agronomy, woods and forests. Completely different to

Africa where political independence was given before they had been trained for taking on responsibility.

The great social changes in India are chiefly due to the influence of Gandhi, who had a dynamic personality and set himself to remove the social and religious abuses in India. He had a vast power of moral appeal to the four hundred million people of India. That power did not depend on any external force, or material wealth or worldly power, but on spiritual power. He became the embodiment of their own idea of goodness.

In attacking these age-long social abuses he taught the village people by a simple parable of hand and wrist, which those simple people could remember. He suggested that the five fingers represent the essential things without which India cannot receive her freedom from age-long abuses. The first, the thumb, is Hindu – Mohammedan unity. No united India could be built up without that. The first finger is the removal of 'untouchabilty', which is equally necessary if India is to be one people. The middle finger stands for equality between man and woman. That is fundamental. On the other side, the third finger, is the prohibition of the drug and liquor traffic which is ruining the morals of the people. Last is the promotion of village industries, especially hand-spinning and hand-weaving. Then the uniting force, the wrist, which binds the five fingers of the hand together, stands for non-violence, or 'Ahimsa', non-violence in thought, word and deed. This 'Ahimsa', which is called the soul-force, combines all the social and economic aspects of the one national programme and makes it a living and organised whole with a moral purpose behind it.

Now if you examine that closely you see that moral factors predominate and separate it entirely from any political programme. Its object is nothing less than the regeneration of the whole Indian people, from within; and with Gandhi, it is deeds which count the most. Nobody was more severe than he was with regard to the hypocrisy of profession without practice. It can be said that nowhere in the world are abuses being swept away so quickly as in India, and in no country are political ideals so high.

There were forty million 'untouchables' in India. They were denied elementary social rights, such as the use of public wells, and were treated as less than human beings. In the extreme South this oppression was carried to such lengths that, even the shadow of an 'untouchable' was supposed to pollute a high caste man. In British India the more inhuman restrictions, such as the ban on the use of public transport and the denial of all education had disappeared. In the territories administered by the Indian Princes, these oppressive customs still held sway. But even in British India the 'untouchables' suffered from many disabilities: they were forced to live in special areas outside the village and were confined to menial and degrading occupations.

Gandhi, who was a high born Brahman, was determined to stop this and to free the 'untouchables'. By choice he lived in 'untouchable' colonies and had 'untouchables' to stay with him. After Independence when the Constituent Assembly met they passed a resolution that 'untouchability' was to be abolished forthwith. The Untouchability Offences Act came into force all over India. Formerly they were not admitted into Hindu Temples, or allowed to bathe in the same tanks as others, or enter restaurants or hotels. Anyone who encourages 'untouchability' can now be prosecuted under this Act.

If it were only a question of Law, this age-long custom would still have survived in the more inaccessible rural areas. What has made it impossible to survive in any shape has been the working of democratic institutions. There are forty million 'untouchables' and their votes generally determine the results of an election. Therefore the political parties usually appear as champions of the backward classes. Also, because of the tradition inherited from Gandhi, and because of their voting strength, members of the these classes are included in the cabinets of the Central and Provincial Governments.

These democratic institutions have brought a great shift in social balance. Broadly speaking, political power has shifted from the landowners and professional classes who produced the leadership in the past, to 'new people' who had no voice in public affairs before. For instance, in Rajasthan, the Rajputs, who are the landowners and used to rule that State, have not even one representative in the cabinet, whereas the Jat cultivators, who were the labourers for the Rajputs have become the most important group in the legislature. In Madras, the chief citadel of Brahman power, the Ministry does not contain a single Brahman member. The Chief Minister was once an 'untouchable'.

Everywhere the emergence of 'new people' has been the notable feature. In the past, the intellectual and political life of India drew its strength from a very small minority. To-day, the most important fact in India's life is the release of the energies and intellectual potential of vast masses of people. It is, in fact, a major revolution.

Next, equality between men and women. Formerly girls were married at the age of eleven or twelve. Their first babies were weaklings and continued to be weaklings. Women were kept in purdah and could not inherit property. It all went to their husbands. The life of a widow was a miserable one. She was the slave of the family and was not allowed to marry again. As she was betrothed at the age of three or four, and thus considered to be married, she might become a widow when still a child. Purdah and no education were now swept away.

Economic changes cannot be described, like the social changes, as a major revolution, but they are very great indeed. The poverty of India has always been proverbial and the vast majority of the population have always lived at starvation level. We made big strides in increasing the yield of crops by irrigation, especially in the North. But it was always offset by a corresponding increase in population breeding to starvation level again. The population increased by five million a year i.e. a hundred million in twenty years. We could do little to stop it because it was all bound up in their religion. Another great drain on the peasantry was the semi-feudal landlordism in most parts of the country. The landlords charged a large rent, the intermediaries had their rake-off, the land was let and sub-let until the wretched peasant was in great poverty. This was particularly practised in the Princely States. The reform of land tenure was therefore a problem of great urgency, not only from a political point of view, but also from the necessity of increasing agricultural production.

The new Government of India, by Indians, were very cautious in their land reform. They had a five year plan for the Provinces in which they eliminated all intermediaries and got rid of the middle man. They also recommended it to the Princes. That did not touch the heart of the problem of producing more food. In the second five year plan the Government enforced cooperative methods, so eliminating the evils of fragmentation of holdings and ancient techniques of cultivation. Under the old system a man who had four sons would divide his holding into four. If each of these had four sons this fragmentation went to such an extent that no man had sufficient to keep his family alive. Then, the wooden plough, which only dug a few inches of soil was replaced by the iron plough and by tractors. Cooperation enabled fertilizers and seeds to be bought at low prices, subsidised by the Government. Far more land was put under cultivation by irrigation. Far more power was produced by hydro-electric works and a great increase of industry, notably in steel production, machinery, aluminium and phosphates. The National Income was raised by 30%. Education, advanced and technical training, health, housing and welfare were also included in this five-year plan so that, at the end of it, India may be said to have laid the foundation of a modern state.

The most extraordinary and successful movement in India in modern times is known as Bhoodan (B.H.O.O.D.A.N.), associated with a man named Vinoba Bhave. His object has been to awaken villagers to the social and moral purposes of owning land. Vinoba was a disciple of Ghandi in his social work. He is wedded to a life of austerity. He believes in natural cure for illness. He dislikes travelling by car or train and walks from village to village. He started in Hyderabad and succeeded in persuading those rich landowners who had a superfluity amount of land to distribute it to the landless. But he soon realised that the question was not one of distribution of plots of land to the poor, and the new policy which he initiated was the surrender of the entire village land for the cultivation of the village as a whole. It has awakened the conscience of the whole nation to the land problem as a whole, and it has popularised the idea of voluntary effort in cooperative cultivation.

Vinoba, in the genuine tradition of Mahatma Ghandi, walks from village to village, preaching his message and making the people realise not only the moral issue involved but also the great economic value of cooperative effort in cultivation. It is all done by non-violent means – no laws, no Government orders, no police – but by awakening the conscience of the whole nation and making them see the economic value of cooperative action. He has also introduced village industries, such as spinning home spun cloth, making furniture, building etc., and above all happy cooperative villages.

The Indian Government is trying to develop India's industries, especially heavy industries and produce her own machinery and capital goods, but these must be in or near urban centres and will not absorb more than 10% of her population. The vast majority will continue to live in the countryside. To buy capital goods she has had to depend on foreign loans and credits from Britain, America and Russia, and has already become highly industrialised.

Many people in England think that India, by being friendly to China, a communist country, and also friendly to Russia, is letting down the Commonwealth. Few English people can fully understand India's point of view. We are too prejudiced. India is not in the least unfriendly to us. Her attitude is quite simple. Because of her Gandhian background and her own immediate interest she is wedded to a policy of peace. The cold war, as Nehru has never ceased to emphasise, means 'thinking all the time in terms of war; in terms of preparation for war and the risk of having the hot war'.

To India, especially with social and industrial problems of unparalleled magnitude staring her in the face, this constant talk of war and of preparation for war seems to be suicidal. Apart from all other considerations, the maintenance of a peaceful atmosphere seems to India to be the first necessity and consequently from the very beginning she refused to align herself with either party in the cold war. That does not mean that India has a greater sympathy with the Soviet Union than with the Western Alliance. In fact India, while recognising the right of the Communists to propagate their views, just as much as any other ideology or religion can propagate their views, has never tolerated any policy of subversion and has consistently taken a firm attitude in regard to internal intervention by Communists from outside. All that India emphasises is that she is not content to follow other people's judgement on international issues, and will not be committed to partisanship, but must decide her own policy based on her own judgement.

When India declared that she would remain in the Commonwealth it was a declaration that, in becoming independent, India was not going to forswear the British political and social traditions, and intellectual traditions which she had developed during her period of association with the West. It was a declaration of faith in parliamentary democracy and in the institutions associated with it, in a social pattern based on equality and justice and liberty, and in an economic system which, while guaranteeing freedom, ensures the fullest development of natural resources. Further, the evolution of the Commonwealth from the British Empire into its present multi-racial association of States seemed to be a desirable ideal.

India's relations with the Commonwealth have had great and severe strains. Britain, India and Pakistan recognised China. Canada, Australia and South Africa recognised Chiang-Kai-Shek. In the war in Korea, India took an attitude different to that of Britain and other members of the Commonwealth. Finally came the Middle Eastern issue, the greatest strain which the Commonwealth has had to undergo, in which members of the Commonwealth were ranged squarely on opposite sides. That it has survived so great a strain shows its vitality. To-day, India's association with the Commonwealth is not anywhere questioned.

The great question to-day is, will democratic institutions survive in India? They have broken down in other countries in Asia.

Appendix IV

A Christmas Charade
(written by Puck for the annual Christmas party in 1957, shortly after the Russians launched Sputnik)

Pa is Puck; John is John Strover; Peter is Peter Tapsell,
staying with the family for Christmas; Dick is Dick Strover;
Ma is Rosalind

Scene 1
John enters and announces: the first scene is in the Kremlin.
Enter Cashchief, Veryshyoff, Nickelin and Bulkgaining, in
    that order.

Cashchief (Pa): Ah! Here we are. That's where they put the vodka.
    Can't do anything without vodka (offering glasses).
    Bulkgaining, Veryshyoff, Nickelen. 'Varshiss daroviah'. All
    reply: 'Varshiss daroviah'. Now Nickelin, when will it be ready?
Nickelin (John): It goes up on Wednesday.
Cashchief: Well now, who shall we put inside it? Bulk, what
    about you?
Nickelin: No, no room for Bulk. He's too fat.
Veryshyoff (Peter): The best propaganda would be to send the
    most important man in the Soviet State.
Cashchief: What do you mean? You don't think I'm going up do
    you. Who would run the State?
Bulkgaining (Dick): What about Newkoff? He's been getting
    a bit above himself lately. The best cure is to put him up a
    bit higher.

Vershyoff: He'd get awfully bored, poor chap, whizzing round the earth with nothing to do.

Cashchief: Oh! I don't know. He'd have a television set, and a very powerful electronic Telescope. He'd be able to see what's going on all over the world and report back to us.

Nickelin: As a matter of fact there's only room for a good-sized dog, as before.

Bulk: We'd get a lot of criticisms and dispute from Britain. The Newspapers reported Lady Munnings as saying that we ought to send up criminals instead.

Cashchief: Tell her that she can go instead of the dog if she likes. Volunteers only, if they are small enough, and they will be national heroes.

Veryshyoff: Molotov is pretty small, but he has got rather fat with all the foreign embassy Dinners he has consumed.

Cashchief: Can't make a national hero out of Molotov. It wouldn't do.

Bulk: Well if it's criminals you want. We are all criminals.

Cashchief: Ha! Ha! There's many a true word spoken in jest. But you mustn't give that away to the world. In our propaganda we are a kindly, generous people, saving the backward countries from the iron heel of the Western capitalists who grind the faces of the poor. Workers of the world unite! Down with the blood-sucking capitalists. Bring your glasses into dinner!

Scene 2

John announces: the second scene is in the White House, Washington.
Enter Wisendower, Dullass, Nickson and Hellroy in that order.

Wisendower (Pa): Wonderful putt of yours Hellroy – just got the winning point. That'll put your pecker up, Nickson. No American likes being beaten.

Nickson (John): That's what I've been trying to tell you. The Russians have beaten us good and proper with their satellites.

Dullass (Peter): We've got enough troubles here on earth. Who wants to go to the moon?

Wisendower: Yes, our people know it's only propaganda.

Nickson: What do you know of our people with your golf-playing business men? Our people know darned well it's a long-term research by first-class scientists.

Hellroy (Dick): And the smaller countries are going to kow-tow to where they know the power is.

Wisendower: Well, Nickson, you are more in touch with our people than I am. What do you say Dullass?

Dullass: The money they spend on these satellites would have given their homeless people a million houses, not even bungalows but with stairs to a second floor. It's all a stunt. (Pause). Of course, on the other hand, if the smaller countries are going to turn to Russia we'll have to do something about it. On the other hand we don't want to waste the tax-payers' money. On the other hand, we can frighten the tax-payer to back us up. On the other hand it pays to tell the truth.

Scene 3

John announces: the third scene is in the Earl of Rutlandshire's stately home.

Sight-seers are being shown round by the Earl at half-a-crown each. Enter the Butler (Pa) with tray, Mr. and Mrs. Snooks (John and Ma) with Ernie (Dick).

Butler: Half-a-crown please Madam – thank you Madam. Half-a-crown please Sir – thank you Sir. Half-a-crown please Sir – thank you Sir.

Enter the Earl (Peter).

Earl: This is the Great Hall. Above you is a portrait of the 4th Earl – painted by Kneller.

Mrs. Snooks: Wipe your nose, Ernie.

Earl: Above is the minstrel's gallery. It was in this hall that Sir Francis Drake came to stay with his friend when he arrived home in the Golden Hind.

Mrs. Snooks: Sailors, I says to her, is all very well, I says, but you watch your step, my girl, I says.

Earl: We will now go upstairs and see the bedroom in which Queen Elizabeth the First stayed and the four-poster bed in which she slept. The room is kept very much the same as when she slept there four centuries ago.

Outside Crash!!!

Earl: What on earth's that?

Mrs. Snooks: Sounds like what 'appens in our kitchen when me 'usband comes 'ome...

Enter Butler.

Butler: My Lord, the Russian Sputnik has fallen in our garden, in the rose bed.

Earl: In my rose bed! Come on! Let's see it!

Rushes off followed by everyone except the Butler.

Butler: What lack of dignity! Running to see a foreign toy! What would his grand-father have said! The 10th Earl must have turned in his grave.

Takes up tray of half-crowns and walks off with dignity.

The Charade word is 'Upstairs'.
The red herring is 'Sputnik'.

Appendix V

Great Snakes
from *The Times*, 27 March 1956

Never have I enjoyed the warmth and beauty of summer so much as in a garden in Rhodesia after leaving London in a blizzard two days before. Even the swallows which circled around seemed to be saying: 'What fools people and birds are to stay in England in the winter.'

My nephew, who was a doctor, and with whom I was staying, was away for most of the day. My great-nephews, who were home from school, wore only a pair of trousers and shoes, and their bodies were a rich golden-brown. They were on their horses for half the day, with their dogs, hunting, shooting, and capturing animals and insects and making pets of them. They would look these up in their books, and sometimes draw and paint them.

A Real Expert

The eight horses kept by the family were looked after by one African groom and a boy. But my great-nephews took their share in the work. In the early morning they took the temperatures of their horses. This is essential because of central African horse-sickness. If a horse has a temperature he must be inoculated at once, otherwise he may quickly sicken and die. They clean their own saddles and bridles and help to feed, water, and groom the horses.

The second boy, Ian, loved snakes. He was a genuine expert on snakes and had discovered a new kind which had been sent to America. His method of capturing them was with a loop of wire hanging from the end of a stick. Directly the head of the snake went through the loop he gave the stick a jerk upwards and the wire loop tightened behind the snake's head. He then ran his hand up the snake from the tail and held it behind the head so that it could not bite him.

He thus caught the most venomous snakes without harm. As a precaution he carried a strong anti-toxin in a hypo-dermic syringe. One day he came back in triumph with a puff-adder which he had safely bestowed in a box. His father, one of the most generous of men, thought this was going too far and said so in no unmeasured terms: 'Do you realize that one bite from that and you'll be dead in ten minutes?' 'I've thought it all out, Daddy, and I'll keep him in a pit.'

Pit for the Adders

Ian eventually won the day. He dug a square pit four feet deep, and covered it with doors which stopped every possible egress. The puff-adder was lowered in beside a saucer of egg and milk. It moved very slowly and relished its meal. Ian said it looked at him with an affectionate eye. Although accustomed to Ian's curious tastes, the whole family regarded his latest adventure with apprehension. My own attitude was one of horror and dread and I only moved in the garden clad in a pair of riding boots which I had sent out in advance.

After a few days Ian, who had gone out before breakfast to feed his pet, came running back to the house in wild excitement. 'Mummy, Mummee!! There are 30 baby snakes in the pit!'

It produced an uproar. We all knew that puff-adders do not lay eggs. They produce their young like mammals. In fact, all their characteristics had been discussed as far as we knew from books. There was a rush from the house, led by Ian. I brought up the rear, having paused to put on my riding boots. There they were in the pit, 30 tiny puff-adders, each one, as we knew, a harbinger of death from its birth. Never have I seen a boy so delighted as Ian, except perhaps, my own youngest son who did six cartwheels on the lawn when he heard that his housemaster was leaving.

Ian's days were spent in feeding and watching his progeny and reading everything he could find in the Salisbury library on the subject of puff-adders. He discovered that by making it bite the inside of a tumbler he could collect the poison and sell it at an enormous price. He also saw an advertisement offering 25s. a foot for puff-adders and a rapid calculation showed him that, when the babies were grown up, he would be able to buy an expensive polo pony. But he discovered some things which no book had shown him and which no money could buy.

One early morning he rushed in, 'Mummy! Mummee!! the babies are mewing like kittens.' We hurried out in the same order and heard, without any doubt, those kittenish mews.

Termtime Tragedy

The time came when Ian had to return to school. He left his pets with sad regret and begged us to look after them properly, leaving full notes on their diet and times of feeding. We carried out his instructions loyally and with great care, particularly when we opened the horizontal folding doors above the pit which were made of wood and wire mosquito-proof gauze. The youngsters grew apace and did their best to get out. But Ian had done his work well and there was no possible exit.

At Easter we had a small house party. They all came to church on Easter Sunday, and then went off to play their games, coming back to lunch. Then we all went to see the puff-adders of which our visitors had heard so much. On arrival at the pit we saw a gaping hole in one of the doors.

One of the horses had broken loose during the night for a short time. He must have put his foot through the door. On opening it and counting, one snake was missing. It was essential to find it and we looked around very cautiously. How glad I was for my riding boots! Suddenly one of the ladies shrieked to her husband: 'Johnny, behind you!' Johnny leapt forward and there, within a yard of where his foot had been, was the missing puff-adder. It was too much. By unanimous consent guns were brought and a massacre ensued. Far away at school, Ian wept many tears.

Appendix VI

A short story: 'Staying on in India'

It was a particularly happy gathering at the bar of the club that evening as the hot weather began to remind us of its devastating approach. It was happy because the majority were planning their leave home. Even those who had to endure six months of scorching heat were planning their leave for next year or consoling themselves with the memories of their last summer in England. Bill Johnson, who was always an individualist and something of an iconoclast, broke the general trend of agreement by announcing that he was spending his six months' leave in India.

'Good Lord! What are you going to do?'

'Fishing.'

'I know you're keen on fishing, but you haven't been home for three years and won't for another three.'

'You won't have another white man to talk to. Very bad for you Bill, and you'll get horribly bored.'

'Bill, you're mad.'

'Well, I don't know, I'm not married and my parents are not alive, so I've no particular reason to go home. I suppose I shall retire to England. But I shall never get such fishing as I can get out here and it's a pity not to take advantage of it while I can.'

'Yes, that's all very well, but you'll get frightfully fed up in the evenings with no one to talk to.'

'Well, of course, I should be delighted if any of you chaps came with me. But I know you won't. And I'm very much interested in these hill tribes. They're grand fellows to do any "Shikar" with, and it's the best way to learn the language. Besides I read, I paint and I sometimes write. I shan't be bored. I can promise you that.'

'Well, well, "Chacun son gout", but give me England any time.'

'So say all of us.'

Thus it came about that Bill Johnson set out with his retinue of men, ponies, tents, baggage and stores late in April and began to climb the foothills of the Himalayas on his long trek to the upper reaches of the river, which he heard of as very good fishing, but a long way to go. Striding ahead, he had a glowing feeling of freedom, having shaken off the shackles of civilisation and being able to go where he liked, when he liked and how he liked. Hour after hour they climbed under the sweltering sun. The men, who were mountaineers, and the ponies were more exhausted by the heat than he was and he had to cheer and lead them through the sweltering afternoon and evening until they reached the 'dak' bungalow in which they were to spend the night.

Day after day they climbed until they crossed a pass and were revived by the cool breezes which blew from the snows. Then down, down as the steep rocky descent became a more gentle slope and the river widened to flow through a lovely valley. Here the vivid green of the grass, extending on each side of the river to the pine woods, was covered with blue irises. Above the dark woods were mountains with snow, cut like cameos against the blue sky. But, much as he revelled in the scenery which he intended to paint, it was the fishing for which he had come.

So, he instructed the leader of his drivers to enquire about the fishing from every man they met on the road as they approached the village which they could now see at the bottom of the valley on the banks of the river. Although the grass was luscious there were not many cattle. There were cows to give milk and oxen to pull the ploughs and carts. He was soon to know the reason.

'These people are all Hindus, Sahib. They do not kill the cattle and cannot eat beef. They do not bother much with sheep and goats which are kept by the tribes in the mountains. They depend for their meat on the fish.'

That was enough for Bill. He pitched his camp above the village in order to get unpolluted water, had his longed-for tea and, feeling mightily refreshed and in great spirits, sent for the headman of the village. He treated him with great courtesy, offering him a camp chair while the other villagers who came with him and his drivers stood listening to the conversation and sometimes joining in, but with the perfect manners which Hindus always show. Bill never failed to admire and enjoy the courtesy of these 'jungli' folk. The headman told him a great deal about the fishing.

Apparently the village lived on fish for most of the year. There was very good fishing for the next two months. After that the water dried up, the fish went down stream, and there was no fishing until the monsoon brought the water gushing down from the mountains in September. He offered to supply milk, eggs and vegetables, which Bill had rather counted on. Before he left Bill gave him an umbrella which gave the headman enormous pleasure and pride!

Next morning, just as Bill was getting his tackle together for his first day's sport, a good looking young man appeared at his camp and announced that he was Bill's 'Shikari', sent by the headman. His name was 'Shuratan', and both his father and grandfather had been recognised as outstanding fishermen. He carried all Bill's kit and lunch and a blanket which he insisted that the sahib must have to sit on.

Bill preferred to be on his own, to use his own cunning and to learn by trial and error. But he soon realised the value of Shuratan who seemed to know the habits and haunts of the fish and their fears and suspicions. From him he learned the language, so that he was able to walk down to the village in the evening and talk to the men as they sat together.

The children, too, became friendly but Bill made it quite clear that they must not come up to his camp. A wise precaution of which their fathers fully approved. He began to love these people and their simple care-free life, their health, their happiness and what our 'civilisation' would call poverty.

He began to realise that such poverty carried with it freedom from the tyranny of possessions. Being Hindus, they had their religion, their superstitions, their images which they worshipped naturally and easily, their gods and their images being the same. But they sat lightly to the fear of which the Hindu religion abounds. Living in that beautiful country they could not help feeling that Brahma, the Creator, created beauty and was so much greater than Vishnu, the destroyer. The children, particularly, in and out of the river, playing about in their little boats which they had helped their fathers to make, the boys helping in the fields and with the cows, the girls helping their mothers in the house and all of them fishing in the evenings were some of the happiest children he had ever seen in any part of the world.

Bill supplied a good deal of fish to the village. He was chiefly there to catch mahseer, a species of salmon with a hard mouth. He learned a great deal about the habits of the mahseer, the best time and the best weather and the best places to fish. He caught several over fifteen pounds, but was out for something bigger. Normally, in this fast moving river, he fished with a spoon, but the villagers pulled out the smaller mahseers with a mulberry of which there was a plentiful supply in the valley. Occasionally he caught a rainbow trout in the tributaries higher up. They gave him great fun and he need all his skill to get them. He went higher up the stream as the summer wore on and the flood water from the melted snows began to subside. There came a time in July when the river became low and the fish began to disappear. He was told that for the next two months until the monsoon came there would be no more fish.

'But how do they live', he asked Shuratan.

'They just live on chapattis and Ghi (unleavened bread and butter), but they do not feel so well, sahib, or have the same strength'.

'There are fish higher up the stream where it flows fast between the rocks. Have you been up there?'

'Yes, sahib, near the top there is a lake but no one may fish there.'

'Why not?'

'Because, sahib, the priests say that, if you fish there, you will die.'

'Nonsense, I shall go there tomorrow, and you will come with me.'

'I will come with you, sahib, but I will not fish.'

So they started up the gorge where the river still came down in rapid flow, sometimes bubbling happily over the stones, sometimes rushing between the boulders. As they climbed, wild flowers, moss and shrubs appeared near the water's edge. The higher they climbed the more beautiful the surroundings. Then, as they climbed on to the plateau one of those beautiful mountain lakes opened out before them. It was scorching hot in the sun and quite cold in the shade. It was evening and the sun was dipping below the mountain top. As he looked, Bill saw fish rising to the flies which were in profusion.

Carefully selecting a fly he made a cast, and almost immediately pulled out a rainbow trout. Again and again he got a bite until he filled his fishing basket. Shuraton, who stood watching at a distance, expecting his master to fall dead, was still frightened but came a little closer as he saw Bill very much alive, and enjoying sport such as he had never had before. At last he stopped because they could not carry any more fish. They struggled down to the village with their load. The villagers were horrified when they heard of their adventures but were not averse to eating the longed-for food.

Next morning, Shuraton arrived at Bill's camp and was overjoyed to find Bill very much alive and looking forward to another day's sport. Bill pulled his leg and twitted him on his cowardice and superstition until Shuraton took his rod and said that he would join him. Throwing discretion to the winds he enjoyed the best day's sport of his life and they took back an even larger supply to the village. Bill suggested that some of the villagers might like to join them next day and Shuraton enthusiastically backed him up. The elders of the village shook their white beards and reminded them of the legend and the words of the priests.

Bill assured them that he and Shuraton were in the best of health and some of the keener young fishermen said that they would come and join them. On the following evening several came. They returned home with their blankets full, eager to continue. Day by day more joined in. Some of them carried a small boat and were able to throw their lines in any part of the lake. Thus the hottest part of the year passed, with Bill still enjoying his life and not at all anxious to move. The river by the village was very low and the ground was hard and baked.

At last, to everyone's relief, the monsoon broke and the rain came pouring down on the thirsty soil and drenching the river and camp, for which they had prepared by channelling to the river. The tributaries swelled into torrents, the river rose to a flood and surged down to the plains below. As the first rains diminished and the floods subsided, they began to fish in the river as before. But they had very little sport. Day after day they tried the waters which had given them the greatest success, but they came back empty handed. The whole village found the same. They went up to the mountain lake which had yielded so abundantly. But even here there were very few. Bill became worried. A great fear came into his heart. Had he led these simple people to destroy the fish which would have bred the generation which could have supplied their needs this year? Had the priests been right after all?

With hundreds of years, thousands of years of experiences behind them, was there not wisdom in that which he had taken to be superstition?

Bill felt like a murderer, a destroyer of the people whom he had grown to love. They must know now. The old man must have said, 'We told you so', and they must have realised the truth. What a terrible prospect for them! He hardly dared face them and yet, face them he must. But he could not face them without a creative plan to save their lives. Hour after hour he spent that night awake in bed, thinking out what he must do, spurred on by the fear of the consequences if he did nothing.

It would be cowardly not to face the village. He could not just say to them that he was sorry but he would compensate them with money. It went much deeper than that. He had defied their priests. He had defied their gods. Worse even than that, he had led the younger generation away from the religion in which they had been brought up. That religion was more than a tradition to the older men and women. They had practised it all their lives and had a natural reverence for their priests. To them, disobedience had been rightly punished by their gods. But it was those who had been led away who were punished and their parents with them.

The sins of the sons were being visited on the fathers. To them, Bill was the evil one and the consequences of evil were now obvious to everyone. How could he face them? For a white man to eat humble pie before an Indian villager was against the grain, against all his upbringing.

He was prepared to do that and to offer them money. What would be their reaction? They would say, 'What use is your money to us? It will not bring us back our fish. Go away! You have made us disobey our gods. You have brought us starvation. All our lives we have eaten fish and we cannot live without it. Go away before you bring more evil on us'. And he would have to slink away, crushed, miserable, feeling like a murderer for the rest of his life. No, at all costs he must bring back the fish.

Bill knew that in Kashmir there were breeding places for rainbow trout and mahseer, created and protected by the Government. He knew the man in charge. He had heard that the young fish could be sent in sealed tanks so that they could be transported by ponies to the upper streams of the lower Himalayas. But he knew that the cost was very high. Like most men in the Indian Army he had no capital except his polo ponies and equipment. He was in his regimental polo team and polo had occupied most of his leisure time. That must all go. He must sell all that he had and borrow more rather than let this village starve.

Even then, it would be long time before the new fish began to fill the river. How were the people to be fed meanwhile? They would not eat beef. They had no goats or sheep. Fortunately, Bill had brought several months' pay with him and had spent very little. He decided to buy a herd of mountain goats from a neighbouring tribe.

In the early morning he wrote out a long telegram to his friend in Kashmir stressing the urgent need to stock this river at all costs and asking the time it would take, giving him times of his own journey. He sent one of his men with this over the pass to the nearest post office which was twelve miles away. He told him to wait until an answer came.

It was a depressing day. Rain came up from the South West but he could not stay all day in the tent, with his thoughts inevitably returning again and again to the terrible consequences if, as he dreaded, he was unable to restock the river. Also, he felt that he could not meet any of the villagers, not even the faithful Shuratan, should they come to see him. So he set out on a long climb in the mountains, picking his way between the many mountain streams which had formed since the monsoons broke.

In the evening he returned tired, soaked to the skin and anxious, to find that no reply to his telegram had arrived. However, a hot bath and a meal was soon ready for him which brought back some of his normal, buoyant spirits. Surely an answer must come soon. It was only a four hour journey over the pass to the next village with its telegraph office. Then the dread of the impossibility to comply with his request came upon him and he finally went to bed weary in mind and body, where nature took control and 'ravelled up the sleeve of care'.

He woke up late with a start. Beside his bed was standing a man with a telegram. He tore it open and read, 'Can supply your needs but consider you should accompany the expedition, wire time of arrival.' A wave of gratitude came over him. He dressed quickly and sent for the headman of the village.

As he waited for him, he calculated the time required to complete this bold and extravagant enterprise. It would take three weeks to reach the Kashmir breeding water and, possibly, three to four weeks to get the expedition up here. He only had two more months leave, so he must make forced marches both ways. As for the cost, he dared not think of it.

The headman arrived, obviously terribly distressed. If there was anger and resentment, it did not appear, his courtesy was unchanged. Bill, who by this time could speak the language well, received him with sympathy and humble apology, which he felt most deeply. He then explained to him the action he had already taken to restock the river. Finally he gave him a thousand rupees to buy a herd of goats.

The headman was deeply moved. To be humbly apologised to by a white man was an experience which he had never known or dreamed possible. To consider even the possibility of the river being restocked had seemed to be fantastic. Finally to be given, without interest, after exorbitant interest demanded by money-lenders, to be completely and whole-heartedly given such an enormous sum, to him, as a thousand rupees, overwhelmed him. In spite of everything he trusted Bill as simply as a child when he said that he could restock the river. He said that he would hand over the money to the village 'Panchayat' (group of five men to whom authority and a good deal of power was delegated by the government). He went away happily to spread the news.

Bill gave orders to move at once, travelling lightly with a small bivouac tent and leaving his camp standing. He would take only two ponies and two men with another bivouac tent and basic food supplies. Then he moved fast, sometimes doing two marches a day. He moved by the shortest route, following a map, helped by the knowledge of his men, and directed by the headmen of the villages through which they passed. He completed his journey in less than a fortnight, having notified his friend by wire that he hoped to do so. On arrival, he found the expedition ready, his friend co-operative but very firm and meticulous in his instructions. The cost staggered him, yet it was almost with a feeling of elation that he handed over the cheque. 'There goes my polo', he said, 'probably for ever.'

Bill made the journey back in less than three weeks and poured the fish into the mountain lake, taking with him the headman and many of the villagers. Then he packed up the camp and left at once for his regiment, duty and civilisation. The whole village turned out to bid him farewell with most genuine affection and regret at his departure. Many of them frankly wept and begged him to return next year. Bill, on his side, had never known such affection for any people.

Bill had experienced happiness, tragedy, humility, remorse and thankfulness. He had spent all that he had and crippled himself for many years for these people. But he had achieved something great which he did not yet realise and which would make an immeasurable difference to his character, his influence and usefulness during the remainder of his life, especially in India.

Index

Index

Index

Index